Women of China

Imperialism and Women's Resistance 1900-1949

Bobby Siu

Zed Press, 57 Caledonian Road, London N1 9DN

Women of China was first published by Zed
Press, 57 Caledonian Road, London N1 9DN
in 1982.

Typeset by Lyn Caldwell
Proofread by Penelope Fryxell
Cover design Jan Brown
Printed by Redwood Burn, Trowbridge, Wiltshire

U.S. Distributor:
Lawrence Hill & Co., 520 Riverside Avenue,
Westport, Conn. 06880, U.S.A.

**British Library Cataloguing in Publication
Data**

Siu, Bobby
   Women of China.
     1. Feminism – China – History –
      20th century
     I. Title
     305. 4'2'0951   HQ1736
ISBN 0 905762 58 4 Hb
ISBN 0 905762 63 0 Pb

Contents

List of Tables

Statistical Appendix

Dedication

To Stephanie Holbik

Note on Romanization

I have used the Hanyu Pinyin system of romanization in this book. This system is the official system used in the People's Republic of China, and Asian scholars are increasingly using it to romanize the Chinese language. The only exceptions are the names of Chinese authors and institutions previously romanized using other systems.

Acknowledgements

My interest in social movements, especially women's movements, dates back ten years ago to the cafeteria at Champlain College of Trent University. Students gathered there and spent many days and nights talking about the evils of the system and debating the best strategies for effecting social change. Although I was the quiet observer type, their conversations gradually led me to an interest in social movements and social change. Amongst these concerned students were several women who saw the liberation of women as an integral part of the larger social transformation. Their views were quite refreshing, since in Xianggang (Hong Kong) such scepticism was unheard of. That was in 1969-70, when the Canadian women's liberation movement was still in its infancy. This book, in the final analysis, owes a great debt to those students.

When I started working on the Chinese women's movements seven years ago, the material available was far from extensive. The libraries of the Canadian universities I visited did not even have a section on Women's Movements, let alone one on the women's movements in China. After spending a year locating and reading through the materials available in these libraries on the Chinese women's movements, I found they were not sufficient either in quality or quantity even to write a term paper for an undergraduate course. The general lack of knowledge of the pre-Revolutionary women's movements in China is very disheartening, especially since this ignorance is not limited to my friends, but is found among historians, sociologists, anthropologists, and even among Chinese scholars — male and female alike. It has been quite painful and difficult to demonstrate that my study was viable and to actually dig through piles of dusty newspapers and unread historical documents in dark corners of libraries in remote countries. This experience would have been even more difficult if Stephanie Holbik had not stood by my side during the past seven years. She was a greatly needed source of intellectual and emotional support.

Throughout my research, several people proved to be of great help to me. Professor Janet Salaff's critical insight into Chinese society, theory and methodology helped shape my investigation, especially in the initial stages. My conversation and correspondence with Professor Norma Diamond also furthered my understanding of the political situation in China.

During my research in Xianggang, Sister Margaret Ho (of Chu Hai College) provided useful guidance in locating sources on Chinese women. Marjorie Topley (of the Centre of Asian Studies, University of Hong Kong) shared her research expertise in the area of Chinese history with me. Two women whom I met in 1975 deserve special mention: Matilda Ng (of the Hong Kong Council of Women), who enlightened me with her first-hand experience of the historical development of Chinese women's movements and their difficulties in organizing and mobilizing women in Xianggang; and Teresa Ng (of the International Feminist League), who told me about her experience as a feminist in a male-oriented society.

While doing research in Taiwan, I came to know several people who deserve more than mere acknowledgement: John Ku was most helpful and introduced me to different scholars in my area of research. Bessie Shih, a 'traditional' Chinese woman, provided me with her view of why Chinese women do not 'need' to be liberated. Professor Chialin Pao and Weihong Lin (of the National University of Taiwan) provided me with valuable insights into certain areas of the Chinese women's movements before 1912. Lin's insistence on the high status of women in Taiwan should be noted, even though I finally remained unconvinced. Professor Yufa Chang (of the Institute of Modern History, Academia Sinica) suggested several sources of data which I was unaware of.

Chorman Ching, whose assistance was greatly needed, speeded the completion of this book. Our Christmas dinner of 1977 will be remembered by me for years to come.

Wherever I went, I needed the expertise and guidance of many librarians. The staff of the following libraries were particularly helpful: the East Asian Library of the University of Toronto, the Asian Studies Library of the University of British Columbia, John Robarts Library of the University of Toronto, Harvard-Yenching Library, East-Asian Library of Columbia University, Fung Ping Shan Library of the University of Hong Kong, the Union Research Institute Library, the Central Library of the Chinese University of Hong Kong, the Hong Kong City Hall Library, the Reference Library of the Public Record Office of Hong Kong, the Sun Yat Sen Library, the University Service Centre of Xianggang, the Party Archives Commission of Guomindang under the Guomindang Central Committee, the Institute of Modern History of the Academic Sinica, the Intelligence Bureau of the Ministry of National Defence, the Taiwan National University Library (Graduate Library), and the National Central Library of Taiwan. Two librarians deserve special mention: Kuangmei Lin of the Taiwan National University Library and P.C. Yu of the Asian Studies Library of the University of British Columbia.

Some of the material included in this book was presented as academic papers in different conferences: 'The Impact of Foreign Textile Goods on the Peasant Economy in Nineteenth-Century China with Special Reference to the Status of Women' (Annual meeting of the Canadian Society for Asian Studies, 1978) is included in Chapters Two and Three; '"Anti-Imperialism" in Chinese Women's Journals, 1900-1949' (Annual meeting of the Canadian Society for

Asian Studies, 1978) is part of Chapter Four; 'Repression, Institutionaliz-
ation, and the Women's Anti-Imperialist Movement in China, 1900-1949'
(Annual meeting of the Canadian Asian Studies Association, 1979) is incor-
porated in Chapter Five; and 'Mobilizing Peasant Women' (Workshop on
Asian Peasants, University of British Columbia, 1978) is contained in Chapter
Six. All of these papers have been modified.

Preface

History is always in the process of becoming. By the early 20th Century, the colonial phase of British and European capitalism was already in decline and a new phase of imperialism was in the ascendant. It was at this time that the global hegemony of Britain was gradually replaced by that of the United States. Imperialist rivalry had an impact on China as well as on other Third World countries. Political interference, economic exploitation and social oppression were and are a daily phenomenon in the underdeveloped countries. Early currents of anti-imperialism in China were merely previews of contemporary waves of national liberation struggle in Africa, Latin America and, sooner or later South East Asia. More and more people in these countries are beginning to realize the human consequences of imperialism and are determined to eradicate it, just as Chinese men and women did over 30 years ago. Working-class and peasant men and women are fighting against foreign powers and their puppet governments in order to liberate their countries and themselves.

Meanwhile, within the capitalist countries, the internal contradictions of capitalism have created near uncontrollable economic crisis — mounting unemployment and inflation, growing poverty, continuous proletarianization of the labour force, intensification of political surveillance, erosion of democracy and freedom, mismanagement of the state apparatus, militarization of the police force, irreconcilable labour disputes, radicalization of workers and a new militancy of dissidents on all fronts. The rising activism of women in both reformist and revolutionary politics since the late 1960s is a part of the general radicalization of young people through the Vietnam War and the deterioration of the capitalist economies. Whilst trying to claim their basic right to political, economic and social equality, women have to confront a shrinking economy. The state apparatus and the corporations have placed a few women in top posts as tokens in order to satisfy feminists; but this cannot hide the continued lower status of women generally and the fact that certain structural constraints within capitalism prevent the bringing about of any form of human equality.

It is within these historical and structural conjunctures that women of both capitalist and Third World countries began to look for alternative routes to human liberty and equality. It is not an historical accident that many feminists have turned to China as a focus of research. Of course, experience of the Chinese women's movements cannot be replicated, but it may offer some suggestions, some inspiration and some hope for those who are concerned with human liberation.

Bobby Siu

Introduction

On 1 April 1937, Zhuang Ming wrote a poem entitled 'The Marching Song of Women':

> Look, the iron hoofs of imperialism have pounded our soil;
> Look, the black hands of feudalism are still threatening our sisters.
> Come quickly, come quickly, come quickly and get rid of all these
> tigers and foxes, and sweep away all obstacles.
> We, we, we are the free masters of our country, and not born slaves.
> Come, come, dear sisters,
> Unite together and march forward,
> How can loose sands be solid?
> Come, come, dear sisters,
> And unite together as one heart,
> The last victory belongs to us.
> Work hard,
> Struggle,
> Resist,
> The last victory belongs to us.[1]

Zhuang Ming's poem was not the first or the last cry of Chinese women in the midst of feudalism and imperialism, but it epitomizes that mix of desperation, anger, determination and hope felt by Chinese women in the 20th Century. Their cries took a variety of forms, and revealed a range of human emotions and thought arising in a context of profound oppression. The oppression of women is not novel in Chinese history, nor, for that matter, in world history. For centuries, Chinese women were bound by feudal and male-imposed restrictions, and the changes in the Chinese economy and political system in the 19th and 20th Centuries made the situation of women even worse. In addition to feudalism and male chauvinism, women in China suffered the consequences of imperialism, an historical force which exceeded the comprehension of most Chinese men and women, at least for a substantial period in contemporary China. But imperialism was also, finally, a self-destructive force which revealed its inner mechanisms to the oppressed under its dominance.

It is the central thesis of this book that the Chinese women's resistance was

1

an offspring of the contradictions of imperialism. It was part of a radical historical force which began in resistance to imperialism and ended in socialist revolution.

The history of China is a history of Chinese men and women; this is especially the case in 20th Century China. However, many historians in the past have ignored the contribution of women to history-making. We read records and documents which glorify the roles of Sun Yixian in overthrowing the Manchu Dynasty, of Jiang Jieshi (Chiang Kai-shek) in leading the Northern Expedition, of Mao Zedong (Mao Tse-tung) in northern China, and of thousands and millions of men engaged in anti-Japanese resistance. But we seldom hear of women's participation in these epoch-making activities. It may come as a surprise to many people, historians and Sinologists included, to learn that women *did* engage in anti-Manchu activities, in anti-warlord struggles, in boycotts of foreign goods, in anti-imperialist wars, in guerrilla fights, in espionage, in planting mines and throwing grenades, in fighting at the front against the Japanese, in rent-reduction campaigns, in the Long March, etc. Chinese women, as we will see in this book, were *not* passive and docile beings who clung to the men or did nothing more than needlework or poetry readings. They were and are actively engaged in the making of history and deserve more than the mere token mention of their names. It is one of the central tasks of this book to take up the neglected task of systematically documenting the role of women in anti-imperialist struggle and revolution in China.

Social movements which undermine and challenge the *status quo* do not usually follow a smooth path. They are faced not only with internal debates and factions, but they also have to confront the repressive measures imposed by the State apparatus. The Chinese women's movements were no exception to this rule. Chinese women criticized government policies on women's status, domestic customs and foreign relations, attacking not only internal institutions but also foreign powers. This resulted in government harassment, policing, spying, co-option, institutionalization, intimidation and military coercion. On top of this, the Chinese women's resistance was faced with foreign troops and foreign political interference.

A study of the variety of strategies and tactics used by Chinese women to combat this repression should produce insights for other women engaged in struggles in both capitalist and underdeveloped countries. Since women's movements in these countries confront similar kinds of repression, they may be able to learn from the experience of the Chinese women who spent 50 years struggling to gain their rights and establish the preconditions for human liberation. It is important not only to know that Chinese women participated in resistance and revolution, but also to learn from their struggles.

The tasks of this book are: (1) to show the linkages between imperialism and the Chinese women's struggle; (2) to give a systematic account of women's role in social change; and (3) to illustrate the inter-relationship between repression and struggle.

There were a variety of women's movements in China in the first half of this century, including movements for educational reforms, suffrage, antifootbinding, anti-Manchuism, free love and marriage reforms, family and child-care reforms, women's legal rights, economic reforms and many others. It is impossible to document all of them thoroughly in one book. The women's anti-imperialist and revolutionary movements were selected for analysis in this book because of their monumental social, political and economic impact on women as well as on the whole of China. While the social reform movements were effective in their way, compared with women's resistance to imperialism and their efforts to build a socialist China, they appear insubstantial and cannot compare with the tremendous transformation of China after 1949.

We shall focus on the first half of this century for two reasons. First, because it was during this period that the women's movement emerged and developed as a historical force. Although there were a few sporadic women's struggles, both individual and collective, in the 19th Century, they were not organized and co-ordinated. It was not until the first decade of this century that the growth of the first organized women's movement could be observed. Secondly, the first half of the 20th Century was a time of transition for China: from a colonial-feudal-capitalist society to a socialist one. As far as contemporary Chinese history is concerned, the Republican period (1911-49) is the least studied and least understood by historians, Sinologists and political scientists. Such neglect by Western and Taiwanese scholars is largely political, for it is just this period of Chinese history which reveals not only the corruption and impotence of the Guomindang (Kuomintang or K.M.T.) but also the escalating interference of foreign powers, especially the United States, in the politics and economy of China.

At this stage of our knowledge the lack of or unavailability of materials makes it impossible to do a complete study of women's movements in all regions, while variation in regions makes it difficult to generalize local or regional findings to the rest of China. Nonetheless, this book will attempt to paint a national picture of the movements using data on several cities and regions: Shanghai, Beijing (Peking), Chongqing, Jiangxi and northern China in general. While the selection of these regions may be unwittingly biased, they do show the variations between urban and rural areas necessary for a study of women's movements.

The following chapter will discuss the imperialist invasion of China in the 19th and 20th Centuries. After a brief outline of the global context of imperialism and the situation of China before the invasion, it will focus on various processes of imperialism: military, political, economic and cultural; and how these processes varied through time.

Chapter Two will show how imperialism affected the Chinese industrial and agricultural systems by looking specifically at the cotton textile industry. We will also examine how the K.M.T. Government policies affected the economy.

Chapter Three will deal with the way the above-mentioned structural changes *vis-a-vis* imperialism made an impact on the life-situations of women. We will show that imperialism has human consequences and affects women

3

differently according to their class positions, placing particular attention on the study of peasant and working-class women. An analysis will first be made of the life-chances of these classes under imperialism, and then of the situations of women of these classes, particularly with respect to their 'problems' as women.

Chapter Four will investigate anti-imperialist ideas in women's literature, classifying them as to their themes, rationales, strategies and tactics. Once again, special attention will be placed on peasant and working-class women. This chapter will also trace the changing patterns of emphasis in anti-imperialist ideas and the way these patterns were, in turn, related to the changing structural context.

Chapter Five will examine the responses of women to imperialism in terms of their political activities, which are, in turn, responses to foreign interventions and government policies of repression and institutionalization. Again, these responses are put into the context of general class reactions and the different responses of women in different classes are then discussed. This chapter will also outline the various repressive measures that the government and foreign powers used in suppressing or 'cooling off' women's activism.

Chapter Six will discuss the policies on women of the Chinese Communist Party (C.C.P.) and the Guomindang (K.M.T.): their mobilization strategies and tactics as well as their positions on women's status within and outside the family. It will compare these policies and tactics to see why the C.C.P. succeeded, where the K.M.T. failed, in mobilizing women.

Chapter Seven will summarize the previous discussion and draw out the lessons that can be learnt from the Chinese women's movements.

References

1.   Zhuang Ming, 'The Marching Song of Women', *Women's Life*, Vol. IV, No. vi, 1937, p.34.

1. The Faces of Imperialism

We cannot begin to understand the origin and development of the Chinese women's movements without first placing them in the context of structural changes in China in the 19th and 20th Centuries. And structural changes in China cannot themselves be understood without a prior examination of the changing world economy.

The task of this chapter, therefore, is to answer two related questions: (1) what were the structural forces compelling foreign powers to dominate China in the 19th and 20th Centuries? and (2) what forms did this domination take? To answer the first question, we will examine the changing economic structures of several imperialist countries which exerted the main impact on China, namely Britain, Japan and the United States. As for the second question, we shall examine military invasion, political influence, economic domination and cultural intrusion as they affected China.

The Development of Imperialism

Britain

During the 16th to 18th Centuries, several European powers, especially Britain, Spain, Holland and Portugal, built up colonial empires through military plunder and economic exploitation. These colonies yielded large amounts of capital for these European countries. Between 1757 and 1780, for example, Britain extracted roughly £40 million from India alone.[1]

These shipments of money and commercial capital made possible the industrial revolution in Britain, although initially this capital was used for buying landed estates and not for industrial purposes.[2] However, in the 18th Century, a series of factors continued to stimulate industry: the expanding colonial market, government initiatives in ammunition production, a rise in population, the decline of domestic workshops, the commercialization of farming, the enclosure movement, improvement of transportation systems and banking facilities, as well as technological innovations.[3]

The textile industry may be taken as representative, both because of the extent of its expansion in Britain in the 18th Century and its eventual effects on the Chinese economy. Its rise was connected with several breakthroughs in textile technology, for example: Kay's flying shuttle (1730s), Paul's carding machine (1748) and Hargreaves' spinning-jenny (1764). But the most significant was the invention of Arkwright's water-frame (1769), which produced strong cotton yarn serving as both warp and weft. This development was soon followed by Crompton's mule (1779) and Boulton and Watt's steam engine (1785), which together made spinning mills a possibility. By the turn of the 19th Century, the power-loom had begun to displace the hand-loom, thus paving the way for the handicraft workshops to be replaced by a factory system.[4] The enclosure movement and the resultant migration of peasants to urban settings provided the necessary labour force for the factory system to expand — for, however important the technical innovations, the factory system depended absolutely upon the exploitation of workers by the lengthening of working hours, while maintaining bare subsistence wages.

Thus, the establishment of a factory system meant the beginning of industrial capitalism. Through the two methods of increasing surplus value — lengthening working hours and improving productive technology — the bourgeoisie was able to produce commodities in great quantities at low consumer prices. In 1779, for instance, the price of a certain quantity of No.40 cotton thread was 16 shillings; by 1830, it was 1s 2½d.[5] The increase in production may be seen in the rise of raw cotton consumed between 1781 and 1818: from 5 million to 164 million pounds respectively.[6]

But productive capacity gradually exceeded demand in the British economy. In 1802, cotton manufacture constituted 4 to 5% of the national income of Britain, but by 1830, it grew to more than half of the British home-produced exports.[7] Markets in other countries were needed to absorb the surplus of commodities. The conquest of world markets was undertaken through military invasion and political pressure. Trade relations once achieved, the ideology of 'free trade' could be used to justify the ruin of the indigenous development of industry in overseas countries. In addition to being passive markets for exported commodities, the colonies also served as sources of raw materials, and hence their competitive potential was doubly undermined.

The cotton textile industry in Britain illustrates the significance of trade in the expansion of capitalism. The Lancashire industry was established in the mid-18th Century. Between 1700 and 1780, imports of raw cotton increased from 1 to 5 million pounds (weight), and by 1789 they had increased to 32.5 million pounds. Export of cotton commodities increased ten times from 1750 to 1769.[8] British trade expanded at a tremendous rate and by the second half of the 19th Century British exports went to every corner of the earth.

In order to maintain the maximum rate of profit, the capital accumulated through trade had to be invested either in the home country or overseas, or both. To do this, the bourgeoisie was forced to invest capital in other sectors of the economy, to incorporate other firms in the same trade — which led to monopolization — and to export capital to other countries, a further development of imperialism which will be discussed in the following section.

Foreign investment had become such an established phenomenon of the British economy by 1870, increasing from £785 million in 1871 to £3,500 million in 1911, that 'annual net foreign investments were frequently greater than gross domestic fixed investments'.[9] Foreign investment reached its peak of £4,000 million in 1913, and since then has been on the decline (see Appendix, Table A). Most of British investments overseas were in railways and the extraction of raw materials. The export of capital also took the form of state loans to foreign countries, loans whose terms required them to buy goods from the imperialist powers, thus creating guaranteed purchasers to stablize the home economy during economic slumps. In short, it is all too clear that Britain's overseas trade and investment was not based on any altruistic interest in developing industry in other countries.[10]

Beside exporting capital, establishing markets for commodities and searching for raw materials, capitalist countries sought to establish spheres of control in other parts of the world in order to lessen internal contradictions in their own countries — the key one being the contradiction between capitalists and workers. The rise in labour movements forms an immense obstacle to profit-making and exploitation through demands for higher wages, better fringe benefits, healthier working conditions, stricter pollution legislation and so on. In Britain, trade unions began to be organized in the 1750s; since then, the country has experienced riots, sabotage, slow-downs and strikes. The bourgeoisie has found it convenient to export capital to overseas countries where there is no (strong) labour movement, and little restriction on pollution, exploitation, etc.

Thus, British imperialism was based on the maximization of profit and the export of internal contradictions. With the expansion of the cotton textile industry and other British industries in the first half of the 19th Century, it is not surprising that Britain turned to overseas markets, especially to China with its mass of potential customers. This economic motive is quite explicit in R.M. Martin's 'Minute on the British Positions and Prospects in China' (1845). R.M. Martin was the Treasurer for the Colonial, Consular, and Diplomatic Service in China and a member of the Hong Kong Legislative Council when he wrote: ' . . . To the British Colonial Possession and to new unexplored regions must England look for the increase of her commerce. . . . . The opening therefore of the vast and populous territories on the borders of the Northern Pacific is a matter of vital consequence to Britain.'[11]

This was especially true of the cotton textile industry in Britain. One of the British plenipotentiaries who signed the Treaty of Nanjing in 1842 informed the British people that he had opened up a country so big 'that all the mills of Lancashire could not make stocking stuff enough for one of its provinces.'[12]

Another of R.M. Martin's writings indicates how philanthropic and religious arguments were used to justify the economic (and military) invasion of China:

> Britain cannot remain stationary; she must either retrograde or advance. Happily her advancement rightly directed is beneficial to all mankind, by enabling her to maintain the peace of the world, to promote

civilization, to reclaim the savage, to till the waste regions of the earth, and to fulfill her high vocation by a widespread dissemination of the inestimable blessings of Christianity.

A Republic of nations is as Utopian in the existing selfishness of mankind as a Republic of individuals and the maintenance of one Kingdom sufficiently supreme to protect weaker Kingdoms, to preserve order, to uphold the reign of law, and to inculcate by precept and by example the duties which the possession of Great Power involves is essential to the steady and triumphant progress of true civilization. No nation is so well adapted for this supreme control as Britain by reason of her insularity, her tolerant religion, her free institutions, her distant and varied Colonial Possessions, her non-alliance with continental intrigues, her obvious policy to maintain peace, and her maritime superiority which leaves no desire for continental aggrandizement in Europe.[13]

Such blatant convictions of superiority can also be seen in their specific effects of rationalization of aggression if we take, for instance, what Lieutenant Colonel G.J. Wolseley wrote about the 1860 war with China: ' . . . Before the Asiatic world can be led to believe in the justice of our policy, or before it will be applicable to Eastern nations, it will be necessary first to raise them up to our standard of knowledge, and enable them to reason in the same logical manner with ourselves.'[14]

British imperialism attempted to open up China during the mid-19th Century, reaching a peak of activity during the First World War. Cotton and woollen textile exports dropped from 39% to 31% of British exports from 1896 to 1913,[15] and after the war, British exports never regained their old prosperity. By 1930, exports of Lancashire's cotton goods were only one-third those of 1913, and later they dropped even lower.[16]

With respect to the export of capital (foreign investment), Britain continued to top other countries, although it began to decline in 1930 and by the end of the Second World War was overtaken by the United States (see Table 1.1).

The United States
Examining American and Japanese imperialism is as significant for understanding China in the 20th Century as a study of British imperialism is for comprehending the 19th Century. As in Britain, the U.S. factory system began with the cotton textile industry, but in the late 19th Century its industrial output still lagged behind that of Britain. After 1900, however, the U.S. surpassed Britain in its share of world industrial output (see Table 1.2). In the second half of the 19th Century, the U.S. experienced its period of greatest growth: on average, the value of manufactured producers' durables increased yearly by roughly 30%, and manufacturing capital grew from $1.6 billion in 1869 to $5.7 billion in 1889. Between 1850 and 1890, there was roughly a 750% increase in the value added by manufacturing; and during the same period, manufactured goods jumped from 16.3% to 20.7% of their share in

Table 1.1
Foreign Investment, 1862-1960 (billions of gold francs of 1913)*

Year	Britain	France	Germany	U.S.A.	Japan
1862	3.6	–	–	–	–
1870	20	10**	—	–	–
1885	30	15***	6.5	–.	–
1902	62	30	12.5	3****	–
1914	87	40	30	15	1
1930	90	20	5.6	75	4.5
1938	85	15	–	48	9
1948	40	3	–	69	–
1957	46	6	2	120	–
1960	60	?	4	150	1

*　　£1 = $5 = 20 RM = 25 francs
**　　1869 figure
***　　1880 figure
****　　1900 figure
Source: Ernest Mandel, *Marxist Economic Theory*, London, Merlin Press, 1971, p.450.

Table 1.2
U.S. and U.K. Share of World Industrial Output, 1820–1950

Year	Percentage of Total Output	
	U.S.A.	England
1820	10	50
1850	15	39
1880	28	28
1900	31	18
1920	47	14
1937	35	9
1950	39	7

Source: M. Weinberg, 'American Economic Development', in V.B. Singh, *Patterns of Economic Development*, New York: Allied Pub. Private Ltd., 1970, p.185.

total exports, and dropped from 63.0% to 45.5% in their share of total imports.[17]

This period of expansion also involved an upsurge of monopolization, beginning with the American Brass Association in 1853 and reaching a peak in the last two decades in the 19th Century with over 5,000 companies consolidating into about 300 trusts.[18] In the five-year period between 1898 and 1902, there were 276 mergers resulting in a capitalization of $5.6 billion.[19]

While the tremendous pace of consolidation appears to have declined after the turn of the century (as witnessed in the reduced numbers of mergers in manufacturing and mining (see Appendix, Table B), monopoly capitalism had become the dominant phenomenon in the U.S. For example, 32% of industrial production and 40% of mining production (excluding the oil industry) had been monopolized.[20] The total number of national banks jumped from 3,732 in 1900 to 8,030 in 1920, then fell to 7,536 in 1929 and 5,021 in 1945. The number of companies manufacturing automobiles dropped from 265 in 1909 to six in 1955.[21] By 1947, one firm alone produced 85% of the fire extinguishers, two firms produced 85% of industrial gases, three firms produced 90% of domestic cotton threads, and so on.[22]

But this overall industrial expansion and monopolization in the 20th Century should not mask the fact that economic growth has been slower in this century than the last one. (Table C in the Appendix shows the declining rates of per capita growth in the 19th and 20th Centuries.) Although total profits for the increasingly monopolized manufacturing industry were increasing, the actual rate of profit was dropping, as witnessed in Table D in the Appendix.

This, of course, posed a serious problem for the industrial bourgeoisie, whose key aim was to accumulate profits at a maximum rate, but was eased somewhat by the export of capital — the route that Britain took in the 19th Century. Before 1895, it was the 'independent and isolated entrepreneurs' who made most of the foreign investments. As of 1897, their investment overseas was roughly $684.5 millions, most of it in Latin America and Canada. However, after 1895, the export of capital came mainly from the monopolies. As Table 1.3 illustrates, the majority of these investments took the form of 'direct' investments and all rose through time (except in 1939). By 1969, U.S. companies accounted for an estimated 60 to 65% of all foreign direct investment.[23] There is no doubt that the U.S. had emerged as the super-imperialist power in the 20th Century.

However, the development of American capitalism has not been smooth. By 1929, the accumulated capital had become so enormous that it was no longer profitable to invest abroad or in production at home. New markets had to be opened for the export of commodities. Yet between 1929 and 1933, the already-limited market shrank to such an extent that there was actually a 30% fall in gross national product. There were some recoveries between 1933 and 1937, but they never reached the 1929 level. Beginning in September 1937, there was a nine-month depression-within-a-depression, the worst in the history of American capitalism. As M. Weinberg states:

> Industrial production declined by 33 per cent and durable goods production by over 50 per cent; national income declined by 13 per cent and payrolls by 35 per cent; industrial stock average declined by over

7-1958 ($millions)

(...net)	Short-term Credits	Total
	—	684.5
	—	3,513.8
	1,617.0	17,009.6
	1,060.0	12,445.0
	1,516.0	19,004.0
	3,488.0	40,824.0

...nic Development', p.196.

...ne in five months; profits fell by 78 per ...yment declined by 23 per cent. At the ...s tended to be resistant, although prices ...l per cent.[24]

...of 1908-15, a world war ended the de- ...nd Paul Sweezy aptly argue, the war ...or the under-utilized capacities and ...d ammunition industry.[25] They also ...oth world wars provided investment ...civilian use cleared up the backlogs of consumer demands — and absorbed a large amount of surplus. The effects of a war economy for capitalism may be judged from the fact that between 1939 and 1957 the United States Government expanded its investment by two-thirds of a trillion dollars on military goods and services. During the most intense period of the Second World War — 1941-45 — the U.S. donated some $41 billion to its allies, principally to England and Soviet Union.[26]

But U.S. hegemony was challenged by the rise of socialism in the Soviet Union. Under a planned economy, the Soviet Union was able to expand its industry at a pace which shocked the world. (A comparison of the U.S. and Soviet Union's share of world industrial output is given in Table E in the Appendix.) Japan also, as a rising capitalist country, appeared to the U.S. as a threat. Table 1.1 shows that, although Japan was still far behind the U.S. in the export of capital, its share was growing. So in the 1930s, the U.S. Government sought to strengthen its ties with China in order to counter the Soviet Union and Japan in the Far East.[27]

Furthermore, the U.S. intended to open up China as a market for its commodities. Edwin A. Locke, Jr., a banker and President Truman's personal representative for economic affairs in 1945, believed that the U.S. should invest in China so as to create 'a large permanent and growing market for U.S. goods. . . .'[28]

Japan

Unlike Britain and the U.S., Japan's industrialization began through active State initiation and participation. Although before 1868 there were some forms of industry, such as arsenals and engineering works, it was the Meiji Government (formed in 1868) which transformed the Japanese economy by developing military and strategic industries.[29] But the government gradually transferred its enterprises into the hands of the financial oligarchy.

Although the government began with heavy industries, light industries (especially textile) remained significant throughout the latter part of the 19th Century and the first half of the 20th Century. As late as 1930, light industries constituted 58.8% of the national income within the industrial sector, with heavy industries only 41.2%.[30]

Industries expanded at a rapid rate. Take the cotton textile industry as an example. Between 1913 and 1918, there was an increase of 41% in the number of spindles and 23% in yarn output. Other industries expanded at an even greater speed, especially the iron and steel industry.[31] Between the two world wars, 'the index of textile production increased by three times, metals and machinery by eight times, chemicals and ceramics by twelve times, pig-iron by five times, and generation of electricity and gas by fourteen times. The centre of gravity of production shifted from extractive to manufacturing industries.'[32] From another perspective, within the 50-year period of 1885-1935, Japan tripled its per capita production of goods and services.[33]

However, the development of different industries in Japan was uneven. Heavy industry mushroomed in the 1930s under the stimulus of armament spending. Between 1930 and 1936, consumer goods production advanced only 33%, but that of producer goods 83%.[34]

As in other capitalist countries, the process of monopolization was embedded in industrial expansion. This process may be seen in Table F in the Appendix, which traces the control by the Mitsui Trust (one of the Big Four in Japan) in four of the sectors of the economy.

The banking system also went through a process of centralization and concentration between 1914 and 1945. The number of banks fell from 2,155 in 1914 to 61 in 1945. The five biggest banks had 24.3% of all bank deposits in 1926, 41.9% in 1936 and 62% in 1945 (the biggest eight banks).[35]

Although the interests of the Zaibatsu had been mostly industrial, manifested in buying small-scale commerce and manufacturing after the First World War, it nevertheless merged with the financial sector and came to own and control many private banks. In effect the beginning of this century saw the merger of industrial and financial capital in Japan.[36]

The depression of the 1930s provided the conditions for the formation of cartels, which were legally sanctioned by the government with the Major Industrial Law and Industrial Association Law of 1931. After that, monopolization reached a new height.[37] During the Second World War, the four biggest corporations doubled their positions, moving from 12% of total corporate and partnership capital to 24% during the four-year period between 1941 and 1945.[38] Before the end of the war, these four corporate groups almost completely dominated the Japanese economy (see Table G in the Appendix). Monopolization of the financial and industrial sectors also meant the concentration of wealth in a few hands. Although there are variations through time, the trend is obvious: more and more of the national wealth was concentrated in fewer hands, as witnessed in Table H in the Appendix. As Table 1.1 reveals, the export of accumulated capital increased along with the process of monopolization, cartelization, centralization and concentration of wealth. It jumped from one billion gold francs in 1914 to nine billion in 1938, but, compared with other capitalist countries like the U.S., Germany, France, or Britain, the total export of capital was small.

It was in the area of trade, however, that Japan was moving rapidly upwards as a competitor in the world market. Up to 1882, the balance of payments in Japan was unfavourable because of its heavy imports of cotton and woollen goods, raw cotton, sugar and machinery, but the rapid industrialization produced an increase in foreign trade. As Table 1.4 reveals, up to 1931 foreign trade constituted an increasing proportion of the national income. In monetary

Table 1.4
Japanese Foreign Trade as Percentage of National Income

Period	Percentage
1878-82	10.4
1888-92	18.1
1914-17	36.2
1931	20.0

Source: P. Banerji, 'Economic Development of Japan', in V.B. Singh, *Patterns of Economic Development*, p. 30.

terms, the total volume of exports rose from 124 million yen in 1893-97 to 444.9 million yen in 1908-12. During this period, total imports also increased by about 350%.[39]

The First World War provided Japan with a great opportunity to develop the munitions industry, while the disrupted state of the European economy meant that Japanese goods were temporarily free from the competition of European goods. There was an increase in the export of Japanese goods to Asiatic countries, Europe, North and South America and Australia.[40]

The 1920s was a decade of financial instability for Japan, reaching its peak in the financial crisis of 1927. However, the later depression in the Western countries in the 1930s resulted in a booming Japanese economy and markets for her goods. From 1930 to 1936, total exports increased from 1,435 to 2,641 million yen, nearly doubling the volume of exports. Textile manufactures were the dominant items in Japan's exports and by 1936 Japan had become the top exporter of cotton piece goods.[41]

The trade boom which occurred in Japan between 1932 and 1937 signified the formal entry of Japan into the world capitalist system: Japanese commodities were marketed throughout the world and posed an immense threat to severely strained European capitalism.

However, the Second World War greatly limited the Japanese export market. To curtail expansion, restrictions were imposed on Japanese exports, and Japan shifted its production to the heavy industry needed for the war economy. War industry in 1945 accounted for more than 80% of Japan's total industrial output.[42] Military defeat pushed the Japanese economy below its 1919 level of production, completely destroying one-sixth of the national reproducible wealth. Under the influence of the U.S., the Supreme Commander of Allied Powers (SCAP) aimed to 'destroy completely the material basis of Japanese imperialism' between 1945 and 1952.[43]

Although Japan was curtailed in its imperialist expansion after the Second World War, it must be remembered that, since its beginnings in 1868, State-initiated industrialization had gradually changed into full-blown monopoly capitalism not dissimilar to monopoly capitalism in the U.S. and Britain, and was confronted with the same problems of maximization of profits, marketing of goods, export of capital and the capture of raw materials and natural resources (including cheap labour).

By 1890, the Japanese Government (including its armed forces) had come to realize that Japan could remain a sovereign power only by joining the great Western powers in demanding privileges in Asia. Liaodong Peninsula and Formosa had always been the imperialist targets of Japan.[44] In 1902, the Army General Staff concluded that, 'for the long-range planning of our country', it was necessary to make 'Korea part of the Japanese Empire'.[45]

The concern over political sovereignty was based on the Japanese conviction that China's economy had been ruined by imperialist powers. That a U.S. invasion of Japan was seen as a threat is evident in the strategy of the naval planners to establish naval hegemony over the U.S. in the Western Pacific. Admiral Fukudome noted, 'In 1907, the Imperial navy made the United States its sole strategic enemy.'[46] Furthermore, the Japanese Government was also concerned with the expansion of Russia to the north of Japan, and hence the government took steps to strengthen the army to meet this challenge.[47]

This concern with national sovereignty gradually combined with economic imperialism and world hegemony as monopoly capitalism in Japan took its shape. China, a vast country full of potential consumers and natural resources, became the target of Japanese imperialism. The following quotation is taken from a memorandum written by Premier Tanaka to the Emperor of Japan on 25 July, 1927. It is worth quoting at length for all that it reveals of the imperialist ambitions of Japan:

> In order to conquer China we must first conquer Manchuria and Mongolia. In order to conquer the world, we must first conquer China. If we succeed in conquering China the rest of the Asiatic countries and the South Sea countries will fear us and surrender to us. Then the world will realize that Eastern Asia is ours and will not dare to violate our rights.

. . . Our best policy lies in the direction of taking positive steps to secure rights and privileges in Manchuria and Mongolia. These will enable us to develop our trade. This will not only forestall China's own industrial development, but also prevent the penetration of European Powers. This is the best policy possible!

The way to gain actual rights in Manchuria and Mongolia is to use this region as a base and under the pretence of trade and commerce penetrate the rest of China. Armed by the rights already secured we shall seize the resources all over the country. Having China's entire resources at our disposal we shall proceed to conquer India, the Archipelago, Asia Minor, Central Asia, and even Europe.[48]

The Logic of Imperialism

In the previous pages, we have traced the development of capitalism in three countries: Britain, the U.S. and Japan. The central argument is based on Lenin's theory that imperialism grows out of monopoly capitalism because of the problem of the falling rate of profit. The bourgeoisie requires markets, first, for its commodities and then for the export of capital in order to maintain maximum profits.[49] Britain, the U.S. and Japan intensified their search for and conquest of markets at various periods in the 19th and 20th Centuries. In their scramble for world territories, Britain dominated South East Asia, Southern Africa, North America, Australia and New Zealand; the U.S. supervised parts of South America and became increasingly interested in other parts of the world as well; Japan held islands in the Pacific Ocean and showed increasing interest in dominating South East Asia. France seized Northern Africa and Vietnam; Germany got a few territories in Africa and Asia, and so on. Although we have only discussed the imperialist ambitions of Britain, the U.S. and Japan in Chinese territories and their relation to capitalist expansion at home, similar processes took place in other European capitalist countries.[50] The formation of international capitalist monopolies and the territorial division of the world are the key characteristics of imperialism according to Lenin, and in the second half of this chapter we will see how they are linked to the partitioning of China. As Jules Ferry — the great promoter of French colonial expansion — once said in his book *Le Tonkin et la Mere Patrie* (Tongking and the Mother Country), 'The nations of Europe have long since realized that the conquest of China, of its 400 millions of consumers, must be undertaken exclusively by and for the producers of Europe.'[51]

Imperialism and China

Driven by economic necessity and internal contradictions, the imperialist powers descended upon China one after another. Using techniques of intrusion, interference, manipulation and domination, they made interventions in military, cultural, political and economic spheres. Each of them worked to undermine China's autonomy and sovereignty as a nation, and, until the liberation of 1949, reduced China to a state of collapse, chaos and ruin.

Military Forces

China was forced to open her ports to the imperialist powers during the Opium War (1839-42). This war is usually dated from 3 November, 1839, when the Chinese openly confronted the British over the murder of a Chinese named Lin Weixi. Lord Palmerston, the British Foreign Secretary, urged on by the English merchants to make a show of force against China, decided in February 1840 to send a force of British soldiers to deal with the crisis.[52]

All the imperialist powers thereafter used military force or the threat of military force. For instance, the 1858 Treaty of Tianjin provided the legal basis for the presence of gunboats in the rivers and treaty ports and of larger ships along the sea coasts of China. By the end of the 19th Century, several strategic naval bases, for example, Xianggang (Honk Kong), had been ceded by leasehold to various imperialist powers. Military force, even if not used directly, was a threat to China, as evidenced in the frequent appearance of cruisers and battleships in Chinese waters. According to A. Feuerwerker's estimate, 'in 1896, British naval tonnage on the China station totalled 59,000; Russia nearly the same; France 28,000; Germany 23,000; and the U.S. 18,000 tons.'[53]

In addition, foreign municipal police and international militias ('voluntary corps') were allowed to station themselves in several settlements and concessions. After the Boxer Uprising, the imperialist powers maintained armed detachments ('Legation Guards') in Beijing (Peking) and occupied several important points along the railways from Beijing to the sea coast. The Protocol also permitted troops to be stationed in Tianjin, where Chinese soldiers were themselves excluded.

These military presences in Chinese territories were usually legitimized by treaties or agreements which China had to sign at gunpoint. But military forces, such as the Japanese troops occupying the railroad zones in Manchuria and Shandong, were neither legal nor legitimate. Their presence meant that the imperialist powers were ready to deploy force to protect their properties or personnel or to secure what they unilaterally maintained were their rights. Even without the deployment of military force, the very existence of these forces in Chinese territories was an undisguised infringement of China's sovereignty.

There were, of course, many cases in which military force was actually employed to increase privileges and rights in China. The Opium War was only the beginning of a whole series of aggressive wars against China, followed by the Arrow Incident (1856), conflicts between China and Britain and France (1860), the employment of British and French troops in repressing the Taiping rebels in Shanghai (1860), the formation of the foreign-run Ever Victorious Army (1860-63), the occupation of Ili by the Russians during the Muslim Rebellion (1871), the Sino-Japanese War (1894-95), the introduction of Russian forces into Manchuria during the Boxer Uprising (1900), the expeditions by foreign troops to centres of anti-foreign activities (1900-01), the British military missions to Tibet (1904), the use of foreign police and troops to suppress workers' and students' demonstrations and strikes (1920s and 1930s), the Mukden Incident (1931), the landing of Japanese armies at Shanghai (1931), the Japanese infiltration beyond the Great Wall (1935), the Marco-Polo Bridge Incident (1937) and the Sino-Japanese War (1937-45).

These wars and conflicts were not only distressing in themselves, but resulted in further erosions of the political, economic and social autonomy and sovereignty of China through the resulting treaties or agreements. These included the Treaty of Nanjing (with Britain in 1842), the Supplementary Treaty of the Bogue (with Britain in 1843), the Treaty of Wanghai (with the U.S. in 1842), the Treaty of Tainjin (1858), the Treaties of Peijing (1860) and the Boxer Protocol (1901), among others.

Cultural Influence

Imperialism has always had a strong ideological element. From the 1840s the ideology of imperialism took the form of religious indoctrination. European missionaries were sent to China to convert the Chinese to their beliefs and worldview.

It was the contention of many British who came to China in the 19th Century that the Chinese were uncivilized, uneducated and heathen. While such ethnocentrism was widespread among all imperialists, it was particularly manifest in missionary activities in China.

The earliest treaties with the West, such as the treaties of 1842, 1844 and 1860, made it legal for the missionaries to live in the treaty ports and travel to the interior of China. They were also permitted to buy or lease land and build houses or churches after 1860. Due to the most-favoured-nation clauses of the treaties, by which privileges granted to any one nation were automatically extended to others, missionaries of all nationalities had these rights, and could go everywhere in China. By 1919, over 94% of all 'xian' (districts) in China proper and Manchuria reported some Protestant missionary activities.

However, the wide extent of Protestant missionary work masks the concentration of missionaries in the coastal provinces and in the Yangzi Valley provinces. In fact, only 17% worked in the interior of China, and, most were to be found in big cities such as Shanghai, Beijing (Peking), Guangzhou (Canton), Nanjing, Fuzhou and Changsha. Two-thirds of the Protestant missionaries and one-quarter of the communicants lived in 176 cities with a population of 50,000 or more.[54]

Shanghai was the major centre of the missionary activity with the Church of the Holy Trinity, the Union Church, the Baptist Church on the Bund, the Deutsche Evangelische Kirche, and a dozen mission associations. The French and International Settlements in Shanghai contained a variety of Catholic churches.

The 20th Century saw the expansion of missionary work, in the form of missionary societies and such organizations as the Y.M.C.A. and the Salvation Army as well as in the work of the traditional Protestant and Catholic churches.

(For a summary of the growth of the Protestant church in China from 1889 to 1919, see Table I in the Appendix.) These missionary establishments and their personnel came to China to Christianize the Chinese, not to learn from them. Their segregation from the Chinese world has been remarked upon by Paul Cohen:

> From the time they arrived in China until the time they left, the missionaries lived and worked in the highly organized structure of the mission compound, which resulted in their effective segregation — psychological as well as physical — from the surrounding Chinese society . . . . For the missionaries really did not want to enter the Chinese world any more than they had to. Their whole purpose was to get the Chinese to enter theirs.[55]

In the 19th Century, the missionaries concentrated on building schools for the Chinese children, usually as a pretext for preaching the gospel. It was claimed that by 1919, at least 199,694 schools were formed for this purpose (see Table J in the Appendix). These schools were geared towards individual salvation as well as training Chinese in Western and Christian images.

Very soon, the missionaries found that although many Chinese needed to be saved, few were interested in Christianity, and so they began to concern themselves with a total reconstruction of China through the introduction of Western books. Missionaries like Young Allen and Timothy Richard and the Society for Promoting Christian Knowledge diligently translated Western books — and transmitted Western ideas and values to the Chinese, especially to the Chinese elite.[56]

After the turn of the century, the Protestant missionaries shifted their religious/educational concerns to social reforms, opposing the binding of women's feet, and engaging in urban and labour issues, famine relief work and public hygience (such as anti-fly and anti-T.B. campaigns); they established public playgrounds, athletic and recreational programmes, urged the scientific study of agriculture and battled against opium-smoking.[57]

It would be naive to presume that missionaries were concerned only with educational, social, philanthropic and religious matters. Sometimes their connections with politicians and government officials were explicit; for instance, John C. Ferguson, a Methodist missionary who came to China in 1887, presided over the early phase of Nanjing University and developed many contacts with Chinese officials. Another example is Edward T. Williams, who worked in the Foreign Christian Missionary Society between 1887 and 1896 and became the Chinese secretary at the American legation in Shanghai between 1901 and 1908 and later first secretary of the American legation in Beijing in 1911-13.[58] These missionaries did not hesitate to interfere in politics to strengthen their own local positions, and it has been suggested that they were more than willing to share information on local conditions with their consuls. Their activities inland or among the poor may be regarded as outright spying for their consuls.[59]

Political Interventions

It is virtually impossible to document all the means used by foreign powers to influence the Chinese Governments, since interference may occur through such subtle means as friendship networks, favouritism and informal lobbying, which are not mentioned in historical documents written by officials. Political interference may also involve economic measures such as economic blackmail. In this section, we will outline a few of the methods, often quite undisguised, which were used to diminish the political autonomy of China.

One of the most blatant means of political interference was the institution of the 'most-favoured-nation' clause in treaties. This clause was introduced by Britain in the Treaty of Bogue (1843); it allowed all involved countries to share freely and equally in any rights and privileges that China might grant to any one country. As other treaties later contained the same clause, it is obvious that Western powers shared a common interest in exploiting China.

Fifteen countries had the 'most-favoured-nation' clause, including Britain, France, Germany, the U.S., Belgium, Sweden, Russia, Portugal, Denmark, the Netherlands, Spain, Italy, Austria-Hungary and Brazil. Three more nations had treaty relations with China — Peru, Norway and Mexico — making 18 nations in all who benefited from such a clause.

The legalization of such a clause in the treaties reflects the imperialist rivalry among the European powers in the 19th Century. No imperialist nation liked to be excluded from the scramble for territories, privileges, and rights in China. But the clause prevented China from imposing any restriction on the expansion of Western imperialism; furthermore, it violated the fundamental principle of a nation's right to self-determination in political or economic affairs.

Another explicit infringement of Chinese sovereignty was the institutionalization of the 'extra-territoriality' clause in the treaties. The Bogue Treaty sowed the seeds of such a clause, but full extra-territorial privileges were not granted until 1858; then, due to the 'most-favoured-nation' clause, they were granted to all nations signing treaties with China.

Under the extra-territoriality clause, foreign establishments were not subject to Chinese legislation, but were under their own jurisdiction. All foreigners in China carried their extra-territorial rights with them wherever they went. For example, missionary schools were not subject to Chinese government regulations when designing curricula or hiring teachers. Foreign banks issued currency which was not controlled by the Chinese Government. Foreign individuals and corporations were exempt from direct Chinese taxation. The foreign press could, without repercussions, print any information they wished. In fact, Chinese troops were not even allowed to pass through concessions or settlements, though they were Chinese territories, since they were under foreign jurisdiction.[60]

This clause actually deprived China of the right to intervene in any foreign establishments in China. As one American diplomat put it:

The Treaties had come to be interpreted . . . as providing protection to

19

Americans, and other foreigners enjoying extra-territorial rights and privileges, from interference of any sort or degree in their activities by the authorities or agents of the Chinese government. The basic original right of freedom from Chinese court jurisdiction had been extended and broadened to include freedom from Chinese administrative control except in matters explicitly provided for in the treaties.[61]

Although some nations, such as Germany and Austria-Hungary and Russia in 1917, lost their extra-territorial rights in China, many others retained them well into the 20th Century.

'Extra-territoriality' also had certain economic repercussions for China. The very fact that foreign industries were exempt from Chinese taxation gave them a great advantage in accumulating the capital which was urgently needed by native Chinese enterprises. The foreign banks also attracted Chinese capital due to the security provided by the 'extra-territoriality' clause, and thus Chinese capital was transferred to finance foreign industries or used in international trade. Since the Chinese Governments were unable to tax the foreign corporations and their imported goods, they lost a considerable proportion of national revenue necessary for economic or social development.[62]

Another means of political interference was 'foreign aid' or 'loans', that is economic measures with a highly political content. The U.S. was threatened by Japanese imperialism in the Pacific during the 1930s and 1940s, so it sent huge loans and direct cash to the K.M.T. to strengthen its armies against the Japanese. Although a Foreign Service expert — John S. Service — advised the U.S. Government not to support them in 1944-45, the U.S. Government continued to aid the K.M.T. in its fight against the Communists.[63] In fact, the U.S. Government gave more than U.S. $51 billion worth of weaponry and ammunition to the K.M.T. in the three-year period between 1945 and 1947, and in 1948 alone they gave U.S. $4 billion to the K.M.T.[64]

Slightly more subtle forms of political persuasion were also used. The imperialist powers sent advisers to China to influence the decisions of the Chinese Governments. For example, the U.S. Government sent General Joseph W. Stilwell to serve as Jiang Jieshi's (Chiang Kai-Shek) Chief of Staff in 1938, and then urged Jiang to give him command of all Chinese troops.[65] In 1945, it was U.S. foreign policy to persuade the Russians to enter the Pacific War, and to this end the U.S. Government persuaded Jiang to make concessions to the Russians on the Sino-Soviet border.[66]

Thus the mechanisms of political intervention, were complex: at first, in the 19th Century, the imperialist nations used quite direct methods such as extra-territoriality and 'most-favoured-nation' treaty clauses; while latterly, as imperialism changed in the second half of the 20th Century, more indirect methods such as 'foreign aid' and persuasion were employed.

Economic Domination
Earlier in this chapter it was argued that the imperialist powers were interested in China purely for what they could get out of her — the marketing of

commodities, the export of capital, the search for cheap raw materials,and human labour and the migration of the internal contradictions of capitalism. The imposition of military force, cultural influence and political interference were simply the tools for the major goal, the appropriation of China's wealth. In this section, 'economic domination' is used specifically to cover the appropriation of treaty ports, landownership, the narcotics trade, tariffs, indemnities and debts, investments and monetary controls.

Treaty Ports: After the defeat of China in the Opium War (1839-42), treaty ports were established. Rhoads Murphey classified the treaty ports into three levels: the first level consisted of central places and quasi-monopolistic ports for foreign trade for the whole of China, such as Shanghai and Xianggang (Hong Kong); the second level included central places and quasi-monopolistic ports for North, Central, and South China, such as Tianjin, Hankou and Guangzhou (Canton); and the third level consisted of small regional and provincial service centres (such as Changsha, Chongqing and Fuzhou).[67]

In these treaty ports, foreigners had settlements and concessions, and virtually owned the property since they had 99-year leases. Furthermore, they maintained their extra-territorial rights, and thus were able to build factories, banks and firms, and engage in business under their own jurisdiction without interference from the Chinese Governments. Since the Chinese Governments could not control the tariff system at the treaty ports, foreign commodities paid duties only once and were exempt from further payments if re-shipped to other treaty ports.[68] By the end of the 19th Century, these treaty ports became virtual colonial cities in China, monopolizing external trade and machine manufacturing.

Since these colonial pockets had their own autonomous systems independent of the Chinese Governments their very existence undermined Chinese sovereignty. So independent — and arrogant — were the foreigners, they erected a sign saying 'Dogs and Chinese not allowed' in front of parks in Shanghai! Since these treaty ports were also trade and industrial centres in China, the extra-territorial rights harmed the economy of China, as we will see later.

Landownership: Landownership was another means of economic domination by foreign powers. The most common way to acquire lands was through military seizure, and foreign concessions, settlements and leaseholds were all obtained in this way. Afterwards, of course, China was forced to sign treaties and acknowledge the legitimacy of such seizures.

There were foreign concessions and settlements in 16 treaty ports. These were areas in which foreign residents had their own local administration which was financed by local taxes. In Tianjin, Hankou and Guangzhou (Canton), entire areas were leased in perpetuity to imperialist powers, such as the British and French in Guangzhou.[69]

There were also railway and mining concessions to increase the sphere of influence of certain imperialist powers. Before the First World War, Britain held most of the railway and mining concessions and provided, as A. Feuerwerker said, 'the majority of the foreign personnel in the Maritime Customs

Service and the Salt Administration, and accounted for half of the Protestant missionaries.'[70] In this sense, British influence was quite extensive, covering most of China's territories. Japan gained a strong hold in Manchuria when the South Manchurian Railway Concessions were extended to 99 years in 1915.

There was also an international settlement which covered roughly one square mile before 1893, and was extended to 8.35 square miles in 1899. Foreign powers continued to extend this settlement into adjacent areas by building extra-concessional roads, water pipes, electrical lines, etc. By 1925, the area under *de facto* foreign control had been greatly increased.[71]

In addition to concessions and settlements, the foreign powers — Germany, Russia, France and Britain — obtained five leaseholds on territories ceded by China during 1898. For example, Russia obtained a 25-year lease for Liaodong Peninsula, Port Arthur, and Dairen in Southern Manchuria. Germany got a 99-year lease for Jiaozhou Bay in Shandong and surrounding territories. These included a total of 552 square kilometres.

The expansion of the churches is itself an indicator of landownership.[72] Protestant churches increased from 55 in 1885 to 1,223 in 1935 (with 2,261 branches throughout China). Fifty-seven per cent of these churches were owned by the Americans. By 1948, of all the land owned by foreigners in Beijing (Peking), Shanghai, Tianjin, Hankou, Guangzhou (Canton), Qingdao and Harbin, 44.4% belonged to the churches; in these same seven cities, the churches owned 43.2% of all housed owned by foreigners.

The foreign banks also participated enthusiastically in investment in land and houses. A 1936 estimate suggested that foreign banks had invested a total of $132,650,000 (U.S.? Chinese? — the source unfortunately does not specify). Most of these banks were American and British.[73]

During the Sino-Japanese War of 1937-45, some imperialist powers either purchased land in China by bribing local government officials or obtained it through outright robbery. For example, between 1937 and 1940, the Japanese bought 45% of the land in Manchukuo through two Japanese-owned development firms. In Shanghai, 8.4% of the land belonged to the Americans in 1933, but this increased to 20.6% in 1948. A 1946 agreement between the K.M.T. and the U.S. Government arranged for the K.M.T. to buy lands for the Americans with U.S. $35 million 'donated' funds.[75]

Finally, one may investigate the extent to which each country and each social group (governments, missionaries, real estate enterprises, etc.) owned land in China. Although there is no study of the whole of China, the closest estimate is based on a study of land and houses owned by imperialist countries in seven big cities in China: Beijing (Peking), Shanghai, Tianjin, Hankou, Guangzhou (Canton), Qingdao and Harbin.

Table 1.5 illustrates quite clearly that Britain surpassed all other countries in the ownership of lands and houses in the seven cities in China in 1948. Among the British-owned properties, enterprises had most of the share, however, among properties owned by other countries including the U.S. and France), the churches had the most. This suggests that the British enterprises had a long-established history of business in China, much more so than any

Table 1.5
Property Owned by Imperialist Countries in Beijing, Shanghai, Tianjin, Hankou, Guangzhou, Qingdao and Harbin.

	Britain	U.S.A.	France	Others*	Total
I. % owned by each country					
Lands**	42.4	18.8	14.9	23.9	100.0
Houses	37.3	11.8	30.9	20.0	100.0
II. % of lands owned by each social group					
Governments	2.0	2.1	5.2	0.8	2.2
Groups	8.9	2.2	0.5	0.1	4.3
Private	11.9	10.6	9.0	21.9	13.6
Churches***	16.9	53.0	67.4	72.2	44.4
Real Estate	10.6	5.3	6.2	2.8	7.1
Enterprises	49.7	26.8	11.7	2.2	28.4
III. % of houses owned by each social group					
Governments	1.2	3.6	1.2	0.5	1.4
Groups	0.3	5.6	0.1	1.0	0.8
Private	23.0	8.2	4.8	23.0	15.7
Churches	1.0	33.3	82.7	66.0	43.2
Real Estate	48.3	26.5	8.2	9.0	25.4
Enterprises	26.2	22.8	3.0	0.5	13.5

*   'Others' means other capitalist countries. Suburban areas and imperialist army camps are not included.

**   Landownership is calculated in terms of *'mu'* (one *mu* = 0.1647 acre); and houseownership in terms of buildings constructed.

*** 'Churches' includes schools, hospitals and cultural centres sponsored by the churches.

Source: Wu Chengming, *The Investments of Imperialist Countries in Old China,* Beijing: Renmin Chubanshe, 1956, p.69.

other country. And the predominance of church-owned houses and lands suggests that missionaries played an important role in economic domination. *Narcotics:* Another form of economic domination was the narcotics trade, primarily the opium trade, which drained most of China's financial resources. Prior to the opium trade, the Chinese economy was self-sufficient. It had a well-developed internal marketing and production system, as can be seen by the inability of foreign products to penetrate Chinese markets. To balance the trade between Britain and China — Britain was importing Chinese silk and tea in the 19th Century and China was not importing much British-owned Indian cotton or cotton goods – the British introduced opium into China in great quantities. Between 1736 and 1795, the Chinese imported only about 400 chests of opium annually, but from 1796 to 1820 this was raised to roughly 4,000 chests a year.[76] Table 1.6 illustrates the tremendous increase after 1824. By 1870, opium constituted 43% of China's imports and it remained the largest single import item until 1890.[77] After that, the opium imports were second only to imports of cotton manufactured goods. The financial drain created by this trade had enormous implications for China. In the 19 years between 1816 and 1838, Chinese $188,514,393 worth of opium was imported.[78]

Table 1.6
Annual Imports of Opium to China 1795-1838 (in chests)

Periods	Chests
1795-99	4,124
1800-04	3,562
1805-09	4,281
1810-14	4,713
1815-19	4,420
1820-24	7,889
1825-29	12,576
1830-34	20,331
1835-38	35,445

Source: Yan Zhongping, et al., *Selection of Statistical Materials on the History of the Modern Chinese Economy,* Beijing: Kexue Chubanshe, 1955, p.22.

In the 1930s, the Japanese also smuggled narcotics to China on a massive scale, flooding the Chinese markets with heroin made from vast poppy fields in Manchuria. It was through this trade that the Japanese raised funds for their war efforts in the late 1930s.[79]

Indemnities and Loans: Two of the greatest indemnities which the Chinese Government had to pay were the 1895 indemnity of £30 million and the Boxer indemnity of (Chinese ?) $333 million. The Chinese Government borrowed money to pay the 1895 one, which, including interest, amounted to £100 million. As for the Boxer indemnity, the Chinese had to make instalment payments which would have reached, with interest, about (Chinese?) $739 million. (However, part of this debt was reduced after the First World War, then amounting to only $250 million.)[80]

Since 1865, the Chinese Governments had been borrowing money from imperialist powers. Most of the loans were for military purposes, though some were railway loans. (Table 1.7 shows the proportion of these loans over time.) With the exception of 1931-36, military loans far exceeded railway loans,

Table 1.7
Chinese Public Debts 1865-1948 (in U.S. $million)*

| | Military Loans | | Railway Loans | |
	Total	Average per year	Total	Average per year
1865-1902	284.4**	7.5	48.3	1.3
1903-1914	238.3	19.9	205.2	17.1
1915-1930	304.1	19.0	161.5	10.1
1931-1936	35.8	6.0	51.2	8.5
1937-1941	635.9	127.2	18.8	3.8
1942-1949	999.8***	142.8	34.2	4.9
Total	*2,500.3*	*29.8*	*519.2*	*6.2*

*   Except the loans after the Incident of 18 September 1931.
**   Does not include the Boxer Indemnity.
***   Does not include the portion of American 'foreign aid' which was
        classified as 'loans'.

Source: Wu Chengming, *The Investments of Imperialist Countries in Old China,* p.73.

Table 1.8
Chinese Loans from Imperialist Countries, 1902-48 (debts on the year's basis, in U.S. $million)

	1902	1914	1930	1936	1941	1948
Britain	109.4	195.7	162.9	150.1	314.4	318.2
U.S.A.	4.5	7.3	50.8	64.4	223.9	1,008.3*
France	61.0	119.9	102.7	90.0	81.1	71.1
Germany	78.3	127.1	93.6	89.4	93.0	–
Japan	–	37.4	373.3	258.2**	–	–
Italy	–	–	51.5	69.7	–	–
Russia	26.1	45.1	–	–	–	–
Belgium	4.4	18.1	42.3	54.6	113.6	113.6
Holland	–	–	19.1	35.1	17.8	17.8
Denmark	0.6	1.6	0.9	1.7	–	–
Others	–	23.8	–	–	29.1	82.8
Total	*284.3*	*576.0*	*897.1*	*814.1*	*872.9*	*1,611.8*

*   Does not include the portion of foreign aid of the U.S. which was
      classified as 'loans'.
**   Does not include the debt immediately after the Incident of 18
      September 1931.

Source: Wu Chengming, *The Investments of Imperialist Countries in Old China,* p.77.

being on average five times more than the railway loans. This illustrates the extent to which the Chinese Governments borrowed money for military use – a non-productive activity.

In the first half of this century, Britain, Japan, and the U.S. were China's top creditors. The data in Table 1.8 suggest that in the 1900s and 1910s, the Chinese Governments borrowed mainly from Britain, in the 1930s, from Japan; and then, towards the end of the 1940s, from the U.S. To repay these debts, the Chinese Governments allowed the foreign powers to secure revenue from the Maritime Customs and the Salt Administration, and the principal and interest were paid without interruption. Thus, the Chinese Governments lost a main avenue for obtaining revenue for developing the country,

Tariffs: The removal of China's autonomy in the tariff system was both humiliating and economically debilitating. From 1843 to 1930, the imperialist powers imposed their rate of tariff on the Maritime Customs Service. After an initial reduction in tariff after the Treaty of Nanjing (1842) (see Table K in the Appendix), these rates were further reduced from the signing of the Treaty of Tianjin (1858) until the late 1920s. There were some ups and downs in the tariff rates, but they were kept below 5% of the value. Table 1.9 demonstrates this phenomenon of tariff control before 1930.

Table 1.9
Tariff for Imports, 1873-1936

Year	Rates of Imports (%)*
1873	4.9
1883	4.8
1893	3.4
1903	3.3
1911	3.2
1921	3.1
1926	3.8
1927	3.5
1928	3.9
1929	8.5
1930	10.4
1931	14.1
1932	14.5
1933	19.7
1934	25.3
1935	27.2
1936	27.0

* Does not include the rates of importing opium.

Source: Yan Zhongping et al., *Selection of Statistical Materials on the History of the Modern Chinese Economy*, p.61.

The imposition of tariff control worked to the advantage of the imperialist powers, since they could now penetrate and disrupt China's indigenous markets with impunity. In addition, since it had been agreed that the Chinese Customs Service revenue must act as a source of repayment for indemnities and loans, the Customs Service was required to act as a debt-collecting agency for the imperialist powers.

Due to the fact that only a small portion of the customs revenue was available to the Chinese Governments, they did not have enough funds for administration or other expenditures. There is no reliable data on the amount that the Chinese Governments collected before 1912; however, for 1912-27 it is estimated that only about 20% of the total customs revenue went to them. This financial drain formed a vicious circle for China; in order to further economic development or military expenditure, China had to borrow money from foreign powers, and this in turn snowballed into large deficits.

Foreign Investment: Corresponding to the monopoly stage of capitalist development in Western countries, in which the export of capital was the dominant form of expansion, foreign investment in China began to be noticeable around the turn of this century. Table 1.10 shows that while the key investor in the 1900s was Russia, Britain had taken its place by the 1910s, Japan in the 1930s and 1940s, and the U.S. in the late 1940s. If we include

Table 1.10
Foreign Investment in China, 1902-48 (U.S. $billion)

	1902	1914	1930	1936	1941	1948
Britain	344.1	664.6	1,047.0	1,045.9	1,095.3	1,033.7
U.S.A.	79.4	99.1	285.7	340.5	482.4	1,393.3*
France	211.6	282.5	304.8	311.9	285.1	297.3
Germany	300.7	385.7	174.6	136.4	137.0	—
Japan	53.6	290.9	1,411.6	2,096.4	6,829.0**	—
Russia	450.3	440.2	—	—	—	—
Others	69.6	92.7	263.9	354.3	333.0	374.6
Total	*1,509.3*	*2,255.7*	*3,487.6*	*4,285.4*	*9,161.8*	*3,098.9**

*   U.S. foreign aid not classified as 'loans' is not included in these figures. (The latter amounted to $U.S. 4,709 million.)
**   An estimate based on the peak of Japanese foreign investment in 1944.

Source: Wu Chengming, *The Investments of Imperialist Countries in Old China,* p.45.

foreign aid from the U.S. in our calculation, U.S. capital in China in 1948 constituted 80% of all foreign capital.[81] After the Second World War, Japanese capital constituted only 22.5% of all foreign capital in China.[82]

The export of capital from the imperialist powers to China became an important part of economic exploitation in this century. While in 1914 foreign investment constituted 44.3% of all foreign capital (including indemnities) in China, the percentage increased to 56.7 in 1930, 62.9 in 1936, and 77.2 in 1941.[83]

Foreign investment in China did not even promote industrial development, since the capital was largely used in the trade and transportation sectors. Although investment in the manufacturing sector was increasing, by 1948 it reached only 23.3% of all foreign investment. This phenomenon is shown in Table 1.11.

Table 1.11
Foreign Capital in China, 1914-48 (U.S. $ millions)

	1914		1930		1936*		1948	
	$	%	$	%	$	%	$	%
Finance	6.3	0.6	317.1	16.0	310.2	22.6	143.3	20
Trade	142.1	14.2	555.0	28.1	397.7	29.0	96.0	13
Transportation	338.8	33.9	407.2	20.6	169.3	12.4	68.6	9
Mining	59.1	5.9	151.1	7.6	69.8	5.1	55.3	7
Manufacturing	110.6	11.0	312.2	15.8	281.6	20.6	163.0	23
Utilities	26.6	2.7	119.0	6.0	132.3	9.7	172.4	24
Others	316.8	31.7	115.5	5.9	8.4	0.6	−	
Total	1,000.3	100.7	1,977.1	100.0	1,369.3	100.0	698.6	100

* The capital controlled by Japanese enterprises in northeastern China in 1936 was U.S. $13,242,000,000.

Source: Wu Chengming, *The Investments of Imperialist Countries in Old China*, p.60.

While the figures in Table 1.11 give us a picture of the sectors of foreign investment in China, they cannot reveal the fact that in some industries even a small investment is all that is necessary for a foreign company to dominate the field. In the mining sector, for example, foreign-owned firms controlled 99% of iron ore and 76% of coal in 1920. In the transportation sector, monopolization was much more obvious: foreign-owned firms controlled 83% of the steam tonnage, and 78% of China's main internal waterway (the Yangzi River) in 1920. Their control of railways resulted mainly from loans rather than direct investment: foreigners owned 93% of China's railways in 1911, 98% in 1927 and 91% in 1936.[84]

Although their share in manufacturing industries remained low compared with the trade and transportation sectors, it is obvious that foreign firms concentrated on two kinds of industries: food-processing and tobacco, and textiles. There was also some international division of labour: Britain invested most in the food-processing and tobacco industries; the U.S. in machine-making and ship-building; Japan in the textile industry, and so on (see Table 1.12).

Table 1.12
Foreign Capital in Manufacturing Industries, 1936 (U.S. $thousand)

	Machine-making & Ship-building	Chemical	Pottery	Textile	Food-processing & Tobacco	Leather & Pulp/ Paper	Others
Britain	15,704	6,840	2,330	17,531	58,563	4,382	1,986
U.S.A.	5,523	3,744.	1,399	1,857	4,180	2,150	2,146
France	870	1,029	–	–	1,620	–	–
Japan	5,416	4,448	4,067	113,174	6,113	4,104	2,753
Germany	600	360	60	–	1,145	15	624
Others	3,400	1,100	500	–	700	1,000	129
Total	31,573	17,521	8,356	132,562	72,321	11,651	7,638

Source: Wu Chengming, *The Investments of Imperialist Countries in Old China*, p.63.

The mechanisms through which imperialist powers invested their capital varied, but they can be classified into two main types: (1) establishing firms/corporations in China; and (2) working through 'co-operative' economic development programmes with Chinese Governments. Britain used mainly the first mechanism, as testified by the presence of big corporations such as the Hong Kong Shanghai Banking Corporation, Asiatic Petroleum Co. (North and South China) Ltd., the British American Tobacco Co. (China) Ltd., Imperial Chemical Industries (China) Ltd., Jardine, Matheson, and Co. Ltd., and John Sivire and Sons.[85]

The U.S. used the 'co-operative' mechanism increasingly after the First World War. Instead of working through individual corporations, the U.S. Government actively arranged investments through the U.S. Army Head-quarters and the United Nations. The U.S. Government also made agreements with the Chinese Governments regarding foreign investments under programmes such as U.S.-China 'Economic Co-operation', 'Technological Co-operation', or 'Agricultural Co-operation'. Through these programmes, the U.S. Govern-ment helped its corporations to channel their capital into China or export their commodities to the Chinese markets.[86]

The question of whether these foreign investments helped the economic development of China is answered in Table 1.13, which shows that, although between 1894 and 1937 there was an inflow of U.S. $1,035,200,000, the outflow was greater: U.S. $2,009,100,000 — a net loss of U.S. $973,000,000 in this 44-year period! If we include the repayment of loans, the figure is much higher.

During the Sino-Japanese War and the civil war, this pattern of inflow and

Table 1.13
Chinese Government Revenues and Expenditure on the International Market
(U.S. $ million)

| Periods | Inflow | | | Outflow | | |
	Foreign Invest- ment	Loans	Total	Invest- ment Profit	Repay- ment of Loans (interest & principal)	Total
1894-1901	–	85.1	85.1	–	83.6	83.6
1902-1913	290.7	335.7	626.4	381.6	491.0	872.6
1914-1930	651.3	210.6	861.9	1,229.1	628.0	1,857.1
1931-1937*	93.2	69.5	162.7	398.4	226.0	624.4
Total	1,035.2	700.9	1,736.1	2,009.1	1,428.6	3,437.7

* Northeastern China not included.

Source: Wu Chengming, *The Investments of Imperialist Countries in Old China,* p.91.

outflow of capital changed. As mentioned before, this was due to the fact that the U.S. was interested not only in halting the Japanese advance in China, but also in warding off the Communists' victory. Consequently, large amounts of capital poured into China in the form of foreign aid and United Nations Aid, and hence the inflow exceeded the outflow as witnessed in Table 1.14. But, once again, this inflow of capital did not encourage the industrial development of China since its disposal was determined by the U.S. or the United Nations and earmarked for military expenditure or welfare benefits.

Two more factors hindered the economic development of China. One is the fact that most of the inflow of capital was in the form of 'direct investment' which meant that the imperialist powers were able to control the deployment of this investment to their own benefit. (The proportion of 'direct investment' in the total amount of foreign capital increased from 1914 to 1941: 66.3% in 1914, 72.9% in 1930, 80.5% in 1936, and 90.4% in 1941.[87] The other factor was the uneven concentration of foreign investment in China. Most was invested in big cities. (For example, in 1930, 42.8% of foreign investment was in Shanghai, and 33.9% in northeastern China.) Consequently, economic development was restricted to the urban areas and never touched the country-side.[88]

Combined Economic Effects: Taking all these factors into account — tariff control, payment of indemnities and loans, direct investments, narcotics trade and treaty port privileges — suggests that the economic control of China by foreign powers was almost total. Their combined effect was to deprive China of any benefits from trading, and create a severe financial drain in

Table 1.14
Chinese Government Revenues and Expenditure, 1937-47 (U.S. $ million)

Inflow		Outflow	
Public debts	1,008.5	Repayment of debts	254.1
U.S. loans	550.0	Payment of 'surplus goods'	825.0
U.S. 'rental goods'	1,613.9	Payment for 'surplus goods' transportation fees	30.0
United Nations Aids	569.0	Payment for 'rental goods' transportation fees	10.9
U.S. 'surplus goods'	855.0	Payment for United Nations Aids transportation fees	112.5
		Payment for United Nations Aids	21.4
Total	*4,596.4*	*Total*	*1,253.9*

Source: Wu Chengming: *The Investments of Imperialist Countries in Old China,* pp.92-3.

favour of the imperialist countries. Against this, Hou Chiming, in his book *Foreign Investment and Economic Development in China, 1840-1937,* contends that foreign investment did not really harm China's economy.[89] However, despite the great pains he takes to demonstrate that Chinese firms were actually able to co-exist and even grow rapidly in the context of imperialism, he fails to face up to the fact that Chinese firms were always overshadowed by and were unable to outgrow the foreign ones, and that China was not autonomous in its economic development due to the system of extra-territoriality and war indemnities.

The dependence of the Chinese economy on the imperialist powers was especially apparent in the 1910s. When, between 1917 and 1920, the imperialist powers diverted their attention from China to the First World War and to the reconstruction of post-war Europe, native Chinese industries experienced their greatest growth. However, with the return of imperialist powers to China between 1920 and 1922, native Chinese industries suffered a steep decline.[90] Another sign of the dependency relationship is the negative impact of the U.S. Silver Purchase Act of June 1934 when, in order to stablize its own depressed economy, the U.S. purchased silver from all over the world at a high price. Since China's currency was based on silver, this greatly disrupted the Chinese monetary system. Between July and October 1934, there was a $200 million outflow of Chinese silver. Sixteen foreign banks transferred huge sums of capital, both foreign and Chinese, back to their own countries; and the Japanese smuggled silver out of China in great quantities. The resultant drop in consumer prices and increase in bank interest paved the way for the closure of hundreds and thousands of firms and forced up the unemployment rate.[91]

Conclusion

In this chapter, we have argued that the development of capitalism in European countries, the U.S. and Japan led naturally to the need for overseas markets for the export of commodities and capital as well as for sources of cheap labour power and natural resources. This is part of the development of monopoly capitalism which is based on the premise of the maximization of profits. By the mid-19th Century, the British bourgeoisie had reached the point where they had to export their commodities (especially textile goods) in order to maintain maximum profits, while it was not until the turn of the century that the U.S. and the Japanese bourgeoisie felt the need to export their capital (and commodities). For all of them China was merely one of their 'colonies'.

Gunpowder was the basis of imperialism. Although it was British cannons which opened China to economic exploitation, cultural influence and political intervention by the imperialist powers, military force continued to be used to gain rights and privileges in China and to intimidate the Chinese and their governments.

Missionaries were sent to China to Christianize or 'civilize' the Chinese by indoctrinating them with Western ideas and systems of values. Churches and schools were built and Western literature was translated into Chinese — activities soon to be supplemented with missionary work on social reforms. While professing religious and philanthropic ideals, the missionaries managed to acquire land and houses which constituted a significant proportion of foreign holdings. In addition, their close connections with politicians cast certain doubts on their purely 'cultural' functions.

To secure the rights and privileges gained through warfare and intimidation, the imperialist powers used persuasion, economic blackmail and foreign aid in order to shape the political decisions made by the Chinese Governments. Subtle political manoeuvring was combined with such blatant inroads on Chinese autonomy as the institutionalization of extra-territoriality and the 'most-favoured-nation' clauses in treaties. These two clauses restricted the Chinese Governments' ability to regulate foreigners in China and to limit the damage inflicted upon them by imperialist powers.

After the seizure of the treaty ports and allocation of concessions and settlements, the imperialist countries started buying land and houses, or obtaining leaseholds on them. All these were part of the imperialist powers' attempt to carve out pockets of colonies within China.

The introduction of opium by the British and heroin by the Japanese not only produced the social problem of addiction, but also created an enormous drain on Chinese finances. In addition, the Chinese had to pay an astronomical sum in indemnities and loan interest, mainly through the Maritime Customs Service, leaving the Chinese Government without the capital needed to develop its own country.

By controlling the tariff system until the 1930s, the imperialist powers also prevented the Chinese Governments from controlling the influx of commodities in order to protect its own indigenous market. Since the tariff was itself usually kept at a minimum rate of 5%, Chinea was unable to accumulate capital for development.

While these mechanisms were dominant in the 19th Century, foreign investment became significant in the 20th Century for the exploitation of China. Foreign investment was usually concentrated in the trade and transportation sectors and therefore failed to stimulate any significant industrial growth for China. In addition, it took the form of 'direct investment', and the Chinese Government had little say in its deployment. It produced a constant outflow of capital from China with the exception of the Second World War period, when the inflow of capital primarily from the U.S. was used for military technology or social welfare rather than for economic development.

In their plunder of China, the imperialist powers (mainly Britain, Japan and the U.S.) did not hesitate to use all the mechanisms available to them — military, cultural, political and economic. The process of imperialist conquest was at times disguised but, nevertheless, fatal to the economy and society of China. Slowly but surely, it ate away at the very fabric of traditional China and truncated its development. When we consider that the 19th and 20th Centuries saw China bombarded with wars, political intervention, economic exploitation and cultural harassment it is impossible to conclude that imperialism benefited China. However, to understand the social consequences of Western (and Japanese) imperialism in China, it is important to look at the specific changes in the Chinese economy and the way these affected the life-situations of Chinese women under imperialism. This will be done in the next two chapters.

References

1. Ernest Mandel, *Marxist Economic Theory,* London: Merlin Press, 1971, p.444.
2. Christopher Hill, *The Pelican History of Britain, 1530-1780,* Harmondsworth: Penguin Vol. 2, 1969, p.242.
3. Ibid., pp.146, 247-8.
4. Sima Lieberman, *Europe and the Industrial Revolution,* Cambridge: Schenkman, 1972, pp.68-9.
5. Mandel, *Marxist Economic Theory,* p.137.
6. G.D.H. Cole and Raymond Postgate, *The Common People, 1746-1946,* London: Methuen, 1966, p.139.
7. Lieberman, op. cit., p.89.
8. Cole and Postgate, op. cit., pp.337-38.
9. James O'Connor, 'The Meaning of Economic Imperialism' in Robert I. Rhodes, *Imperialism and Underdevelopment: A Reader,* New York: Monthly Review Press, 1970, p.109.
10. Mandel, op. cit., p.472.
11. R.M. Martin, 'Minute on the British positions and prospects in China' (19 April, 1845, Xianggang) in Rhodes Murphey, *Nineteenth Century*

China: Five Imperialist Perspectives, Ann Arbor: Center for Chinese Studies, University of Michigan, 1972, pp.47-59.

12. Rhodes Murphey, *The Treaty Ports and China's Modernization: What Went Wrong?* Ann Arbor, Center for Chinese Studies, University of Michigan, 1970, p.15.
13. R.M. Martin, op. cit., p.48.
14. G.J. Wolseley, 'War with China' in Franz Schurmann and Orville Schell, *Imperial China,* New York: Vintage, 1967, p.158.
15. Cole and Postgate, op. cit., p.499.
16. Ibid., p.621.
17. M. Weinberg, 'American Economic Development' in V.B. Singh, *Patterns of Economic Development,* New York: Allied Pub., 1970.
18. Mandel, op. cit., p.400; Christopher Tugendhat, *The Multinationals,* Harmondsworth: Penguin, 1976, p.35.
19. Weinberg, op. cit.
20. Mandel, op. cit., p.403.
21. Ibid., p.400.
22. Ibid., p.407.
23. Tugendhat, op. cit., p.45.
24. Weinberg, op. cit.
25. Paul Baran and Paul Sweezy, *Monopoly Capital,* Harmondsworth: Penguin, 1975, pp.215-43.
26. Weinberg, op. cit.
27. Stephen Ambrose, *Rise to Globalism: American Foreign Policy since 1938,* Harmondsworth: Penguin, 1971, pp.86-7.
28. Ibid., p.90.
29. E.H. Norman, 'Early Industrialization' in Jon Livingston et al., *Imperial Japan, 1800-1945,* New York: Pantheon Books, 1973, pp.116-22.
30. P. Banerji, 'Economic Development of Japan' in V.B. Singh, op. cit.
31. John Orchard, 'The Effect of the World War on Industrialization' in Livingston, op. cit.
32. Banerji, op. cit.
33. Ray F. Downs, *Japan: Yesterday and Today,* New York: Bantam Books, 1976, p.117.
34. William Lockwood, 'Trade, Armament, Industrial Expansion, 1930-1938' in Livingston, op. cit, pp.371-78.
35. Mandel, op. cit., p.404.
36. William Lockwood, 'Japan's Economy in Transition' in Livingston, op. cit., pp.336-42.
37. Lockwood, 'Trade, Armament, Industrial Expansion, 1930-1938', op. cit., pp.371-8.
38. Eleanor Hadley, 'The Zaibatsu and the War' in Livingston, op. cit., p.453.
39. Banerji, op. cit.
40. Orchard, op. cit., pp.318-22.
41. Lockwood, 'Trade, Armament, Industrial Expansion, 1930-1938', op. cit., pp.371-8.
42. T.A. Bisson, 'Increase of Zaibatsu Predominance in Wartime Japan' in Livingston, op. cit., p.457.
43. Banerji, op. cit.
44. Marlen Mayo, 'Attitudes towards Asia and the Beginnings of Japanese

Empire' in Livingston, op. cit., pp.212-21.

45. James Crowley, 'Creation of an Empire, 1896-1910' in Livingston, op. cit., pp.225-30.

46. Ibid.

47. Ibid.

48. Franz Schurmann and Orville Schell, op. cit., pp.183-4.

49. V.I. Lenin, *Imperialism, the Highest Stage of Capitalism,* Beijing: Foreign Languages Press, 1970.

50. Mandel, op. cit., p.453.

51. Ibid., p.449.

52. Gwenneth Stokes and John Stokes, *The Extreme East: A Modern History,* London: Longmans, 1971, pp.45-8.

53. A. Feuerwerker, *The Foreign Establishment in China in the Early Twentieth Century,* Ann Arbor: Center for Chinese Studies, University of Michigan, 1976, pp.21-3.

54. Ibid., pp.42-4.

55. Ibid., p.48.

56. It has been estimated that in 1918, 1,188 books, 1,152 pamphlets and 1,066 tracts were published by the Protestant Churches. There was some duplication, especially with respect to hymn books and catechisms. The average annual sales in the three-year period between 1915 and 1918 were 633,746 books and 751,873 pamphlets which included 1,524 titles in religion, 168 in history and geography, 149 each in literature and sociology, 109 in science and 103 in medicine. Cf. Feuerwerker, op. cit., p.56.

57. Ibid., p.49.

58. Ibid., pp.28, 104.

59. Andrew J. Nathan, 'Imperialism's Effects on China', *Bulletin of Concerned Asian Scholars,* Vol. IV, No. iv, 1972, pp.3-8.

60. Feuerwerker, op. cit., pp.5, 18-21.

61. Ibid., pp.18-21.

62. Joseph Esherick, 'Harvard on China' the Apologetics of Imperialism', *Bulletin of Concerned Asian Scholars,* Vol. IV, No.iv, 1972, pp.9-15.

63. Joseph Esherick, *Lost Chance in China,* New York: Vintage Books, 1974, p.xviii.

64. Meng Xianzhang, *Teaching Materials for the History of Chinese Modern Economy (Zhongguo jindai jingji shi jiaocheng),* Shanghai: Zhonghua Shudian, 1951, pp.319-22.

65. Ambrose, op. cit., p.89.

66. Ibid., p.97.

67. Murphey, op. cit., p.50.

68. Feuerwerker, op. cit., p.2.

69. Ibid., pp.2-3.

70. Ibid., p.14.

71. Ibid., pp.3-4.

72. Wu Chengming, *The Investments of Imperialist Powers in Old China (Diguozhuyi zai jiu Zhongguo de touzi),* Beijing: Renmin Chubanshe, 1956, pp.65-8.

73. Ibid., p.66.

74. Ibid., p.68.

75. Meng, op. cit., pp.319-22; Wu, op. cit., p.68.
76. Tsing Ting-fu, 'The English and the Opium Trade' in Schurmann and Schell, op. cit., p.133.
77. Esherick, op. cit., pp.9-16.
78. Yan Zhongping et al., *Selection of Statistical Materials on the History of the Modern China (Zhongguo jindai jingjishi tongji ziliao xuanji)*, Beijing: Kexue Chubanshe, 1955, p.23.
79. Jonathan Marshall, 'Opium and the Politics of Gangsterism in Nationalist China, 1927-1945', *Bulletin of Concerned Asian Scholars,* Vol. VIII, No.iii, 1976, p.41.
80. Nathan, 'Imperialism's Effects on China', pp.3-8.
81. Wu, op. cit., p.3.
82. Ibid., p.60.
83. Ibid.
84. Esherick, op. cit., pp.9-15.
85. Stephen Lyon Endicott, *Diplomacy and Enterprise: British China Policy, 1933-1937,* Vancouver: University of British Colombia Press, 1975.
86. Wu, op. cit., pp.48-51.
87. Ibid., p.55.
88. Ibid., pp.58-9.
89. Hou Chi-ming, *Foreign Investment and Economic Development in China, 1840-1937,* Cambridge Mass. : Harvard University Press, 1965.
90. Esherick, op. cit., pp.9-15.
91. Meng, op. cit., pp.163-4.

2. Imperialism and the Chinese Economy

While Chapter One set out some of the general features of the historical development of imperialism, in the present chapter its devastating consequences for the Chinese economy will be demonstrated by looking in particular at the cotton textile industry. In addition, we will outline the way certain feudalistic elements in China hindered the development of the economy, especially in the agricultural sector. In fact, cotton and agriculture form an important nexus determining the peasant way of life, as textile work was an often vital supplement to the average poor farmer's income.

We shall begin then by looking at the cotton textile industry, both in its handicraft phase and later as a manufacturing industry. In both phases it was a 'women's' industry, and in both phases it was women who were thus particularly hard hit by the effects of imperialism on the Chinese cotton textile industry. However, given the relation between textiles and agriculture, it is also necessary to consider the wider context of the peasant economy.

Finally, this chapter will investigate the role that the K.M.T. Government played in the decline of the Chinese economy, a role consisting essentially of mismanagement in the areas of militarization, famine and inflation.

The Cotton Textile Handicraft Industry

The importance of cotton production in China can be gauged by the fact that by the end of the 16th Century (according to the tribute record of the Ming Dynasty) nearly every prefecture produced cotton cloth. This was due partly to government encouragement and partly to the peasants' need for a supplementary income. In the 17th Century, it was claimed that 'cotton cloth can be found everywhere' and 'weaving looms can be seen in every home'.[1] Cotton handicrafts were particularly concentrated in the Yangzi Valley provinces.[2]

The growth of the cotton textile handicraft industry should not be taken to indicate any advance in technology. Although the Ming and Qing Governments encouraged weaving, they never encouraged the invention of more efficient machines, so the instruments used to spin and weave in China were still very primitive. For example, as late as the 19th Century it was not uncommon to spin without a spinning wheel. A piece of wood about four and a half inches long and one and a half inches thick with a small forked tree-branch cut to form a hook was all that was required. More efficient than this was a stand with an axle and a reel revolving it. This one-spindle spinning wheel could produce one-quarter catty of yarn (that is, 0.33 pounds or 0.15 kilograms) every ten hours if three persons worked simultaneously.

Much faster than this was a multi-spindle spinning wheel although, in the Qing period, it was still limited to three spindles. (Some very skilled workers could work with four spindles.) According to a Japanese study (1899), mentioned by Hommel in *China at Work,* this three-spindle spinning wheel could only produce half a catty of yarn every day.

The most common loom used in China was very similar to the European hand loom and had a warp, which could be guided downward and under a horizontal beam and passed to the front of the loom. With this loom, the most skilled labourer in China could produce ten yards of cloth (one foot wide) in a day. These methods of spinning and weaving were still widely used in the 19th Century.[3]

This low level of technology persisted for centuries in China because there was no economic need to increase productivity for markets. The cotton textile handicraft industry was aimed at the self-sufficiency of peasant families, and its products did not face foreign competition until the 19th Century. The primitive level of the tools of production explain, at least partially, why the Chinese cotton textile handicraft industry could not survive the onslaught of Western (and Japanese) imperialism.

Indigenous Structural Changes

In the Chinese traditional peasant economy, *all the work related to production was done within the family.* This included not only the production of cotton textile goods, but also making the instruments for spinning and weaving, and growing the cotton itself. Family enterprises were quite common throughout the 17th and 18th Centuries. In Jiangsu, Zhejiang, Guangdong, Shandong, Sichuan, Jiangxi and Fujian.[4] Although this mode of production was changing, one can still find evidence of it in Zhejiang in 1869 in the *Return of Trade and Trade Reports.* 'The peasants in Zhejiang grow their own cotton or exchange cotton for their farm products; make their own tools, and gin, bow, spin and weave their own cotton yarn. Except for family members, no one can join in these operations.'[5]

In the 18th Century, however, the self-sufficiency of the peasant economy began to crumble, beginning with the *separation of agriculture and handicraft industry.* Instead of remaining secondary, spinning and weaving became for some people the main occupation, especially for the widows of peasants, who turned to full-time spinning and weaving in order to support their families.[6] Gradually this division of labour became more regular and some people even specialized in *either* spinning *or* weaving, a specialization which was later operative at the level of entire villages and regions. (At the beginning of the 19th Century, for instance, there were villages in Guizhou specializing in one or the other.)[7]

The growing separation of agriculture and the handicraft industry and the attendant specialization at the regional level was inseparable from the commercialization of agricultural and handicraft products. There were some people who 'sold only cotton yarn for living' and some 'women who took cotton yarn to the market in the morning to exchange it for raw cotton'.[8] Cotton handicrafts, at the village and then provincial level, were sold to merchants in exchange for cotton, cash or other products. Even as early as the 18th Century, inter-regional trade of cotton and cotton handicraft goods was very common, and there is evidence that international trade (with Britain and the U.S.) had already begun in the early 19th Century.[9]

As more and more peasants were affected by this commercialization, the merchants gained a greater degree of control over the market, partly by acting as 'bankers' providing high-interest loans to the peasants and handicraft labourers.[10] On the other hand, as early as 1817 guilds were formed to protect the interests of weavers (and tailors).[11] These guilds would determine the quantity, quality and retail prices of the handicrafts and employ apprentices. It is uncertain whether it was the merchants or the guilds who established the handicraft workshops, which by 1833 had already appeared in Guangdong. There were approximately 2,500 workshops employing roughly 50,000 workers, with 20 workers to a workshop on average.[12]

Thus, it is obvious that, even before the arrival of Western capitalism, some rudimentary forms of capitalism were developing in China. These workshops continued to expand, and by the end of the 19th Century there were cotton textile handicraft workshops in Sichuan, Hubei, Fujian and Guangdong.[13]

Between 1760 and 1800 India and China continued to be the world's key providers of textile goods. In 1819, for example, China exported close to 3.5 million pieces of cotton products, while its imports were minimal.[14] However, the acceleration of the industrial revolution in Britain at the beginning of the 18th Century gave her a technological advantage over other countries and created an excess of British cotton textile products. Some of the surplus found its way to China. Between 1775-79 and 1830-33, the importing of British cotton textile commodities rose almost sixfold in monetary value,[15] a trend which is vividly demonstrated in Table L in the Appendix.

As long as the import of British textile goods was still less than the export of Chinese textile goods to Britain, the balance of payments continued to be in China's favour. However, beginning in 1831, the pattern was reversed and this led to a deficit in the Chinese balance of payments.[16]

After the Opium War (1839-42), the English expected that the opening of the treaty ports and the lowering of tariffs would open up a large market for British cotton products. Even though, as Table M demonstrates, exports to China did not increase consistently, this fluctuation did not last long. After the signing of the treaties of 1858-60, China opened additional treaty ports (including three on the Yangzi River). The imperialist powers also gained the right to inland steam navigation in China as well as the use of the Suez Canal in 1869, which lowered shipping costs from Europe. Consequently, Chinese imports of foreign cotton textile goods increased significantly in the 1850s and 1860s.[17]

Between 1871 and 1910, the quantity of yarn imports increased much more drastically than that of cotton piece goods, as is shown in Table 2.1.

Table 2.1
Estimated Yarn and Cloth Consumed in China, 1871-80 and 1901-10

	Cotton Yarn			
	Piculs (dan)* 1871-80	%	Piculs (dan) 1901-10	%
Domestic mills	–	–	1,055,040	17.98
Handicraft	4,644,881	97.9	2,449,715	41.75
Imports	97,451	2.1	2,363,715	40.27
Total	4,742,332	100.0	5,867,755	100.0

	Cotton Cloth			
	Square Yards 1871-1880	%	Square Yards 1901-1910	%
Domestic mills	–	–	24,494,000	0.97
Handicraft	1,532,970,680	80.30	1,849,680,000	73.16
Imports	376,165,000	19.70	654,200,000	25.87
Total	1,909,135,680	100.00	2,528,374,000	100.00

* 1 *picul* = 100 catties; 20 *piculs* = 1 metric ton.

Source: A. Feuerwerker, *The Chinese Economy, ca. 1870-1911*, Ann Arbor: Center for Chinese Studies, University of Michigan, 1969, p.28.

A comparison of the average annual amounts for 1871-80 and 1901-10 shows that the quantity of cotton *yarn* imports increased by 24 times — from 97,451 to 2,363,000 *piculs*. However, the cotton *piece goods* imports did not increase as spectacularly: from 376,165,000 square yards to 654,200,000 square yards — a roughly twofold increase. The statistics on the percentage of imports of cotton goods in the overall consumption of yarn and cloth are much more interesting: both the imports of yarn and cloth had increased during these four decades, but the percentage of imported yarn (40.27) was higher than that of imported cloth (25.87). The alarming fact was that by 1910 foreign yarn constituted almost half the yarn consumed in China, and foreign cotton cloth one-quarter, even though, in terms of the overall picture of foreign imports in 1909-11, foreign yarn constituted only 12.8% of the value of all foreign imports, and foreign cloth 16.7%. What is significant, however, is their specific effect in gradually taking over the market and edging out the indigenous Chinese cotton textile products.

But this pattern of imports did not last forever. As Chinese domestic machine-production began to gain momentum in the 1910s and 1920s (a theme which will be discussed in greater detail later in this chapter), the import of foreign cotton cloth, and particularly cotton yarn, began to drop as a proportion of the overall imports coming into China, as can be seen in Table 2.2.

Table 2.2
Raw Cotton, Cotton Yarn and Cotton Cloth in Annual Foreign Imports, 1871-1947 (%, total worth of imports = 100)

Periods	Cotton Cloth	Cotton Yarn	Raw Cotton
1871-73	30.2	2.8	3.8
1881-83	22.8	5.8	2.1
1891-93	20.5	14.6	0.9
1901-03	19.7	18.6	0.8
1909-11	16.7	12.8	0.6
1919-21	18.4	9.6	2.6
1929-31	10.0	0.7	10.0
1933	4.3	0.3	7.3
1934	2.6	0.3	8.7
1935	2.3	0.2	4.5
1936	1.3	0.2	3.8
1947	0.2	*	18.5

* Less than 0.05.

Source: Yan Zhongping et al., *Selection of Statistical Materials on the History of the Modern Chinese Economy*, Beijing: Kexue Chubanshe, 1955, p.76.

The Erosion of the Cotton Handicraft Industry
As we have noted, the Chinese did not respond enthusiastically to British-made finished cotton products. One of the central reasons is simply that the Chinese were self-sufficient in cloth, as noted by Abbe Hue, who travelled in China in the 1850s: 'European productions will never have a very extensive market in China. . . . As foreign commerce cannot offer them any article of primary necessity . . . nor even of any real utility. . . . China is a country so vast, so rich, so varied that its internal trade alone would suffice abundantly to occupy that part of the nation which can be devoted to mercantile operations.'[18]

This certainly was not encouraging to the British industrialists or merchants who intended to make China a market for their commodities. The Chinese were so resistant to new goods from the West that G.G. Checkland said, 'little was to be hoped for from the attempt to interest the Chinese in a variety of new and untried things'.[19] This resistance on the part of the Chinese was quite rational, given the superiority of Chinese goods. As a British consul said in 1886 about Chinese resistance to British cloth, 'Ask a Chinaman why this is, and he tells you that the poor wear suits of native cotton, because such clothing last three, four, or five times as long as foreign cloth, because it wears less easily, and because it is much warmer in winter. . . .'[20]

However, the decline in prices of foreign goods soon wore down this resistance (see Table N in the Appendix.) While in the 19th Century it was rich craftsmen and merchants in the cities or towns who bought them, by the end of the 19th Century, according to one estimate, '. . . in the treaty ports and the cities and towns of the interior, only 20 or 30% of the people wear native cloth while 70 or 80% wear foreign cloth.'[21]

Taicang (in Jiangsu) had been specializing in cotton handicrafts, but, with the invasion of foreign cotton commodities, 'the sale of Taicang cloth dropped drastically' in the mid-1840s. On 12 July 1947, *The Report from the Select Committee on Commercial Relations With China* commented, 'The white and strong Chinese cloth is more expensive than our [English] products. Due to the substitution of our cloth, their weaving industry is declining.'[22]

One should also consider the differential aspects of cotton cloth production which meant that where Chinese peasants had been producing 'luxurious cotton cloth for the wealthy, the switch to foreign textile goods as prestige symbols resulted in the capture of these traditional 'luxury' markets by foreign goods; consequently, capital flowed into foreign hands in the treaty ports.

To summarize: *the effects of the importation of foreign textile commodities were twofold: first, native yarn was replaced by foreign yarn; and second, native cloth was replaced by foreign cloth.* The mechanism which initiated and accelerated the whole process of undermining the Chinese indigenous cotton textile handicraft industry was the reduction in the price of foreign goods (see Table N in the Appendix). In addition to low-priced imported cotton yarn, China confronted the problem of the reduced import of raw Indian cotton and the increased export of raw Chinese cotton. This was due to the increased domestic consumption of the expanding Indian textile industry and the demand for Chinese cotton by the Japanese textile industry.

The cotton textile handicraft workers in China began to use foreign yarn instead of Chinese cotton for spinning, as is illustrated by the village of Yichang (in Sichuan): formerly reliant on the cotton of the eastern provinces, the weavers of this village came to depend on foreign yarn in the 1890s because, as they put it, 'the price of Indian cotton yarn and that of (native) raw cotton is more or less the same. Therefore it is more expensive to purchase Chinese cotton and spin yarn than to use foreign yarn.'[23] The effects of such switches to cheap foreign cotton yarn on the Chinese spinning trade may be judged by the case of Wen Changxian (in Hainan) where the whole spinning industry was wiped out between 1882 and 1891.[24]

Further, with more people wearing foreign clothes, the native handicraft industry began to decline. In Taicang, for instance, the sale of clothes was decreasing as early as 1846. 'Recently, foreign clothes have become fashionable. Their prices are one-third of the native ones. Although our village specializes in weaving, one hears that there is no more spinning. The sale of Taicang clothes is half of what it used to be.'[25]

By the end of the 19th Century, the cotton textile handicraft industry in many locations had been destroyed by its inability to compete with foreign goods. It has been estimated that annual employment in spinning fell over 40%, reduced from 5.15 million full-time jobs to 2.9 million. Some argue that many spinners had shifted to weaving, and that home weaving (using cheap imported foreign yarn) provided a significant subsidiary income for the peasants. This may well have been the case for a short period, but the handicraft weavers sooner or later found themselves confronting cheap foreign finished cotton clothes and being drawn into the capitalist system of marketing. In the 1910s and 1920s, there was a boom in cottage weaving, but that ended in the 1930s when the depression reached China.[26]

Even though weaving survived longer than spinning, we find one writer as early as the 19th Century lamenting the collapse of weaving in Dongguan (in Guangdong). 'Sixty years ago, our women lived on spinning and weaving. . . Since foreign yarn was introduced, spinning has declined; and now that foreign clothes prevail, weaving has stopped.'[27]

Even in light of the above information, A. Feuerwerker still maintains that the Chinese indigenous textile handicraft industry as a whole 'was not seriously undermined [by foreign capitalism] between 1870-1911'.[28] In supporting his argument, he notes that in the middle of the 1930s, '61 per cent of the cotton cloth produced in China was woven by handicraft methods. In 1933, the output of handicraft accounted for an estimated 68 per cent of the total value of industrial output.'

Although these figures suggest that the indigenous handicraft industry in China was still doing reasonably well even after almost one century of imperialism, conversely they also show the slow progress of Chinese industrial development even after one century of Western contact! Has it occurred to Feuerwerker that *in spite of* the undermining of the handicraft industry by cheap foreign goods, the Chinese clung to the *traditional* handicraft forms for lack of any other viable means of subsidizing farm income in order to survive? Has it occurred to him that the imperialist powers had no intention of industrializing China to the extent that it would compete with them? These questions should be asked when interpreting Feuerwerker's statistics.

Imperialism and the Chinese Route to Industrialization

In response to the invasion by foreign goods and the consequent deterioration of the indigenous handicraft industry, the Manchu Government instituted a policy of restoring the traditional handicraft industry by establishing schools to train handicraft workers and building handicraft workshops (in some cases, these two institutions overlapped). The reasons behind this Manchu policy appear to have changed, from the 1910s, when a desire to 'catch up' with the West[29] could be pushed through an emphasis on training women to be independent contributors in raising the Chinese economic level,[30] to the more defensive strategy of the depression. As the economy worsened in the 1930s, the Chinese Government advocated the revival of the traditional handicraft industry in the home so as to reduce the unemployment rate.[31]

Data on these 'schools' and 'workshops' are not easily available. Given that the cottage handicraft industry had been declining and that the local merchants had instituted some form of 'putting-out' system for the spinners and weavers, it seems reasonable to see the 'workshop' system as a logical step in the development of classical capitalism. Handicraft workshops emerged as early as the first half of the 19th Century, and by the end of the century they had mushroomed. These workshops varied in size in terms of the capital invested and the number of workers. Table 2.3 is drawn from a sample of such workshops.

Table 2.3
Capital, Looms and Workshops in 142 Handicraft Weaving Workshops, 1899-1913

	Number of Workshops	Total	Average	Largest	Smallest
Capital (Chinese $)	67	660,220	9,854	70,000	200
No. of looms	37	3,307	89	360	12
No. of workers	96	14,972	156	1,264	5

Source: A. Feuerwerker, *The Chinese Economy, ca. 1870-1911*, p.25.

Besides encouraging these 'schools' and 'workshops' in the cotton textile handicraft industry, China did make some attempts to modernize. Although the Chinese Government had concentrated its activity in military industries such as ship-building, machine-making and arsenals, etc. between 1862 and 1881, it thereafter shifted its attention to certain consumer goods industries, such as textiles. The first cotton textile manufacturing firm was built in 1890, and 25 more were founded before 1910.[32] Most of these firms were started in Shanghai, using the money of the official gentry.[33] However, the overall number of factories in China was small, and even in Shanghai the number of factories between 1890 and 1910 only went from one to seven. A survey of six cities (Shanghai, Qingdao, Wuhan, Tianjin, Wuxi and Nantong) shows that the number of spindles increased from 35,000 (1890) to 497,448 (1920) — a 14-fold increase.[34]

After the formation of the Republic (1911-12), there was an increase in the number of spindles in these six big cities, rising from 497,448 (1920) to 2,746,392 (1937) — an almost sixfold increase.[35] In Shanghai alone, the number of factories jumped from seven (1911) to 31 (1936) and the number of spindles from 165,696 (1911) to 1,105,408 (1936).[36]

Yet the growth rate for the period 1890-1910 was higher than that of 1911-36, the acceleration in growth between 1914-22 declining after 1922. Once having consolidated power, the K.M.T. did not seem interested in promoting economic development, and the loss of the Manchurian market after 1931 caused the cotton textile industry to deteriorate further.

During the Sino-Japanese War (1937-45), the textile industry suffered: sixty out of 96 Chinese-owned cotton textile factories were bombed, resulting in a loss of 1,800,000 spindles and 18,000 looms.[37] With the relocation of the textile industry, the combination of the shortage of raw materials, the inefficient transportation system, low morale in production and inflation resulted in a decline in the number of new firms and a decrease in output. A comparison of the output of cotton yarn in the K.M.T.-controlled region between 1933 and 1946 will illustrate the point (see Table 2.4).

Table 2.4
Output of Cotton Yarn in the K.M.T.-Controlled Region, 1933 and 1938-46*

Year	Bags ('000)	Index
1933	1,617	100
1938	25	1
1939	27	2
1940	30	2
1941	112	7
1942	114	7
1943	117	7
1944	115	7
1945	69	4
1946	1,543	95

* Foreign-owned textile industries not included.

Source: Yan Zhongping et al., *Selection of Statistical Materials on the History of the Modern Chinese Economy*, pp.100-01.

After the Sino-Japanese War, a complete breakdown of the cotton textile industry in China occurred as the K.M.T. failed to make plans to take over Japanese industry and restore industrial output.[38]

Features of the Cotton Textile Industry
Capital Investment: Between 1890 and 1910, the largest Chinese-owned factory had only Chinese $1,342,700 in capital.[39] On average, just before the Sino-Japanese War (1937-45), Chinese-owned factories had roughly Chinese $1,500,000.[40] Thus, in general, the factories were founded on a low level of capital.

Location: Most of these factories were located in the coastal regions, in particular in the treaty port cities, and after 1931, in Manchuria. (This applied to the foreign-owned factories as well.) For example, 77% of the cotton textile factories were found in Shanghai, Tainjin and Qingdao. This is in fact a feature of the modern industrial sector as a whole: in 1932, 61% of the factories were founded in Jiangsu; and of the 468 non-mining enterprises founded in the late 1910s and 1920s, 239 were located in treaty port cities and 229 in other areas.[41]

Ownership: A remarkable feature of the Chinese-owned factories is the large number of government officials who owned them. It has been noted that the proportion of gentry funding industries was quite heavy before 1911: while this phenomenon subsided in the 1910s and 1920s, on the eve of the Sino-Japanese War (1937-45), the number of K.M.T.-owned firms began to increase. For example, at the end of 1935, capital for all the Chinese-owned firms amounted to Chinese $250,844,098 of which Chinese $30,199,929 (that is, 11%) belonged to the K.M.T. However, only six years later, in 1941, with the exception of military industry, the K.M.T. owned 50% of Chinese industrial capital (Chinese $8 million out of $16 million).[42]

In the cotton textile industry, the K.M.T.-owned Chinese Textile Development Company *(Zhongguo Fangzhi Jianshe Gongsi)* is an excellent example of monopoly. After 1945, it had 64 factories with 2,116,000 spindles and 39,427 looms, which constituted 40% of all Chinese-owned spindles and 60% of the Chinese looms.[43]

Rate of Exploitation: Chinese-owned textile factories were characterized by high rates of exploitation and profit, as indicated by Table O in the Appendix.

Modernization: We have seen the feeble attempts on the part of the Chinese to modernize the cotton textile industry from 1890 onwards. Although there were some improvements, especially in the 1900s and in 1914-22, after that the Chinese-owned industries as a whole went downhill, as indicated by the declining capital in the Chinese-owned firms (Table 2.5). As Table 2.4 suggests, the output during the war actually worsened. To understand this phenomenon, we have to look at the investments of the imperialist powers in China during this period.

Foreign Interests in the Chinese Economy

Although in a strict legal sense, imperialist powers were not allowed to establish manufacturing firms, they nevertheless existed in foreign concessions (such as Shanghai) and other treaty ports. The Government knew this but could not do much. By 1894, there were already 88 foreign-owned industries with capital of Chinese $19,724,000.[44] Most of these were, however, light manufacturers or processed trading products.[45] There was only one firm which dealt with cotton textiles – the Shanghai Cotton Rolling Factory *(Shanghai Yahua Chang)*. It was founded in Shanghai in 1888 (but closed in 1902) by the joint efforts of the Japanese, British, Americans and Germans.[46]

Table 2.5
Decline of Chinese-Owned Industries, 1928-34 (1928 = 100)

	Factories		Capital Registered		Average Capital per Factory	
Years	No.	Index	Chinese $ (in '000)	Index	Chinese $ (in '000)	Index
1928	250	100.0	117,843	100.0	471	100.0
1929	180	72.0	64,023	54.3	356	75.6
1930	119	47.6	44,947	38.1	378	80.3
1931	113	45.2	27,691	23.5	245	52.0
1932	87	34.8	14,585	12.4	168	35.7
1933	153	61.2	24,399	20.7	159	33.8
1934*	82	32.8	17,810	15.7	217	46.1

* January-June only.

Source: Wu Chengming, *The Investments of Imperialist Countries in Old China,* Beijing: Renmin Chubanshe, 1956, p.113.

With the Treaty of Shimonoseki (1895), foreign industry in the treaty ports was legalized. Immediately following the treaty, one U.S. and three British textile factories were established. Between 1895 and 1913, at least 136 additional foreign-owned industrial enterprises were formed, including 40 joint Sino-foreign firms which, 'for all practical purposes were under foreign control'.[47]

In 1890, the imperialist powers also began to invest in Chinese-owned cotton textile factories, but most of the investment was done in the 1920s. Between 1890 and 1932, the Japanese invested in 11, the British in six, and the Americans in two Chinese-owned factories. The major part of the investment took the form of loans, and when the Chinese could not pay back the principal and interest, some of these factories were sold to the investors.[48]

Another method of gaining control over Chinese-owned factories was the use of mergers. Between 1897 and 1936, mostly in the 1920s and 1930s,[49] at least 22 Chinese-owned factories merged with foreign firms and were eventually entirely owned by foreigners (mainly Japanese, followed by the British and the Americans). Even more straightforward was the simple seizure of property. This was done mainly by the Japanese between 1936 and 1938, when at least 56 Chinese factories were taken over.[50]

The respective strengths of the Chinese- and foreign-owned cotton textile factories can be seen by a comparison of their numbers of spindles and looms. (Table P in the Appendix illustrates the changing pattern of ownership.). The overall pattern indicated is that the foreign-owned spindles had risen in number from one-third (in the 1890s, 1900s and 1910s) to two-fifths (in 1920, 1925, 1930 and 1935) of the total spindles in China. As for looms, while before 1913 foreigners did not possess any, after that, they acquired almost half of the total number. By the mid-1920s, the foreign-owned spinning and weaving industries had also begun to expand.

Of the foreign-owned cotton textile industries, it was the British who had the most spindles and looms before the 1920s, but in the 1920s to 1940s, the Japanese surpassed them. Spindles in Japanese-owned factories increased from 20.6% in 1915 to 44.1% in 1936 of all the spindles in China; British spindles dropped from 23.1% in 1915 to 4.1% in 1936. Similarly, Japanese looms increased from 30.4% in 1915 to 49.5% in 1936 of all the looms in China; while the British declined from 20.2% in 1915 to 6.9% in 1936. The same pattern may be found in the number of Japanese and British factories (see Table Q in the Appendix).

One reason for the Chinese-owned factories' inability to compete with the foreign ones was the high capital investment of the foreign firms. The average capital of a British firm in Shanghai in 1936 was Chinese $3,020,000, and that of an American firm Chinese $1,340,000, and of a Japanese one $1,060,000. Chinese firms (with 30 workers or more) usually had only Chinese $140,000 – seven times less than the Japanese, ten times less than the American, and 21.5 times less than the British! [51]

Due to their greater capital investment and more advanced technology, the foreign firms could manage a higher productivity than the Chinese firms. In 1919 foreign factories spun, on average, five to seven times more than Chinese ones. It is not surprising, therefore, that the foreign firms had higher rates of profit. A study of 18 Chinese and 10 foreign cotton mills between 1905 and 1937 shows that, on average, the rate of profit for the Chinese firms was 14.4%, while that of their foreign counterparts was 24.8%.[52]

One of the basic causes of this 'imperfect competition' between the Chinese and foreign firms was the imperialist powers' control of the economic and political autonomy of China, beginning in the 19th Century and using the method documented in Chapter One. Especially important for the present argument were tariff-control, navigation rights, rights of railway construction, mining rights, and indemnity or loan repayments. These not only drained China's financial resources, but also stopped China from accumulating capital for economic development. The U.S. Silver Purchase Act of June 1934 on Chinese cotton mills was an effective instrument, since the drainage of silver out of the country deprived the small Chinese firms of the necessary funds to keep going. As a result, there was a work-stoppage for 7.55 weeks (in 1934) which increased to 12.31 weeks (in 1935). However, for the Japanese firms in China in the same period there was only 0.32 weeks of work stoppage (in 1934) and 0.36 (in 1935). This suggests that the foreign firms in China were much less hard-hit by the outflow of silver.[53]

Thus the fundamental cause of China's inability to compete with foreign powers and its failure to industrialize was the imperialist domination of China's trade. Imports of cheap cotton yarn and cloth from foreign countries, especially Britain, ruined the traditional Chinese handicraft industry to the point of no return. When China finally attempted to industrialize its textile industry there were few marketing opportunities. In the 20th Century, Chinese exports shifted from tea and silk to more diversified commodities; but these commodities were largely extractive rather than manufactured. Between 1913 and 1936, manufactured or semi-manufactured goods declined from 50.9% to 39.5% of the total value of exports, while beverages, foodstuffs, and raw materials increased from 46.5% to 60.5%. In fact, as Joseph Esherick perceived, '. . . China's foreign trade was increasingly conforming to that pattern so common to underdeveloped nations: she was exporting products the demand for which is relatively inelastic and likely to fall as manufactured substitutes are developed.'[54]

The direct effects of imperialism on China's economy can be demonstrated by looking at the way in which the Second World War actually benefited China's industrial development. The European powers were busy fighting and trade declined (Table 2.6 shows the decrease in foreign ships coming to China to do business). The Chinese were thus given an opportunity to expand production and Chinese cotton mills increased from 32 (1912) to 54 (1919) and the number of spindles jumped from 831,106 (in 1912) to 1,650,000 (in 1919).[55] As Table P in the Appendix shows, the expansion of Chinese-owned firms in the textile industry continued well into the early 1920s. However, as the imperialist powers recovered from the war's disruption and settled the issue of the 'balance of power' at the Versailles Conference, they returned to China, and predictably, from then onwards, the Chinese cotton textile industry rapidly went downhill.

In sum, China's cotton textile industry was unable to stand up on its own for several reasons: (1) China's economic autonomy had been severely undermined since 1842 and China was financially drained; (2) unequal trade exchange had led to China's dependence on foreign manufactured goods such as cotton textile commodities; (3) the small Chinese-owned firms were unable to compete with the capital-intensive foreign firms which yielded higher productivity and profits; and (4) Chinese firms were incorporated by foreign firms through mergers, loans, investments and seizure. Although Chinese cotton textile factories generally had a higher proportion of spindles and looms than the foreign ones (see Table P in the Appendix), they were still unable to compete with them. The Sino-Japanese War (1937-45) completed the ruin of the feeble Chinese cotton textile industry.

Agriculture Under Imperialism

In the previous pages, we have discussed the relationship between the arrival of imperialism and both the decline of the traditional cotton handicraft industry and the crippling of the emergent cotton manufacturing industry in China. In this section, we will explain how imperialism directly and indirectly affected the development of agriculture in China. This is of profound importance in the understanding of women's movements in China because, of the 450 million people in China, 350 million of them were peasants and half

Table 2.6
Tonnage of Foreign Ships Trading in China, 1913-18

Years	Tonnage of Ships
1913	100.0
1914	105.0
1915	97.1
1916	94.3
1917	93.1
1918	86.0

Source: Meng Xianzhang, *Teaching Materials for the History of Chinese Modern Economy*, Shanghai: Zhonghua Shudian, 1951, p.110.

of these peasants were women. These peasants produced 65% of the national product.[56]

There were three key phenomena in the agricultural system of 20th Century China: (1) concentration of landownership; (2) shrinkage of farm size; and (3) commoditization of agricultural products.

Concentration of Landownership

Statistics regarding landownership in China are inadequate and the degree of concentration of landownership in different areas varies greatly. However, in general, agricultural land was more concentrated in southern and central China where the land was more fertile [57] (see Table R in the Appendix). The percentage of peasants owning their own land also decreased over time. Table 2.7 shows percentages for three locations. A study by the K.M.T. of the proportion of non-tenant peasants owning land in 22 provinces shows that it dropped from 49% (in 1912) to 46% (in 1931) and to 42% (in 1947).[58]

Table 2.7
Decline of Non-Tenant Peasants Owning Land in Three Provinces, 1905-24

Years	Kunshan	Nantong	Xiu Xian
1905	26.0	20.2	59.5
1914	11.7	15.8	42.5
1924	8.3	13.0	44.0

Source: Yan Zhongping, et al., *Selection of Statistical Materials on the History of the Modern Chinese Economy*, p.276.

These tables show the tendency toward the concentration of ownership of land and suggest that the percentage of landless peasants and tenant peasants (who owned the top level of soil and rented the bottom ones from landowners) increased through time. Between 1912 and 1933, 'tenant peasants' increased from 28% to 32% of all peasants.[59] Such an increase suggests that more and more peasants were selling their lands to big landowners.

Another way to look at the change in tenancy in China is to examine the change in the stratification system in the countryside. Table 2.8 illustrates that within a short period of time (1928-33) a higher proportion of peasants became either landowners or poor hired peasants – a sign of class polarization, which is further accentuated if we look at the actual quantities of land owned by these peasants. Although Table 2.9 gives a few examples which show the unequal distribution of land, with the great concentration of land in the hands

Table 2.8
Changes in Social Stratification, 1928-33

Districts	Landowners		Rich Peasants		Middle Peasants		Poor Hired Peasants		Others	
	1928	1933	1928	1933	1928	1933	1928	1933	1928	1933
Weinan (Shaanxi)	1.5	1.4	7.4	6.4	32.9	26.3	55.9	62.7	2.4	3.2
Changshu (Jiangsu)	1.3	1.3	2.0	1.9	28.1	25.3	60.1	65.6	8.5	5.9
Panyu (Guangdong)	2.6	2.9	9.3	8.8	17.3	16.0	49.2	51.6	21.6	20.7

Source: Yan Zhongping et al., *Selection of Statistical Materials on the History of the Modern Chinese Economy,* p.265.

of landowners, it fails to portray the extreme cases. In some places, such as Linhe (in Suiyuan), 90% of the land in 1933 belonged to landowners.[60] Jack Belden once said of the concentration of landownership in Henan, south of the Yellow River, 'one might ride a donkey cart past scores of villages for a whole day and still be on the same family's land'. This was the situation in the 1930s and 1940s.[61]

Concentration of landownership also resulted from the privatization of 'public'lands, which began at the end of the 16th Century, and appears to have accelerated in the late 19th and early 20th Centuries (see Table S in the Appendix). In general, half of the Chinese peasants worked with less than ten *mu* (one *mu* = 0.1647 acre = approximately 7,260 square feet), and three-quarters of them had less than 30 *mu* by 1934.[62] Further, the well-off peasants and landowners tended to occupy land of superior quality. For example in Zanhuang (in Hebei) and Xiyang and Pingshun (in Shaanxi) in 1937, 40% of the landowners and only 12% of the poor peasants owned first-rate land. This inequality in land distribution is summarized by Chow Tsetung: 'It is hardly an exaggeration, however, to say that in the second and third decades of the twentieth century, half of the Chinese peasants were

Table 2.9
Distribution of Land, 1933

Districts	Resident Landowners		Rich Peasants		Middle Peasants		Poor Hire Peasants		Others	
	House-holds	Lands	House-holds	Lands	House-holds	Lands	House-holds	Lands	House-holds	Lands
Suide* (Shaanxi)	1.5	16.9	3.3	22.9	11.4	28.4	79.8	31.8	4.0	—
Changshu (Jiangsu)**	1.3	28.2	1.9	31.3	25.3	17.6	65.6	22.4	5.9	0.5
Panyu (Guangdong)***	2.9	18.6	8.8	38.6	16.0	21.9	51.6	17.2	20.7	3.8

*   includes 4 villages
**   Includes 7 villages
*** includes 10 villages

Source: Yan Zhongping et al., *Selection of Statistical Materials on the History of the Modern Chinese Economy*, pp.270-1.

landless, and that among those who owned land, half of them were poor and middle peasants, holding from one to thirty Chinese acres. (A Chinese acre "mou" [*mu*], is regarded at Shanghai by custom as equivalent to one-sixth of an English acre [7,260 square feet], but it varies throughout China from 3,840 square feet to 9,964 square feet . . .)'[63]

Shrinkage of Farm Size
There was also a tendency for farm size to diminish through time, a decline more pronounced in the north than in central or southern China. Table 2.10 illustrates the decreasing sizes of wheat and rice farms between 1890 and 1933.

Table 2.10
Farm Size, 1890-1933

| Districts | *Average Farm Sizes (shi mu = 0.1647 acres)* | | |
	1890	*1910*	*1933*
Average	20.25	15.90	13.80
Wheat zones	26.55	19.80	16.50
Rice zones	12.15	11.55	10.80

Source: Yan Zhongping et al., *Selection of Statistical Material on the History of the Modern Chinese Economy,* p.286.

Commoditization of Agricultural Products
Besides concentration of landownership and shrinkage in farm size, there was one more important trend in agriculture — the commoditization of agriculture. The self-sufficiency of the peasant economy was gradually broken down by the invasion of foreign goods as well as by the emergence of capitalist relationships in the countryside. Instead of merely supplying and providing for themselves, peasants gradually found themselves dependent on the larger market economy. A study in northern and central-eastern China shows that by the 1930s the average peasant sold about half their produce and bought one-third of their daily necessities from the markets (see Table 2.11).

But the degree of commoditization varied according to the position of the peasants in the stratification system. In general, the wealthier ones *sold* more of their produce to the markets than their poorer counterparts; while poor peasants *bought* more of their daily food and beverages in the markets than the richer ones (see Table 2.12).

The self-sufficiency of the peasant economy was also affected by China's trade with other countries. Silk and tea were the key export items in the 19th Century, constituting 92% of China's exports in 1842, 93.5% in 1868 and 64.5% in 1890. In response to this demand, many peasants shifted their energies from food crops to the cultivation of mulberry trees and tea. However, by the Second World War, silk and tea had almost completely disappeared as items for export, the result of a further shift in farming (occurring in the late

Table 2.11
Commoditization of the Peasant Economy, 1921-25

Districts	Agricultural Produce		Daily Family Necessities	
	Self-use (%)	Sell to Markets (%)	Self-provided (%)	Purchase from Markets (%)
Northern China*	56.5	43.5	73.3	26.7
Central/ Eastern China**	37.2	62.8	58.1	41.9
Average	*47.4*	*52.6*	*65.9*	*34.1*

*   Includes Northern Anhui, Hebei, Henan and Shanxi.
**   Includes Southern Anhui, Zhejiang, Fujian and Jiangsu.

Source: Yan Zhongping et al., *Selection of Statistical Materials on the History of the Modern Chinese Economy*, p.328.

Table 2.12
Dependence of Peasant Households on the Market Economy in Heilongiang, 1922-23

Farm Size of Each Household (in shang)*	% of Produce per 'Shang' for Marketing	Purchased Portion of Food as a % of Total Annual Cost per Person
Below 15	56.9	58.7
15-30	55.5	16.4
30-75	58.2	15.2
Above 75	61.9	6.4

* *Shang:* one *shang* = 15 *mu* in northeastern China and = 3-5 *mu* in north-western China; one *mu* = 0.1647 acre

Source: Yan Zhongping et al., *Selection of Statistical Materials on the History of the Modern Chinese Economy*, p.329.

19th and early 20th Centuries) to cash crops, involving a 'progressive substitution of corn, sweet potatoes, and sesame for barley, kaoliang and millet as food crops'.[64] Also important was cotton for the expanding textile industry in Shanghai and Tainjin.

In the last decades of the 19th Century, the domestic growing of opium was definitely on the rise. Until the 1880s opium had been the largest single import item to China in terms of monetary value, when £13 million of foreign opium were consumed every year. By 1900, however, Chinese domestic production of opium had surpassed foreign production.

With the continued increase in the number of Chinese who smoked opium, demand also increased, despite the Chinese Government's campaign against it in 1906. The proportion of opium-smokers remained high — more than one-third of the Chinese smoked at least occasionally — and by 1928, 90% of adult males smoked and 'many babies were born as addicts, having acquired their habits in the wombs of addicted mothers'.[65] It is hardly surprising that the peasants began to adopt it as the main crop; by 1923, China produced 30 million pounds of opium a year. It became the top opium-grower in the world as India produced only 2 million pounds a year, and the rest of the Far East and Near East only 1.15 million.[66]

Thus, at the end of the 19th Century and the beginning of the 20th Century, peasants shifted their cultivation from superior food crops to inferior ones, and from food crops to cash crops. This shift is very important for the understanding of the famines which occurred frequently in China in this century.

Concentrated landownership, diminishing farm size and the commoditization of the peasant economy have been explained in a variety of ways, but one of the commonest explanations is the thesis of overpopulation (see Table 2.13).

Table 2.13
Index Numbers of Change in Rural Population and Area of Farm Land,
1873-1933 (1873 = 100)

Years	Population	Farm Land
1873	100	100
1893	108	101
1913	117	101
1933	131	101

Source: A. Feuerwerker: *The Chinese Economy, ca. 1870-1911,* pp.4-5.

In the context of partible inheritance — equal division of land among sons after the head of the family is dead — the relative increase in available farm land (see Table 2.13), although slight in terms of index numbers, was accompanied by a much greater increase in population. Not only were farms thus subject to increasing parcellization, they 'tended to be broken up into several non-adjacent parcels', and 'considerable land was wasted in boundary strips'.[67]

As the argument goes, these small parcels of land were not conducive to an efficient system of irrigation and thus impeded one of the most significant means of raising productivity. Consequently, in times of drought and floods, the peasants on these small pieces of land found themselves near bare subsistence level, in turn forcing them to become much less self-sufficient and to enter the market economy — selling their produce in exchange for daily necessities or selling their lands to richer peasants or landowners.

Even in its brief presentation here, we can see that this argument puts forward an essentially non-social (ecological/demographic) cause for the deterioration of the peasant economy and the unequal distribution of land. What it *fails* to take into account are *social* factors such as loan-sharking, rent increases, price-manipulation, etc., mechanisms of exploitation whose effects were exacerbated by the context of imperialism.

Mechanisms of Exploitation

With the opening of treaty ports and the rise of commercial activities in the coastal regions after 1842, there emerged in China a new breed of merchants and entrepreneurs who benefited from contact with government officials and acted as investors 'of new opportunities for profit offered by foreign innovation in the steamships, mining, banking, and factory production in the treaty ports'.[68] These entrepreneurs, compradors and local merchants were later joined by the new merchants and industrialists at the end of the 19th Century. The growth of this new group in the 20th Century is shown in Table T in the Appendix.

In some hinterland provinces, the rise of these merchants was even more remarkable. In Shanxi, for example, there were only 20 Chambers of Commerce and 4,220 members in 1912, but by 1918, they had grown to 104 and 7,878 respectively; and in Shandong, while there were 47 Chambers of Commerce with a membership of 6,043 in 1912, by 1918 these numbers had risen to 101 and 14,160 respectively.[69]

After 1930, a new brand of bourgeoisie combining officialdom and business emerged in China, consisting of the senior and junior government officials who owned a growing share of the commercial and industrial sectors. The greatest ones were the Four Families — Jiang Jieshi, Kong Xiangxi, Song Ziwer and Chen Guofu and Chen Lifu — who owned more than 70% of the national productive capital.[70]

Rent: This new bourgeoisie, be they compradors in the treaty ports or indigenous industrialists or bureaucrat-capitalists, were all interested in investing profits in land, as is shown by the increase in absentee landownership after 1842. They entrusted their lands and tenants to the landlord 'bursary', usually members of the local gentry who were able to exercise political muscle when collecting rents and taxes in return for a share. In times of high taxes (such as during wartime), landlord bursary owners squeezed even more from the tenants. The rise in bursary income from rents between 1905 and 1917 suggests that the local gentry was able to pass much of the burden of increased taxation to their tenants.[71]

The linkages between landowners and bourgeoisie may also be seen in Table 2.14 which documents the occupations of big landlords in Jiangsu in 1930. The category 'military and political officers' requires some comment. It is unclear whether these officers also engaged in business, but they did have an increasing share of landownership, especially during the Sino-Japanese War (1937-45). Studies of Jiangsu in this area are not available, but a study of Guanyang in Guangxi shows that they bought close to 70% of the land on the market, while the rest was purchased by the old feudal landowners and rich peasants in 1939-46. [72]

Table 2.14
Occupations of Big Landlords in Jiangsu, 1930

Districts	Military and Political Officers (%)	Loansharks (%)	Businessmen (%)	Industrialists (%)
Southern Jiangsu	27.3	42.9	22.4	7.4
Northern Jiangsu	57.3	28.2	14.5	—

Source: Yan Zhongping et al., *Selection of Statistical Materials on the History of the Modern Chinese Economy*, p.264.

These landlords — working alone or through the local elite — employed a variety of forms of rent payment. One of the most common was fixed rate rent-in-kind (*ding'e shiwu dizu*) which required the tenants to hand over a definite amount of their harvest, irrespective of 'good' or 'bad' harvests. There were, of course, regional variations in rent-in-kind, but in general, it was roughly 40% of the harvest. Table 2.15 documents the range of these rents in different regions.

Table 2.15
Fixed Rate Rent-in-Kind in Three Regions, 1934.

Districts	% of Rents in Total Value of Production Lowest	Highest
Yangzi River	38.64	44.86
Pearl River	39.34	44.20
Yellow River	43.89	51.15

Source: Yan Zhongping et al., *Selection of Statistical Materials on the History of the Modern Chinese Economy*, p.303.

Another kind of rent, rent-in-cash, in 1934, accounted for roughly 21.2% of the value of the land in 22 provinces in China. But this figure obscures the wide range of rents charged. Among these 22 provinces, Hubei had the highest rent-in-cash (52.3%) and Guangxi had the lowest (6.3%). [73]

It appears that, towards the end of the 1940s — just before the establishment of the People's Republic of China — rents had been increasing at rates higher than the prices of produce. (Table 2.16 documents these relative rates in Sichuan.)

Galloping rent increases certainly imposed a burden on peasants who had to pay rent-in-kind. On the eve of the Land Reform Movement of China (1948-50), most of the surveyed locations in seven provinces had rent-in-kind exceeding more than half of their production. At that time rent-in-kind ranged from 33.3% (in Macheng of Hubei) to 96% (in Shaxian of Fujian).[74]

Table 2.16
Index Numbers of Prices of Produce and Rents in Sichuan, 1937-42
(1937 = 100)

Years	Prices of Produce	Rents
1937	100	100
1938	130	140
1939	275	330
1940	900	1,125
1941	2,750	3,000
1942	4,000	4,500

Source: Meng Xianzhang, *Teaching Materials for the History of Chinese Modern Economy*, p.229.

There was a third kind of rent called rent-in-labour. Peasants usually had three alternatives: (1) they worked for a fixed number of days without pay; (2) they worked for an unlimited number of days without pay; or (3) they worked for an unlimited number of days with an undetermined wage. In general, the second was the most common in the 1930s.[75] Where the first option was taken, the fixed number of days was usually 10-12 days. But it could be as low as one day (as in Laiyuan of Hebei) or as high as 60 days (as in Baoshan of Jiangsu).

Other kinds of rent included forms of service to the landlord, which varied in different parts of China. Sometimes landlords required the tenants to pay rent-in-advance one year ahead,[76] or made them and their families perform household chores, transport goods, repair houses, deliver mail and so on. The tenants were also expected to give gifts (such as fish, chickens, noodles, moon-cakes) to the landlords during the festivals of New Year, and the Mid-Autumn, etc. All these 'extras', of course, were of maximum advantage to the landlords.[77]

As rent-in-kind was quite common in China, it is important to point out that the landlords and bourgeoisie exploited the peasant tenants even further by instituting a variety of measures which may be crudely labelled 'price-adjustments'. This involved lowering the prices of the products peasants sold, while raising the prices of the basic necessities which they had to buy. In some cases, it also meant seasonal adjustments, lowering the prices of agricultural produce during the harvest season and raising the prices of the same products between harvests. Using cotton and rice as well as salt, vegetable cakes and fuels as examples, Table 2.17 shows that from 1907 to 1932 the rate of increase for the commodities that peasants purchased was higher than the rate of increase for those which they sold. Vegetable cakes had the highest rate of increase and rice crops the lowest. There is evidence to show that this imbalance in price increase was even more severe in other parts of China.[78] The seasonal adjustment of prices of agricultural produce by merchants and landlords sometimes even meant that peasants had to buy back some of the produce for their own needs. (Table U in the Appendix shows the variations in prices for several essential products in 1936.)

Table 2.17
Changing Price Index of Commodities in Nancheng (in Jiangxi), 1907-32
(1926 = 100)

| | Price Indices of Commodities Sold by Peasants | | Price Indices of Commodities Purchased by Peasants | | |
| | | | | | |
Years	Raw Cotton	Rice Crops	Salt	Vegetable Cakes	Fuels
1907	16	24	17	6	16
1912	23	26	35	15	11
1917	40	31	35	25	28
1922	50	52	52	39	53
1927	100	107	148	118	139
1932	113	141	178	145	165

Source: Yan Zhongping et al., *Selection of Statistical Materials on the History of the Modern Chinese Economy*, p.337.

The transport of agricultural produce from the farms to the marketplace was another point of exploitation as the middlemen (merchants and local entrepreneurs) extracted a certain amount of profit and consequently the price paid by consumers was higher than what the peasant producers actually received (see Table 2.18).

Loan-sharking: As well as oppressive rent structures and the manipulation of prices, the landlords and bourgeoisie (money-lenders, usurers, bankers, merchants, etc.) involved the peasants in high-interest loans to pay off their debts. There were two main kinds of private loans: cash loans, and loans-in-kind, including the pre-harvest sale.[79] (There was, of course, great variation in these loan services.[80])

The interest rate for these loans was unusually high, usually 85% for 'loans-in-kind' and 20 to 40% for 'loans-in-cash'. (Two-thirds of the loans-in-cash' paid 20-40% interest rate, slightly over two-fifths paid over 40% and about one-tenth paid less than 20%). The reason why interest rates for loans-in-kind were much higher than those for loans-in-cash was simply that those

Table 2.18
Proportion of Prices of Marketed Commodities Received by Peasants,
1926-35

Commodities	Areas of Production	Terminal Markets	% of Market Prices Received by the Producers	Dates of Data
Raw Cotton	Donglin	Tianjin	64.7	1926
Tobacco leaves	Shangcheng	Shanghai	69.7	1933
Rice	Linchuan	Shanghai	49.6	1935
Dry cocoons	Jiaxing	Shanghai	72.0	1935 (June)
Rice	Changxing	Hangzhou	74.4	1934-36
Rice	Wuyi	Ningbo	68.5	1932-36
Rice	Shaowu	Fuzhou	53.6	1935 (June-O

Source: Yan Zhongping et al., *Selection of Statistical Materials on the History of the Modern Chinese Economy*, p.335.

Table 2.19
Distribution of Loans among Peasants in Canqsong (in Guangxi), 1934

Strata	Households Borrowing Loans-in-Kind(%)	Households Borrowing Loans-in-Cash (%)	Total
Rich peasants	33.3	66.7	100.0
Middle peasants	50.0	50.0	100.0
Poor peasants	71.6	28.4	100.0
Average	68.8	31.2	100.0

Source: Yan Zhongping et al., *Selection of Statistical Materials on the History of the Modern Chinese Economy*, p.343.

reduced to loans-in-kind were poor peasants with little alternative.[81] (see Table 2.19).

About half of the loan services demanded collateral (property pledged as a guarantee of repayment) and about one-third demanded guarantors; the rest were based on individual promises. Among the poor peasants most loans were based on collateral security.[82]

Most money-lenders demanded that both the loan and the interest be repaid within a year. About 77% of loans were for one year; close to one-tenth were for one to three years; the rest were either for three years and over or for an unspecified period.[83]

During and after the Sino-Japanese War (1937-45), credit was tighter with increased interest rates and shorter repayment periods. In 1938, most (59%) of the loans were for a period of 10 to 12 months, but by 1946 the percentage had dropped to 36. Meanwhile, those for a period of less than three months increased from 9% of all loans (in 1938) to 41% (in 1946). Interest rates increased three to five times during the nine-year period, 1938-46. The interest rate for loans-in-cash based on collateral security jumped from 2.3% per month (in 1938) to 9.4% (in 1946). The interest rate of loans-in-kind increased at a rate similar to those of loans-in-cash, but, seeing they were already more expensive, this meant an enormous total increase. For example, the interest rate for a seven-month loan in 1938 was 39%, but by 1946, it had reached 192%.[84]

In China as a whole, the percentage of households borrowing loans-in-cash (56%) was slightly higher than those borrowing loans-in-kind (48%), Most of those who borrowed were tenant peasants, followed by the semi-tenant peasants and non-tenant peasants,[85] with the poor tenants relying on the more exploitative loans-in-kind. A study done in 1933-44 shows that the majority of debtors were poor peasants, followed by middle and rich peasants (see Table 2.20). The 1944 figures for Sichuan suggest that after the war, the position of the middle peasants deteriorated and they tended to borrow more.

Table 2.20
Distribution of Debtors among Peasants in Four Districts, 1933-44

Districts	Dates of Data	Rich Peasants	Middle Peasants	Poor Peasants	Total
Dingxian (Hebei)	1933	13.0	24.0	63.0	100
Panyu (Guangdon)	1933	11.0	21.6	67.4	100
Cangwu (Guangxi)	1934	1.7	8.7	89.6	100
Sien (Guangxi)	1934	4.6	10.6	84.8	100
Bishan (Sichuan)	1944	4.0	29.2	66.8	100

Source: Yan Zhongping et al., *Selection of Statistical Materials on the History of Modern Chinese Economy*, p.343.

But the trend towards greater debt for an increasing number of peasants began as early as the 1920s. A study in Dingxian (in Hebei) in 1929-31 shows a rapid rise in the number of households in debt and the amount of money borrowed (see Table 2.21).

Most of the loans were borrowed to meet non-productive family needs, the most important of which was food (followed by bridal gifts). A study of loans in four provinces (Henan, Hubei, Anhui and Jiangxi) in 1934-35 suggests that 60.3% of the loans obtained by tenant peasants went on food,

Table 2.21
Changing Pattern of Indebted Peasants in Dingxian (Hebei), 1929-31

| | Households in Debts | | Borrowing Loans | | Loans Borrowed | |
Years	%	Index	Times	Index	Amount	Index
1929	33	100	335	100	$21,026	100
1930	44	135	466	139	$34,401	164
1931	58	178	726	217	$48,944	233

Source: Yan Zhongping, et al., *Selection of Statistical Materials on the History of Modern Chinese Economy*, p.344.

Table 2.22
Sources of Loans for Peasants, 1934

Sources	%
Merchants	25.0
Landlords	24.2
Rich Peasants	18.4
Village Stores	13.1
Pawnshops	8.8
Native Banks	5.5
Cooperatives	2.6
Banks	2.4
Total	*100.0*

Source: Yan Zhongping et al., *Selection of Statistical Materials on the History of Modern Chinese Economy*, p.345.

and even non-tenant peasants used one-quarter of their loans on food. In other words, loans were necessary just for basic survival.[86]

In the 1930s, most of the loans came from merchants and landlords. Table 2.22 gives a breakdown of the sources of loans in 1934 in China as a whole. But this pattern of money-lending changed when China entered the Sino-Japanese War (1937-45). During the first few years of war, merchants, landlords and rich peasants remained the key sources of loans; however, their places were soon taken over by the co-operatives and banks, as demonstrated by Table V in the Appendix. Beginning in the early 1930s, the city banks found they had a surplus of capital which could not be absorbed in the urban areas, and so they turned to the countryside, providing loans under the banner of 'Save the Peasants' and 'Restore the Countryside'. The interest rates were high and when the peasants could not pay back the loan in time, the banks simply took over their lands or their agricultural produce.

To summarize: The dominant patterns in the countryside were the concentration of landownership, shrinking farm sizes and the commoditization of agriculture, all indicating the deterioration of the peasants' status from self-sufficiency to dependency. To understand why such a deterioration occurred, we looked at three mechanisms of exploitation: rents, price-manipulation and loan-sharking, whose combined result was a poorer peasantry, perpetually burdened with debt. Gradually these poor peasants became the tenants or 'serfs' of wealthy landlords and the bourgeoisie.

However, there were other, extra-economic, kinds of oppression. Landlords sometimes forced tenants to sign agreements to provide them with services and to make future generations 'tenants-for-ever'. In some places, landlords tortured their tenants with beatings, whippings, rapes, etc., and robbed them of property such as poultry, pigs, cattle and houses. These extra-economic means of oppression were imposed upon tenants who failed to pay rent or repay a loan.[87]

Kuomintang Mismanagement: Militarization, Famine and Inflation

In the 19th Century and the first half of the 20th Century, a series of structural trends undermined the political sovereignty and economic fabric of Chinese society. We have already examined the impact of imperialism and the subsequent decline of the handicraft industry, the retardation of the modern manufacturing industry and the deterioration in the peasant economy. These phenomena were further exacerbated by mismanagement by the K.M.T., which hastened the collapse of the national economy and the deterioration of the standard of living. Three areas can be pinpointed: militarization, famine and inflation.

Militarization
Between 1911 and 1949, the Chinese Government was preoccupied with militarization, beginning with the Manchu Government's loans from imperialist powers for the purpose of strengthening its armies. During the Taiping Rebellion (1850-64), Manchu armies were used to suppress the dissidents and, towards the end of their regime, the Manchus increasingly resorted to armed force to solve their internal problems. As a result, after 1911, troop movements became much more frequent due to the power struggles among warlords and political parties and the local uprisings of banditry.[88]

The consolidation of power by the K.M.T. in 1927 further accentuated this trend towards militarization. Military expenditure, along with loan and indemnity services, accounted for 67 to 85% of the total expenditure of the K.M.T., leaving little for welfare, education and public works.[89] At this point, military expenditure was based on the K.M.T.'s fear of the Communists, with campaign after campaign launched to suppress and wipe out the C.C.P. and its remnants.

The growing attacks by the Japanese in the 1930s further escalated this process of militarization; conscription was introduced, picking out those from poor families and thus creating much resentment. The K.M.T. slogan, 'Those Who Have Money, Give Money; Those Who Have Strength, Give Strength', summarizes K.M.T. sentiment. The poor, of course, realized the class basis of conscription directly contradicted the democratic ideas of universal military service.[90] They saw that rich people could avoid conscription by making payments, by going to school or by getting minor posts in local governments.[91]

Militarization had other side-effects, such as the looting of peasants' property. The K.M.T. soldiers, underpaid, half-starved and low in morale, would steal and loot wherever and whenever they could. Army discipline was almost nonexistent during the Sino-Japanese War. Contempt for K.M.T. soldiers was reflected in Albert C. Wedemeyer's remarks before the Joint Meeting of State Council and All Ministers of the National Government (22 August 1947): 'Today, after several months of experience with these Central Government armies, the people experience a feeling of hatred and distrust because the officers and enlisted men were arrogant and rude. Also they stole and looted freely. . . .'[92]

The military strategies of the K.M.T. sometimes caused more harm to the indigenous people than the Japanese. On one occasion, the K.M.T.'s strategy resulted in the death of thousands of people and the destruction of a multitude of towns and villages: in June 1938 when the K.M.T. armies were forced to retreat before the advancing Japanese, the K.M.T. sought to halt their progress by demolishing a dam on the Yellow River. The water flooded over 40 townships in Henan, Anhui and Jiangsu, and drowned 2,980,302 persons in Anhui, 325,598 in Henan and 559,900 in Jiangsu. A further 1,860,157 persons were forced to leave as refugees, over 13 million *mu* (one *mu* = 0.1647 acres) of farms were flooded and over one million houses ruined. This tremendous loss of lives and property heaped extra hardship on the heads of the peasants and inflamed their hatred towards the K.M.T.[93]

Famine

Famines were not new to China; between 108 B.C. and A.D. 1911, there were 1,828 famines in China, or one nearly every year in one of the provinces.[94] Famines in the 19th and 20th Centuries, however, became much more frequent and large scale. In 1850, it was reported that 20.22% of villages had a below-normal harvest, but by 1900, over half of the villages in nine provinces had below-normal harvests.[95] There were some great famines, especially in north-west China in 1877-78, 1892-94 and 1900.

Conventional explanations usually attributed them simply to drought and floods,[96] but it seems likely that famines were caused more by imperialism and the K.M.T.'s mismanagement than by natural causes. As we have seen, trade with the imperialist powers after the Opium War turned many of the food cropgrowing lands to the production of cash crops (planting mulberry trees for silkworms, tea and poppy plants for opium). The floods or droughts are undoubtedly important but cannot be isolated from the social context, which also includes the decline of the rural handicraft industry and the exploitative rental and taxation systems, as well as the shift to cash crops.[97]

The famines of the 20th Century are due to two main factors: (1) the spread of opium-growing; (2) the militarization policy of the K.M.T. The greatest famine in this century was the 1919-21 north China famine, described as 'the worst that has ever visited China'. It covered all of Hebei, and large parts of Shandong, Henan, Shanxi and Shaanxi;[97] over 500,000 people died and, at its height, roughly 20 million people were destitute.[98] After many years of below-normal harvests, Shaanxi lost 40% of its population (due to death or migration) by 1928.[99] There were famines in central China in 1925, in Shaanxi in 1928-33, in Sichuan in 1934, and many others which affected more than 16 provinces prior to the onset of the Sino-Japanese War.[100] The 1928 famine alone affected over 30 million people in eight provinces.

The series of events was as follows: high taxation and rent increasingly drove peasants to produce for the market where the prices of food fluctuated beyond their control. When prices fell, they still had to pay taxes and rents, and this forced them to borrow money, even though the interest rates on loans were high. Once in debt, the peasants lost their self-sufficiency and had to resort to cash crop production, devoting vast areas of land to the production of opium, so that, by the turn of this century, China had the dubious virtue of self-sufficiency in opium.

After investigating the famine of Shaanxi in 1928, American Red Cross investigators concluded that it was mainly caused by the cultivation of the poppy. The best land in Shaanxi had been devoted to the production of opium and, consequently, there was a serious shortage of wheat, millet and corn (the staple cereals of the north-west). Similarly, the China International Famine Relief Commission found that land, bought at extremely low prices by landowners during the famine, had been put under irrigation in order to produce poppies rather than food crops. It was observed that 'eight out of every ten mou (*mu*) of land reached by irrigation had come under poppy cultivation'.[101]

Between 1937 and 1949, famines occurred on a regular basis. It has been estimated that 10 to 15 million peasants died of starvation in this period, and it was not uncommon for three or four members of a family of seven to starve to death.[102] As the war proceeded, more and more land and foodstuffs were destroyed. By 1939, over half of the cultivable land was ruined and one-third of the cattle killed. As for food crops, the minimum loss for any area was 19% and the maximum was over 80%. With such a high casualty rate, food had become a serious problem in China.[103] In Henan, for example, the 1942 spring wheat harvest was only about 20% of the normal harvest, and it was not uncommon to see corpses of starving refugees next to the road.[104]

The Japanese should certainly share some responsibility for the famines in China during this period, but the K.M.T. demand that the people feed the soldiers first, combined with their failure to take any positive steps to stimulate production, clearly indicate irresponsibility and mismanagement on the part of the K.M.T. The K.M.T. Government was not interested in feeding the local peasants or refugees. In many districts where the harvest was insufficient to feed both the peasants and the soldiers stationed in these areas, the peasants were just left to die of hunger.[105]   Requirements for 'military grains' were superimposed on the already burdensome taxation and rents of the peasants. The taxation rates were based on a normal harvest, rather than the actual yield for any one year, and thus the poorer the harvest, the larger the proportion taken from the peasants. The peasants were also forced to construct roads, often without pay or food.

Inflation

Inflation is a structural feature of capitalism. In China in the late 1930s, it climbed at a rapid rate and beyond the control of the government, since most of China's wealth lay in Japanese hands; thus the K.M.T. Government was unable to finance the war by selling government bonds or raising taxes.

To cover the cost of the war, the K.M.T. resorted to issuing paper currency,[106] beginning gradually but, towards the end of the war, increasing so rapidly that China had runaway inflation (see Table 2.23).

Table 2.23
Note Issue and Price Index, 1937-48

Year	Note Issue Outstanding (in Chinese $ million)	Price Index (Jan-June 1937 = 100)
1937	2,060	100
1938	2,740	176
1939	4,770	323
1940	8,440	724
1941	15,810	1,980
1942	35,100	6,620
1943	75,400	22,800
1944	189,500	75,500
1945	1,031,900	249,100
1946	3,726,100	627,210
1947	33,188,500	10,340,000
1948	374,762,200	237,700,000

Source: A. Feuerwerker, *The Chinese Economy, 1912-1948,* pp.58-62.

The basic cause of this runaway inflation was the continued fiscal deficit of the K.M.T. Government. With the exceptions of 1938 and 1943, the deficit increased every year. The Government reacted to this by printing more money (see Table 2.24).

Inflation hurt not only the peasants and the working class but also those on fixed incomes, such as school teachers, college professors, government employees and so on. The standard of living naturally deteriorated as purchasing power dropped and, as Table 2.24 shows, the price index after 1937 increased at a galloping rate. From 1944 to 1946, annual price increases

Table 2.24
Wartime Deficits, 1937-45 (in billions of Chinese dollars)

Year	Expenditure	Revenue	Deficit
1937	15	10	5
1938*	9	5	4
1939	19	5	14
1940	46	6	40
1941	107	17	90
1942	283	85	198
1943	362	232	130
1944	1,820	314***	?
1945**	4,987	785***	?

*	July-December only
**	January-August only
***	Taxes only

Source: Meng Xianzhang, *Teaching Materials for the History of Chinese Modern Economy*, p.250.

Table 2.25
Purchasing Power Index, 1937-45

Year	Purchasing Power Index (%)
Dec. 1937	101.72
Dec. 1938	60.97
Dec. 1939	28.13
Dec. 1940	7.85
Dec. 1941	3.65
Dec. 1942	1.28
Dec. 1943	0.47
Dec. 1944	0.17
Dec. 1945	0.04

Source: Meng Xianzhang, *Teaching Materials for the History of Chinese Modern Economy*, pp.255-56.

averaged 300% and, during the postwar period, the price index jumped at an unprecedented rate. Table 2.25 shows the overall decline in purchasing power from 1937 to 1945. For example, the value of a $100 bill declined to only four cents!

This decline in purchasing power can be expressed in another way. On 20 July 1945, the price of rice in Kunming was 8,000 times higher than before the war; cloth was 13,000 times its pre-war price; yarn, 110,000 times; pork 9,000 times; U.S. dollars, 900 times; and gold, 1,000 times. As the editor of *Kunming Weekly (Kuntming Zhoukan)* said, 'The price increases were so fast that it was impossible for the writers' pens and typewriters' fingers, and people's words and thoughts to keep up with them.'[107]

Conclusion

The development of capitalism forced various countries to penetrate China in the 19th and 20th Centuries; this chapter has concentrated on the effects of this penetration on the Chinese economy, in particular the changes which occurred in the cotton textile handicraft and manufacturing industries as well as in the agricultural system. Among the detrimental consequences of foreign domination, we have stressed the way the import of cheap cotton yarn, and later cotton cloth, completely ruined the self-sufficiency of the peasant economy and put the traditional handicraft industry in a disadvantaged position when competing with foreign goods.

The Chinese Governments' lack of success in revitalizing the handicraft industry, and later in industrializing the cotton textile industry, was due to the domination of foreigners over China's sovereignty and economic growth. First of all, foreign goods captured the Chinese indigenous market. Then, due to their low capital investment, Chinese firms and factories were unable to compete with the capital-intensive foreign ones. As a result, the Chinese companies were gradually incorporated into the foreign ones through mergers, investments and seizure of property by physical force. Statistics quoted in this chapter vividly demonstrate that while China's manufacturing industry grew at a rapid rate in the period 1890-1910, it gradually slowed down in 1911-36 and finally collapsed during and after the Sino-Japanese War.

The rise of the bourgeoisie in the cities and treaty ports affected the development of the countryside. Money was invested in lands and, due to the merging of the landlords and the bourgeoisie, landownership became much more concentrated than before. Together, they exploited the peasants through the rental and loan systems as well as through price-adjustments. Once the peasants could not pay their rent or repay loans, they found themselves constantly in debt, and hence in the power of the landlords. Their poverty forced them to grow cash crops rather than food crops, which, in turn, placed them in a dependent position in the market economy.

It is difficult to give an exhaustive account of the deteriorating situation of the peasantry, but undoubtedly both imperialism and the surviving feudal relationships had important effects. The self-sufficiency of the peasant economy broke down in the 19th Century due to capitalist forces which were prevented from carrying through into an indigenous development of capitalism; equally, the import of cheap foreign goods prevented either effective competition or a return to self-sufficiency. The growing number of poor peasants might have been absorbed by modern industries in the cities; but, as a result of imperialist domination, the indigenous manufacturing industries could not compete with the foreign industries or with foreign goods, and so poor peasants had little alternative but to stay in the countryside and struggle with their poverty and debt. No doubt, the mechanisms of exploitation (rents, taxes, loans and price-manipulation), which furthered the deterioration of the peasantry, were aspects of feudalism in China. But exploitation could not have accelerated at such a rapid rate if (1) the economy had not been under the control of foreign powers; (2) Chinese indigenous industry had been allowed to accumulate capital; (3) China had not come under constant military attack or threats of attack (which, in turn, made the Chinese Government increase taxes, which were ultimately passed down to the peasantry or the working class); and (4) there had not been collusion of government officials, the bourgeoisie and landlords in exploiting the masses. Historical facts show that imperialist powers, indigenous capitalists *and* feudal landlords were all interested in sharing the pie. While the latter two played a minor role compared to the imperialist powers, all of them were, of course, responsible for the decline of the Chinese economy.

Given that profit was the common goal of K.M.T. Government officers, the indigenous bourgeoisie and the imperialist powers, the rapid deterioration of the life situation of the peasants and working class is understandable. An examination of militarization, famines and inflation shows that the K.M.T. mismanaged the whole economy: troop movements did not have to disturb the countryside, conscription need not have been undemocratic, the flooding of the peasants' houses and the killing of people had no justification, 'military grain' requirements need not have been imposed and cash crops such as opium need not have been encouraged. This mismanagement occurred at a time when the negative effects of imperialism were being deeply felt by the working class and peasants. One can conclude that the decline of the Chinese economy in the 19th and 20th Centuries was due to the brutal penetration of imperialism aided by the Chinese Governments.

The next chapter describes the human consequences of the impact of these structural forces and how they affected the working class and peasantry, especially the women in these two social groups.

References

1. Yan Zhongping, *A Draft on the History of the Chinese Cotton Textile, 1289-1937,* Beijing: Kexue Xhubanshe, 1963, p.6.
2. A. Feuerwerker, *The Chinese Economy, ca. 1870-1911,* Ann Arbor: University of Michigan, 1969, p.18.
3. Peng Zeyi, *Materials on the Modern Chinese Handicraft Industry, 1840-1949,* Beijing: Zanlian Shuju, Vol. I, 1957, pp.3-10; Yan, op. cit., pp.6-14; R.P. Hommel, *China at Work,* New York: John Day, 1937, pp.165-89.
4. Peng, op. cit., Vol.1, pp.228-34.

5. Yan, op. cit., pp.20-21.
6. Peng, op. cit., Vol. 1, pp.234-8.
7. Yan, op. cit., p.25.
8. Ibid., pp.25-6.
9. Franz Schurmann and Orville Schell, *Imperial China*, New York: Vintage Books, 1967, p.75; Peng, op. cit., Vol. 1, pp.246-49.
10. Fan Baichuan, 'The Experience and Fate of the Chinese Handicraft Industry after the Invasion of Foreign Capitalism, *Historical Research (Lishi Yanjiu)*, Vol. 3, pp.89-90; Peng, op. cit., Vol. 1, pp.239-46.
11. Peng, op. cit., Vol. 1, p.186.
12. Yan, op. cit., p.27.
13. Peng, op. cit., Vol. 2, pp.258-60.
14. Ernest Mandel, *Marxist Economic Theory*, London: Merlin Press, 1971, p.446.
15. Yan Zhongping et al., *Selection of Statistical Materials on the History of Modern China*, Beijing: Kexue Chubanshe, 1955, p.11.
16. Ibid., p.16.
17. Feuerwerker, op. cit., p.21.
18. Rhodes Murphey, *The Treaty Ports and China's Modernization: What Went Wrong?*, Ann Arbor: Center for Chinese Studies, University of Michigan, 1970, p.41.
19. Ibid., p.19.
20. Feuerwerker, op. cit., p.26.
21. Ibid., p.20.
22. Peng, op. cit., Vol. 1, pp.494-5.
23. Yan, op. cit., 1963, p.65.
24. Peng, op. cit., Vol. 2, pp.201-20.
25. Yan, op. cit., 1963, pp.66-7.
26. Frederick Wakeman, 'Rebellion and Revolution: The Study of Popular Movements in China', *Journal of Asian Studies*, Vol. XXXVI, No.2, 1977, p.215.
27. Peng, op. cit., Vol. 2, p.224.
28. Feuerwerker, op. cit., p.17.
29. Tang Caichang, *A Reader of Xiangbao*, Shanghai: Zhonghuo Bianyi Yinshuguan, 1902, Vol. 6, p.24; Vol. 7, pp.3-5; *The Alarming Bell Daily News (Jingzhong ribao)*, 1 March 1904, p.3; 29 April 1904, p.3; 10 May 1904, p.4; 14 May 1904, p.3; 26 May 1904, p.3; 10 June 1904, p.4; 28 September 1904, p.4; 3 November 1904, pp.1, 4; 22 November 1904, p.2; 1 December 1904, pp.2, 3; 2 December 1904, p.3; 21 December 1904, p.4; 8 January 1905, p.4.
30. *The Chinese New Newspaper*, 3 February 1917, p.3.
31. *The Chinese Language Daily Newspaper*, 7 February 1936, section 2, p.2.
32. Yan, op. cit., 1955, pp.98-9.
33. Meng Xianzhang, *Teaching Materials for the History of Modern Chinese Economy*, Shanghai: Zhonghua shuchian, 1951, pp.96-7.
34. Yan, op. cit., 1955, pp.108, 162.
35. Ibid., pp.108-09.
36. Ibid., pp.162-3.
37. Meng, op. cit., p.195.
38. A.Feuerwerker, *The Chinese Economy, 1912-1949*, Ann Arbor: Center

for Chinese Studies, University of Michigan, 1968, pp.19-25.

39. Yan, op. cit., 1955, pp.98-9.
40. Meng, op. cit., pp.181-3.
41. Feuerwerker, op. cit., 1968, pp.13-19; Feuerwerker, op. cit., 1969, pp.33-41.
42. Meng, op. cit., p.237.
43. Wu Chengming, *The Investments of Imperialist Powers in Old China*, Beijing: Renmin chubanshe, 1956, pp.120-8.
44. Yan, op. cit., 1955, pp.116-22. An estimate by Yan shows that there were 101 foreign-owned firms in China before 1894.
45. Feuerwerker, op. cit., 1969, p.32.
46. Yan, op. cit., 1955, p.121.
47. Feuerwerker, op. cit., 1969, p.32.
48. Yan, op. cit., 1955, p.137.
49. Ibid., p.138.
50. Ibid., pp.144-5.
51. Wu, op. cit., pp.112-20.
52. Yan, op. cit., 1955, p.168.
53. Wu, op. cit., pp.112-20.
54. Joseph Esherick, 'Harvard on China: the Apologetics of Imperialism', *Bulletin of Concerned Asian Scholars*, Vol. IV, No. iv, 1972, pp.9-15.
55. Meng, op. cit., p.110.
56. J. Belden, 'The Land Problem' in Schurmann and Schell, *Republican China*, New York: Vintage Books, 1967, p.311; Feuerwerker, op. cit., 1968, p.2.
57. Chow Tse-tung, *The May Fourth Movement*, Cambridge, Mass.: Harvard University Press, 1960, pp.381-3.
58. Yan, op. cit., 1955, p.276. The 22 provinces are: Jiangsu, Zhejiang, Jiangxi, Anhui, Henan, Hubei, Hunan, Sichuan, Yunnan, Guizhou, Fujian, Guangdong, Guangxi, Shaanxi, Hebei, Shandong, Shanxi, Gansu, Suiyuan, Ningxia, Chahaer and Quinghai. (The year 1931 does not include Ningxia.)
59. Chow, op. cit., pp.381-3.
60. Yan, op. cit., 1955, p.272.
61. Belden, op. cit., p.312.
62. Yan, op. cit., 1955, pp.264, 285; Feuerwerker, op. cit., 1968, pp.31-2.
63. Chow, op. cit., pp.381-3.
64. Feuerwerker, op. cit., 1969, p.7.
65. Marshall, 'Opium and the Politics of Gangsterism in Nationalist China', 1927-1945', *Bulletin of Concerned Asian Scholars*, Vol.VIII, No. iii, 1976, p.20.
66. In his article, Marshall clearly documented Jiang Jieshi's (Chiang Kai-shek's) intimate relationship with the underground world which encouraged opium-smoking. The main purpose underlying such manoeuvres was to accumulate profits for both Jiang and the opium gangsters.
67. Feuerwerker, op. cit., 1969, pp.15-16.
68. Murphey, op. cit., pp.13, 20.
69. Chow, op. cit., p.380.
70. Pan'gu 'Guo-gong Zhenzheng Jishi' Bianxiezu, *The Great Transformation: Record of K.M.T.-C.C.P. Internal War, 1945-1949*, Xianggang:

Pan'qu Chubanshe, 1975, p.17.
71. Feuerwerker, op. cit., 1969, pp.12-14.
72. Yan, op. cit., 1955, p.277.
73. Ibid., p.289. The 22 provinces are listed in reference 58 above.
74. Ibid., p.306. The seven provinces are Jiangsu, Zhejiang, Fujian, Hubei, Jiangxi, Shaanxi and Gansu.
75. Ibid., p.291.
76. Ibid., pp.293, 308.
77. Ibid., pp.295-9.
78. Ibid., p.338.
79. Meng, op. cit., 129-30.
80. Yan, op. cit., 1955, pp.350-1.
81. Ibid., p.348.
82. Ibid., p.347.
83. Ibid.
84. Ibid., p.349.
85. Ibid., p.342.
86. Ibid., p.344.
87. Ibid., p.300.
88. Murphey, op. cit., p.30.
89. Feuerwerker, op. cit., 1968, p.58.
90. Joseph Esherick, *Lost Chance in China*, New York: Vintage Books, 1974, pp.62-74.
91. Ibid., p.6.
92. Albert C. Wedemeyer, 'Summary of Remarks . . . before joint meeting of State Council and All Ministers of the National Government, 22 August 1947' in Schurmann and Schell, *Republican China*, p.336.
93. Meng, op. cit., p.196.
94. Walter H. Mallory, 'China, Land of Famine' in Schurmann and Schell, *Imperial China*, pp.262-63.
95. Feuerwerker, op. cit., 1969, p.8.
96. Ibid., p.3.
97. Murphey, op. cit., p.61.
98. Mallory, op. cit., p.263.
99. Murphey, op. cit., p.62.
100. Meng, op. cit., pp.174-5.
101. Marshall, op. cit., p.24.
102. Belden, op. cit., p.313.
103. Esherick, op. cit., 1974, p.196.
104. Ibid., pp.9-19.
105. Ibid.
106. William C. Bullitt, 'Report to the American People on China', in Shurmann and Schell, *Republican China,* pp.347-8.
107. Meng, op. cit., pp.255-6.

3. The Consequences for Women

Up to this point we have been dealing with the general question of the interaction between imperialism and the Chinese economic and political situation. It is time now to see what effects this had on the lives of rural peasant women and urban working-class women. Perhaps the most obvious effects of imperialism are the brutalities of military invasions, but it is also necessary, and ultimately more important, to examine the deterioration of the rural environment, the decline of the handicraft industry and the conditions of the cotton textile industry as it appeared in its more developed urban form.

The Position of Chinese Women before 1949

Military Intervention

The various military invasions which China suffered affected the whole Chinese people. Not only was the country's sovereignty violated and the economy disrupted, but thousands of individuals were slaughtered, community life was violently disrupted and property at all levels was ruined. However, military invasions meant for women not only unemployment but harassment and rape by foreign soldiers, starvation and suffering.

As we have seen in previous chapters, China began to crumble politically and economically after a series of military attacks in the 19th Century. Sir Robert Hart described the effects of the Sino-Japanese War of 1894-95 in this way: 'Although it is only at a minute spot along the fringe of this big empire that the Chinese had received thrashing after thrashing, it is the shell of the egg that is cracked, and — it seems to me a bad case of Humpty Dumpty.'[1]

The subsequent Sino-Japanese War some 40 years later was also damaging: most of the Japanese attacks occurred in the rice-growing area of China (central China), and hence were known as 'rice-bowl campaigns'. 'The Japanese would concentrate several divisions, plunge deep into the front, ravage the countryside, and then turn back. The Chinese would counter by envelopment; their units would fall back before the thrusts, then close in on the flanks and rear to pinch off the garrison supply posts that the Japanese set up to feed their advance; . . . The result was the permanent exhausting stalemate. . . .'[2]

But the Japanese army rapidly gained ground between 1939 and 1943. Whereas in January 1939, the Japanese held only 21 *xian* in 12 provinces,[3] by October 1943, the occupied *xian* had increased to 70.[4] Although only a small number of *xian* were occupied, the overall effect was devastating. Whole areas were ruined by the Japanese invasions, as part of a policy of deliberate destitution. Theodore H. White and Annalee Jacoby described war-torn China:

> The Japanese had just left, but they had blazed a black scarred trail of devastation across the countryside. You might ride for a day through a series of burned villages that were simply huddles of ruins. In some places the roads were so torn that not even Chinese mountain ponies could carry you down the ditches cut across them. . . . Then there would be a single hut standing by itself in the vastness of the hills; with roof fallen in and timbers burned black, it would stand as a symbol of the desolation that ran from end to end of no man's land.[5]

Since the coastal urban cities were also under attack, the K.M.T. Government ordered a mass migration inland from the coastal cities, in which hundreds of thousands of people left their homes and workplaces and travelled to the countryside 'by foot, sampan, junk, railway and rickshaw'. Lack of food and shelter on top of the diseases picked up from the dead bodies along the way had untold consequences: 'there is no estimate of the number who died of disease, exposure, or hunger on the way; their bones are still whitening on the routes of the march.'[6]

Yet the sufferings produced by the Sino-Japanese War of 1937-45 were themselves not without precedent. For example, in late October 1900 German forces had gone into Gaomi of Shandong and slaughtered the people in 200 to 400 villages;[7] such atrocities were extremely common in the countryside during the war.[8]

During imperialist attacks, the 'lucky' survivors were treated as animals or slaves. It was not unusual to find peasant men 'stripped naked, lashed to carts, and driven forward by the Japanese army'. Peasant women were despised and treated with contempt, as described in an eye-witness account by White and Jacoby:

> In some of the districts through which I passed, every woman caught by the Japanese had been raped without exception. The tales of rape were so sickeningly alike that they were monotonous unless they were relieved by some particular device of fiendishness. Japanese soldiers had been seen copulating with sows in some districts. In places where the villagers had not had time to hide themselves effectively, the Japanese rode cavalry through the high grain to trample the women into showing themselves. The Japanese officers brought their own concubines with them from the large garrison cities — women of Chinese, Russian, Korean or Japanese nationality . . . .[9]

In the city as well, women were frequently harassed by foreign soldiers, policemen or factory supervisors exempt from punishment by the extra-territority clauses. For example, one Sunday night sometime in 1901, eight French soldiers entered a house occupied by a number of women in Shanghai (?) and frightened the occupants. The reporter noted that 'this is not the first time such an occurrence has seriously disturbed the Chinese'.[10] There were also many cases of foreign policemen and soldiers harassing women in the streets,[11] and some women disappeared entirely. Not surprisingly, women refused to walk alone in the streets and when they went to work or back home, they usually held each others' hands and walked in groups.[12]

Rape by foreign soldiers was also quite common in the cities. To pick one of countless examples, two women were reported to have been raped by soldiers in Shanghai in 1919.[13] After the Sino-Japanese War (1937-45), a series of students' strikes and demonstrations in Beijing[14] was sparked off by the alleged rape of women in Tianjin and Beijing by American soldiers.

Like the peasant women, urban women were murdered. In just one month (March 1937), thousands of women and children were murdered by the Japanese in Shanghai.[15] On 14 April 1938, the Japanese bombed the factories in Guangxi, killing more than 200 female child-workers, and wounding a similar number.[16] Women were often killed after they had been raped, and, according to reports, even women over 60 years old were not spared. Sometimes they were just burned to death and sometimes they were hung up in trees with their breasts, stomachs, and/or vaginas mutilated.[17]

Any resistance usually led to being killed by the soldiers.[18] In some cases, both women and men were required to kneel down and kow-tow to the Japanese soldiers in the streets after they had been captured; the unwilling were shot immediately.[19]

Another consequence of military attacks was the closing of factories, which meant unemployment for the urban women. After Shanghai was occupied by the Japanese on 11 November 1937, many textile mills, cigarette companies, etc. were ruined and hence many factory women were put out of a job. By 1940, over half of the 300,000 women workers in factories were unemployed.[20] Even when they were working, 'emergency measures' meant that the capitalists lengthened working hours and reduced wages to half or even one-third of their pre-wartime rate. Half-starved and unable to pay their rent, many working women had to find shelter and food as refugees. Between 13 August and 12 November 1937, there were 101,343 children and over 200,000 adult refugees in Shanghai alone. Of the adult refugees, the majority were women.[21]

Some of these victims of war became prostitutes, overtly or secretly. In parts of Shanghai it was not uncommon to see groups of what were then called 'street angels' roaming the streets soliciting customers.[22]

For women in both the countryside and the city, military attacks and contacts with foreign soldiers resulted in the destruction of their property, the end of their employment and constant harassment of one form or another – kidnap, rape, murder or simply disappearance. Yet, in other respects, their experiences were different.

The Fate of Peasant Women: Poverty and Famine

The *Biographies of Eminant Women (Lienuzhuan),* which recorded the lives of famous women in history, showed that women of early China *did* work in the fields: sowing, cultivating and harvesting grain. However, the ideal of Chinese womanhood gradually changed so that women came to be glorified for their work inside the household.[23]

A study of some of the later Chinese women's classics confirms this. *Words to Girls (Nueryan), Women's Precepts (Nujie), Classics for Girls (Nuerjing),* and the *House Rules of Women's Chambers (Guifan)* all indicate that the ideal woman did not work in the fields. Instead, women were encouraged to do all sorts of housework such as cooking, needlework, cleaning, serving meals, educating children at home and so on – but not farming. In fact, even going outside the household was discouraged, especially at night.[24] As the *Book of Change (Yijing)* stated, 'the proper sphere for women is indoors and does not intervene in that of men'.[25]

In reality, only a small proportion of the female population could afford to live up to the ideal. As Lin Xiaoqing noted of Guangdong (Kwangtong), the wealthy could hire servants to do all the household work including 'farming, animal-husbandry, spinning and weaving, and lumbering'.[26] This phenomenon was not restricted to Guangdong, but before 1949 applied to the rest of the country as well.[27] We may safely assume that women of the gentry did not have to work in the fields.

Whatever the ideal, the harsh realities of life for the rural poor meant that peasant women participated in agriculture in one way or another. Women might work only during certain seasons, such as at harvest time or during sowing. In the field, they might specialize in binding the rice stalks or in transporting or transplanting.[28] The intensity of their work and the sexual division of labour varied so much from region to region that it is impossible to list all the variations in women's work in agriculture. Examples from four provinces will have to suffice. In Wenan (Jiangxi), for example, women only carried fertilizer, irrigated the fields and transported the grain home during the harvest time.[29] However, in Yunnan, with the exception of ploughing, most of the work in the fields was done by women.[30] In Shanghai (Jiangsu), women helped men in the fields with irrigation and harvesting, and during the Qing period they also co-operated with men in the planting of cotton.[31] In many places in Guangdong, women worked in the fields alongside men.[32] In Tianpu, for example 70 to 80% of the women peasants worked in the fields: sowing, adding fertilizers and harvesting. They also took care of the tobacco plants, vegetables, fruits and so on.[33]

In every case under survey, the idea of 'women working along with men' was stressed. This is important in the understanding of the status of peasant women in agriculture. Women's farm work was essentially marginal to the family economy and, while it provided some financial help to the family, never allowed women to form an independent economic base. Marion J.

Levy Jr. described this more clearly:

> Peasant women . . . often laboured outside the household at peak periods of labour demand. Such labour was never carried far, however, and work outside the household never became the principal productive work of Chinese women, save in the case of servants whose household was really part of that in which they worked. . . .
>
> At peak agricultural seasons women assisted in both planting and harvest, but in their assistance the distinctions between the sexes were maintained, and certain jobs were done solely by women and small children. These non-household jobs were not a threat to the family structure because they were neither of sufficient duration nor quantity to provide the woman with a possible basis of economic support alternative to that afforded by the men in her family.[34]

The marginal status of women in agriculture changed somewhat in the 19th and 20th Centuries. The concentration of landownership, the shrinkage of farm size and the commoditization of agriculture outlined in Chapter Two put the peasants in a much more impoverished position. Increasingly, they had to farm for their landlords and participate in a commodity market system, while existing on farms that could not produce enough food to eat. Loan-sharking and extortionate rents were a financial drain and caused much suffering. A study of nine regions in five provinces between 1927 and 1941 shows that most peasant families ran a deficit every year.[35] For example, in Yixing (in Jiangsu), an average family had an income of Chinese $54 from farm produce every year, but their expenditure was Chinese $83, resulting in a deficit of Chinese $28 a year.[36] Many of these deficits were met by borrowing money from landlords or loan-sharks who, with their high interest rates, made the peasants even poorer and more desperate. The peasants in Stone Wall Village in the 1940s described their situation thus:

> Harvest every year; but yearly − nothing;
> Borrow money yearly, yearly still in debt.
> Broken huts, small basins, crooked pots;
> Half an acre of land; a few graves.[37]

When famine struck, the peasants were reduced to a sub-human level. In the famines of the early 1930s and in 1943, peasants were reported to have stripped the bark off trees and dug up the roots of grass to eat. Many peasants were forced to migrate to other provinces to search for food; more than 10,000 people died during migrations in 1943.[38]

Many peasants lived without rice or other grains for days or weeks; some were forced to rob. Their desperation for food can be illustrated by a case of rice-robbery which occurred after the Sino-Japanese War in Dabao (in Hunan). As a ship loaded with 'military grains' was unloading, over 30 people rushed to the ship and stole bags of rice. Immediately they were fired on by the soldiers and three people were killed instantly. When they were examined it was noted that the bullet wounds contained a green substance. Autopsy showed that their stomachs were full of grass and contained not a single grain of rice![39]

But this is only one of the many horror stories about famines. Cannibalism was practised in some places during the famines of 1936. In western Anhui and northern Sichuan, it was reported that some people made soup using human meat and sold it.[40] The destitution and starvation in the countryside in China is summarized by Theodore H. White in his description of the famine in Henan during the winter of 1943:

> What we saw, I now no longer believe — except that my scribbled notes insist I saw what I saw. There were the bodies: the first, no more than an hour out of Loyang [Luoyang] , lying in the snow, a day or two dead, her face shrivelled about the skull; she must have been young; and the snow fell on her eyes; and she would lie unburied until the birds or the dogs cleaned her bones. The dogs were also there along the road, slipping back to their wolf kinship, and they were sleek, well-fed. We stopped to take a picture of dogs digging bodies from sand piles; some were half-eaten, and the dogs had already picked clean one visible skull. Half the villages were deserted; some simply abandoned, others already looted. One saw, as one travelled, people chipped bark from trees, with knives, scythes and meat cleavers; you could find bark and eat it. The trees would then die and be chopped down for firewood; . . .
>
> So I saw these things, but the worst was what I heard, which was about cannibalism. I never saw any man kill another person for meat, but it seemed irrefutably true that people were eating people meat. The usual defence was that the people meat was taken from the dead. In one village a mother was discovered boiling her two-year-old to eat its meat. A father was charged with strangling his two boys to eat them; his defence was that they were already dead. . . .
>
> I concentrated my last week in the famine area on estimating figures. My best estimate was five million dead or dying — which may have been 20 per cent off the mark, one way or the other. But figures that large become statistics, thus forgettable. My sharpest memory is a glimpse, at evening as we were riding, of two people lying in a field sobbing. They were a man and his woman, and they were holding each other in the field where they lay, interwined to give warmth to each other. I knew they would die and I could not stop. . . .[41]

Even though, as we shall see in the next section, the decline in the handicraft industry meant that women participated more in agricultural work, the overall context of increasing poverty and starvation rendered these gains insignificant. As farming itself became less and less important in the contribution to family income, especially in the times of flood and drought and the resultant famines, women's contribution was completely wiped out. Thus, the traditional marginal status of peasant women in agriculture remained effectively the same and perhaps worsened.

Peasant women were peripheral to the rural economy — at least that was how they were defined. According to folklore, their status was usually described as below the level of animals, beings who could be removed at the wave of a fingertip by their husbands:

> Taking care of pigs would provide meats; dogs, house-watching; cats, catching mices; as for [women], what can [we] get?

> The new bride, with small feet, went to the kitchen after three days of marriage, [but] the meal [she] made was not good which made the parents-in-law angry. The father-in-law gave [her] a beating with a club, the mother-in-law gave [her] a whipping, making the bride cry with tears.

Peasant families often solved their financial and survival problems by simply killing off female infants. Miss Fielde commented on the situation in the late 19th Century:

> I find that 160 Chinese women, all over fifty years of age, had borne 631 sons, and 538 daughters. Of the sons, 366, or nearly sixty per cent, had lived more than ten years; while of the daughters only 205, or thirty-eight percent, had lived ten years. The 160 women, according to their own statements, had destroyed 158 of their daughters; but none had ever destroyed a boy. As only four women had reared more than three girls, the probability is that the number of infanticides confessed to is considerably below the truth. I had occasionally been told by a woman that she had forgotten just how many girls she had had, more than she wanted. The greatest number of infanticides owned to by any one woman is eleven.[42]

A demographic study by C.B. Malone and J.B. Taylor of five provinces (Shandong, Anhui, Jiangsu, Zhejiang and Zhili) in 1924 seems to confirm this statement. In these provinces, girls of 10 years of age or under constituted only 43.8 – 47.7% of the regional population.[43] In some regions, the proportion of boys to girls was even more unbalanced.[44]

This unbalanced distribution of males and females in the countryside may be due to other factors, such as foot-binding of girls or lack of parental care, but one cannot dismiss infanticide as an important cause. Drowning baby girls was a common practice, simply done by putting the newly-born baby girls in the wooden sink used for cleaning babies when they first appeared during birth, or by throwing them into rivers or streams. Other methods included poisoning the baby girls when they were a little older.[45]

If they survived infancy, marginal girls or women were sometimes sold in difficult times, either in the market or to landlords. They were sold for low prices as servants, slaves or prostitutes. For example, during the famine of 1936 in Chaoshan, a child cost only ten catties of rice.[46] During the famine period in northern China, the price of young girls ranged from Chinese $3.00 to $150.00.[47] Girls between the ages of three and 18 were popular in the 'woman sale' markets in northern Jaingsu. Since their prices were so cheap, it was not uncommon for families of the gentry or even small shopkeepers or innkeepers to have several maidservants working for them.[48]

It was very common throughout China for peasant girls to be sold as child-wives. In Hunan, for example, girls reaching the age of seven or eight either worked in the home or, if their family was poor or in debt, were given or sold to other people as child-wives. From the perspective of the woman's family, it was one less mouth to feed; from the viewpoint of the husband's family, the adoption of a child-wife was cheap, calling for no expensive ceremonies or banquets, and providing what was in effect an extra servant to take care of household chores and, if necessary, to work in the fields.[49]

A child-wife's mode of existence was far from easy — it has been described as 'absolutely below human level'. Since it was not only the rich who had child-wives, many ended up as 'the hired labourer of a hired labourer', scraping by as 'half-starved and half-dead working slaves'.[50] Abuse of child-wives was quite common. In one case a 12 year-old child wife left her home because her parents-in-law beat her so that her body was covered with teeth marks and bruises. In another case, when a child-wife in a blacksmith's family was found sleeping while working on a fan, her uncle used a red-hot tong to beat her about the head, and ordered her not to stop working.[51]

Child-wives very often had to go to bed with empty stomachs, or at best with a meal of light porridge made out of left-over rice. If they were found stealing food, they were beaten. For example, Liying, who was a seven-year old child-wife, was found stealing some left-over rice. Her grandmother-in-law took a long and thick bamboo stick and beat her, saying: 'Short-lived creature! Trying to steal the food for the chicken!' This is the kind of life that many child-wives had to tolerate.[52]

Slightly better than being a child-wife was being a concubine or wife. In the 1930s, women in northeastern China found it hard to get married because, without enough land to farm, many men were unable to support a wife. So, many women from poor peasant families were willing to put up with anything if a man would marry them:[53] cooking, washing, taking care of children, needlework, spinning, weaving, picking mulberry leaves, rearing silkworms; sometimes they had to help their husbands in ploughing, sowing, weeding the fields, feeding cows and cattle and chopping wood. In the north, women had to grind grain and collect dry dung. In the south, they had to paddle water wheels and transplant rice.[54] Their tasks were so heavy that sometimes they were like serfs or servants to the husbands. One peasant, whose mother and wife opposed his getting a concubine, argued: 'Getting a concubine is like buying a cow, she can give birth to babies [and] she can work, why do you oppose?'[55]

On top of the heavy workload, the life of wives and concubines was further burdened by a family structure which sanctioned the dominant role of the mother-in-law, who was quite free to beat her son's women as she pleased. One woman summarized her position in the family before the Liberation:

> It was too bitter a life. My husband was the son of poor peasants with very little land, so that we were obliged to work for the landlord for very little pay. My mother-in-law gave me a very bad time. In the winter she would send me out to gather fuel in the hills nearby, clad only in thin cotton. When she beat me, my husband also had to beat me to show he was a filial son, even though he didn't like doing it. In those days we accepted everything without question because we thought it was our fate and you can do nothing against Fate. Now we know better.[56]

Living in poverty and under oppressive conditions, the lives of many peasant women were far from enviable. For those who could not tolerate it, suicide was a means of protest and relief, and in some parts of China young women founded secret societies with the intention of committing suicide within a certain time after they had been betrothed or married.[57]

The Decline of the Handicraft Industry and Peasant Women

The Chinese peasant economy was traditionally based on agriculture as the main source of subsistence, supplemented by handicraft industry (for example, pottery, textiles and shoe-making). However, especially for the poorer peasants, this 'supplement' meant the difference between survival and starvation.[58]

Generally speaking, there was a broad sexual division of labour in the Chinese peasant economy: men were involved with farming and women with handicraft production and housework. By extension, in the cotton textile handicraft industry, spinning and weaving were usually regarded as women's tasks. *The Book of Poetry (Shi Jing)* suggested that women should be familiar with the weaving tools even as children:

> Daughters shall be born to him; . . .
> They will have tiles to play with.[59]

('Tiles' are emblems of weaving, because women prepare the fibres of the nettle-hemp and grass-cloth plant for the loom by rubbing them on tiles.)

Banzhao (who died in A.D. 116 was even more explicit. According to her *Women's Precepts (Nujie)*, a woman has four qualities, namely womanly attainments, womanly speech, womanly appearance and womanly skills, and of these skills Banzhao asked women 'to concentrate on spinning and weaving'.[60]

This theme of women's responsibility for spinning and weaving continued in the Tang period (A.D. 705-907); a book called *Notes on Women (Nulunyu)* recommended spinning and weaving as special skills for women:

> All women should learn women's skills, . . .
> In spinning and weaving, do not make haste . . . .
> As weaving materials pile up, they can be sold or sewed for one's usage. . .[61]

Similarly, speaking of the duties of women, the *Classic for Girls (Nuerjing)* addressed women in the following manner:

> You should never dare to shirk.
> Knowing that drawing and embroidering is not all of women's work,
> You should labour at your spinning all the time you have to spare . . .[62]

In the *Biographies of Eminent Women (Lienuzhuan)*, several women were selected to demonstrate how women could contribute economically at home, and it was their keen concern in spinning and weaving which won them the highest praise: The exemplary widow of Chen supported her mother-in-law and herself by spinning and weaving.[63]

Not only women's literature, but also the provincial governments in both the Ming and Qing Dynasties (1436-1911) consistently encouraged women to engage in textile handicraft industry.[64] The following excerpt from a Xinghua (in Jiangsu) government notice issued in the Qing Dynasty in the mid 18th Century illustrates this point: 'Those persons whose daughters are between age 11 and 13, and who are willing to train them in spinning and weaving, please inform the governor and have their names and ages registered. Our district will provide free meals and tuition for those who wish to learn spinning and weaving. Enrolment is limited to 30 students for each five-month term.'[65]

We do not know whether spinning and weaving were extensively practised by the daughters of the gentry, but they at least learnt to sew, weave and embroider, and to supervise household work. Socially, the skills of spinning and weaving made them more marriageable, since they were significant in the ideal of Chinese womanhood. Thus it seems to be safe to assume that the daughters of the gentry at least knew the techniques and practised them for their artistic and social value.[66]

For peasant women, spinning and weaving were significant not as mere accomplishments but for vital economic reasons. Women who could spin and weave were great assets to peasant families, making them desirable wives and giving them a higher price as servants to landlords.

If the peasant family was not in great debt, the skills of the daughters living at home could help support the family, since farming alone was not sufficient to make ends meet. Depending on the region and level of poverty of the peasant families, women spun and wove when they had finished a day's heavy work in the fields, or during their spare time between household tasks. They did this both for family consumption and for sale. The practice of selling child-wives and servants to ease the financial burdens of peasant families[67] made these skills a doubly marketable asset.

The collapse of the cotton textile handicraft industry in the peasant economy (described in detail in Chapter Two) meant that peasants in general went through a process of impoverishment in the 19th and 20th Centuries, and the resultant elimination of women's traditional contribution to the peasant household led to further disruption in the social and economic fabric of the peasantry.

As cheap foreign cotton yarn began to pour into China, women who used to gin, bow and spin cotton had to give up their traditional work. This sad phenomenon may be seen in the following quotations gathered from the provincial or district gazetteers in the second half of the 19th Century:

> The women of poor families depended on spinning for a living. Now that the foreign yarn prevails and the price of cotton cloth has dropped gradually . . . [women] have quit spinning and weaving one after another . . . .

> [In the late 19th Century], the weaving industry began to decline. We can only hear the mourning sighs of women, but not the sound of weaving. Occasionally, some weavers use the foreign yarn as warp and native yarn as woof, or use foreign yarn as both. It is hard to find any clothes similar to those they used to make in old days.

> Since foreign yarn has dominated [the market in Jiangsu], the skills of cotton-ginning, cotton-bowing and spinning seem to be forgotten. And young women do not attempt to learn them.[68]

As a further illustration of this phenomenon, let us take a look at two localities in Jiangsu in 1915 and 1935. Wujiang was located in the southern part of Jiangsu. Traditionally, spinning and weaving were the popular work among women in this area.

> From the rich ladies to the rural women, ginning, bowing and spinning, etc. were considered to be recommendable jobs. Even very late at night, one could still hear the sound of spinning and weaving. The diligence of these women can be comprehended. Those who worked hard could weave enough clothes for themselves and their family, others gained some profit by selling the yarn or clothes. . . . as the foreign yarn and clothes became popularly used in the country, the woman's occupational domain was under great challenge.[69]

The influx of foreign cotton goods had brought drastic changes by the 1910s. 'In the villages of one hundred families and the towns within the five square miles, one could not hear the sound of spinning and weaving, nor could one find stores that sell cotton yarns. Those peasant women who lived on selling native yarn and clothes were greatly reduced in number. As for those yarn wholesalers, they had almost disappeared from the market. . . .'[70]

Women of northern Jiangsu suffered the same fate. In Nantong, Rugao, Donhai and Qidong, before the invasion of foreign cotton goods, cotton was one of the main crops, and 80 to 90% of the peasant women wove. Almost every household had at least one loom. At a rough estimate, there were more than two million looms in northern Jiangsu, and many people lived entirely by weaving. In the 1930s, as the cost of producing native clothes was higher than buying the foreign ones, many weavers stopped weaving and sought other forms of employment.[71]

Towards the end of the last century, more and more women found themselves unemployed, thus creating a vast reservoir of female labour. We have already seen some of the alternatives – to stay on with their families and engage more in agricultural work; to be sold as a child-wife or servant. Of the first alternative and its relation to the decline of the cotton handicraft industry in particular,[72] Ding Fengjia commented: 'As the silk industry had not reached its heyday, and the cotton industry had withered, the only chance for women who were energetic and did not want to leave their villages was to help their husbands or brothers in farming . . . . Those who did not have any fields of their own might offer their help to some farmers in order to get some money.'[73] As for the second, with the accelerating deterioration of the peasant economy, the tradition of the sale of servant girls was revived in areas such as northern Jiangsu, and many girls between three and 18 years of age were traded.[74]

Thus the decline of the handicraft industry meant that peasant women were forced to give up their traditional contribution to the domestic economy of peasantry, to uproot themselves and work in other people's farms, workshops or factories, or in landlords' families as servants – or they had to work harder on the family farm. Women actually experienced a *decline* in status, autonomy and wealth and in the power to determine their own destiny.

Due to the worsening economic situation in the countryside, many peasants left their village and migrated to the cities, in some places as much as 8 to 20% of the rural population.[75] Many spinners and weavers, because of the lack of opportunities in the villages, also moved to the city and searched for jobs. This large-scale migration of women contributed to the development of handicraft workshops (which had begun as early as the first half of the 19th Century) and textile factories (which began in the 1890s).[76]

The Report of the Mission to China of the Blackburn Chamber of Commerce 1896-1897 documents the way that peasant women began leaving their families to work in handicraft workshops in towns or cities, and indicates that their change in life-situation was not particularly enviable. *The Report* described a workshop in Guangzhou (Canton): 'We visited a weaving workshop which employed roughly 30 workers. All of them were women who worked 12 hours a day. Their wages were standardized according to the quality of cloth made and they were paid by piecework. The skilled ones could earn five [Chinese] dollars a month out of which two to two-and-a-half had to be spent on food.'[77] Some women worked in the nearby textile factories, which employed women of both northern and southern Jiangsu. In the following section we examine the life of these urban women.

Exploitation and Oppression of Working-Class Women

Women in the cities engaged in a variety of jobs. In Guangdong (Kwangtung) for example, as well as working in agriculture, women were to be found teaching in schools; working in hospitals as physicians, dentists, nurses; working as theatrical painters, aviators, nuns, silk-reelers, silk-weavers, cotton spinners; working in match, shoe and cigarette factories; working as waitresses in restaurants, as money-lenders, as jewellery brokers, as barmaids, as coolies, as actresses, as singers, etc.[78] Women were involved in similar occupations in big cities like Tianjin and Shanghai.[79] But this does not mean that *all* women in cities had a salaried job — in fact, most of them did not. A study of Guangzhou in 1929 shows that three-quarters of women there had no occupation, while those who did were mostly clustered in the 'labourer' category.[80]

Between 1912 and 1920, women working outside of agriculture constituted roughly 30 to 40% of the labour force, as witnessed in Table 3.1. In later years the percentage of women in the labour force appears to have increased. For instance, a study of 29 cities in nine provinces in 1930 shows that women constituted 46.7% of the labour force, men, 46.4% and children, 6.9%. Another study of 23 cities, carried out three years later, gives a startling figure of 56% for women workers. If these figures are correct, it appears that women constituted more and more of the labour force.[81] Unfortunately, data on the labour force after 1933 are not available.

According to a study of 28 cities in nine provinces (Jiangsu, Zhejiang, Anhui, Jiangxi, Hubei, Shandong, Guangdong, Guangxi and Fujian) in 1930, most of the women workers were to be found in occupations categorized under 'textile industry' — a total of 337,546 out of 363,610. However, there is some debate as to the types of textile industries in which women were most prevalent. Some argue that the silk industry had the most workers; others maintain that it was cotton, at least as far as Shanghai was concerned,[82] and this is substantiated by other statistics (see Table 3.2).

The predominance of women workers in the cotton textile industry in Shanghai was still evident after the Sino-Japanese War (1937-45); a 1947 study shows women workers in cotton textile industry in Shanghai as making up 65 to 70% of all women workers in manufacturing industries.[83]

The wages that these women received were amazingly low. On average, women working in the cotton textile industry received Chinese $0.27 a day in 1914, and $0.54 in 1921. The discrepancies in wages between men and women workers in the cotton textile industries were alarming: Table 3.3 illustrates this inequality.

According to this wage-scale, women's wages were roughly 10 to 45% lower than men's. Take the monthly wage for example: on average, a skilled male worker in the textile industry earned Chinese $26 a month, while a woman

Table 3.1
Women Workers in the Labour Force (except Agriculture), 1912-20.

Years	Number of Workers	Number of Women Workers	% of Women in Labour Force
1912	661,784	239,790	36.2
1913	630,890	212,586	33.7
1914	624,524	233,398	37.4
1915	648,524	245,076	37.8
1916*	576,032	239,954	41.7
1917*	555,592	234,745	42.8
1918*	488,605	181,285	37.1
1919*	410,279	183,589	44.7
1920*	413,040	167,367	40.5

* The figures for these years do not represent the whole of China.

Source: Chen Chongguang: 'The Changing Status of Women in Early Republic,' M.A. Thesis, Sili Zhongguo Wenhua Xueyuan Shixue Yanjiusuo, Taibei, Taiwan, 1972, pp.65-9.

Table 3.2
Women Workers in Manufacturing Industries in Shanghai, 1930

Occupations	Number
Cotton spinning	27,574
Cotton weaving	7,128
Silk reeling	14,643
Silk weaving	566
Egg-making	764
Tobacco	4,401
Paper	270
Printing	288

Source: Biyun, 'The Misfortunes of Contemporary Career Women', *Eastern Miscellany*, Vol.33, No.15, August 1936, pp.112-17.

earned Chinese $12; an unskilled man worker earned Chinese $9 a month, and a woman earned Chinese $7.5 in the 1920s. If women were recruited as apprentices, they were given *no* wages at all.[84] Keep in mind that the wages of women workers in the cotton textile industry were usually higher than those of other industries, while, in general, women's wages in the manufacturing industries were 20 to 30% lower than those of men and their daily wages were much lower.

Table 3.3
Daily Wages of Male and Female Workers in the Cotton Textile Industry
ca. 1929 (Chinese $)

	Men		Women	
	Maximum	*Minimum*	*Maximum*	*Minimum*
Average	1.68	0.40	1.03	0.36
Extreme	2.88	0.32	1.86	0.18

Source: Gu Bingyuan: 'The Issue of Women Workers in Shanghai', *Young Women*, Vol. 8, No. 5; May 1929, pp.4-10.

Despite the fact that these women earned only starvation wages, the factory owners found other ways of exploiting them, deducting sums from their wages for such petty infringements of the factory rules as overstaying their lunch periods (for as little as one minute)[85] and yawning or resting during working hours.[86]

In some factories, the company held back a 'reserve' of two weeks' wages for each employee, which would not be paid if the worker was fired or left the factory. This served as an effective deterrent. In another ploy, the employer 'saved' a certain proportion of workers' wages for them. Saving was, of course, compulsory, and any infraction of the company regulations cancelled this saving. In 1927, the K.M.T. actually legalized such compulsory saving by passing a special regulation called 'Temporary Regulations for Factory Workers' Saving'. The first regulation said that 'Those factories which employ more than 100 workers are required to institute a workers' saving department; and those under 100 workers should follow this example. . . .' When this was substituted by a much more rigorous set of regulations, in 1937, the 25th regulation stated that these savings could only be taken out by workers when 'the workers or their children get married' or when 'the workers or their relatives die'.[87] This legislation was obviously designed for the benefit of the employers, who thus had a permanent no-interest loan fund.

To understand the hardship of women workers in real terms we must compare wages with family expenditure. We have data on the workers in Shanghai. Single unskilled workers spent roughly Chinese $12 a month on food, shelter, fuel, transportation and miscellaneous items and skilled workers spent roughly Chinese $20 a month. Unskilled workers with families of five spent only Chinese $21.34, while skilled workers with families of five spent Chinese $35.86 (see Table 3.4).

It is obvious from the evidence on women's wages and the cost of living that it was almost impossible for a woman worker earning Chinese $7.5 - 12 a month to support herself in Shanghai, since a sum of Chinese $11.85-19.26 a month was required to live on. As a result, these women had to cut down on food and other daily necessities. A study of the housing and living conditions in a slum area in Nanchang Shi in the 1930s vividly illustrates the experience

Table 3.4
Monthly Expenditure of Workers in Shanghai, ca. 1927 (Chinese $)

	Food	Clothing	Rent	Fuels	Tram-fares	Miscel-laneous	Total
Unskilled Workers							
Single	5.46	1.19	0.78	0.47	0.71	2.25	*11.85*
Families of five	11.10	2.13	2.78	1.92	0.85	2.56	*21.34*
Skilled Workers							
Single	7.32	2.31	3.09	0.57	2.12	3.85	*19.26*
Families of five	15.06	3.94	5.42	2.51	2.15	7.17	*35.86*

Source: Huang Junlue, 'The Wage System of China', *Eastern Miscellany,* Vol. 24, No. 18, September 1927, pp.44-5.

of poor working-class women: 'With the exception of a few houses, most of the homes of the slum area of Nanchang Shi are cheaply made huts. [They are] small, damp and poorly ventilated. With the exception of one bed, one table and one chair, all worn out and filthy, there is hardly anything left. [As for] kitchen utensils, they have only one stove, several bowls and several pairs of chop-sticks . . . . The monthly income of these women's families range from Chinese $7-8 to slightly over Chinese $20 . . .'[88]

Hours were long, cotton textile workers in Shanghai working roughly 12 hours a day, and some even working more than 15 hours;[89] some of these women also worked the night shift. With hardly any breaks during their working hours, not even for meals, they had to eat while they were working. A lucky few had 15-30 minute meal breaks.[90]

Holidays were at a minimum. A study of 31 factories in Tianjin in 1927 shows that most of these factory workers (women) had one day of rest every seven days (see Table 3.5). But this varied according to region. For example, in three districts of Shanghai — Zhabei, Honggon and Pudong — most women workers had only two days of rest a month.[91]

These kind of working conditions are even more horrendous when we consider the special situation of women. As a rule, there were no provisions for pre-natal and post-natal leave, even if a woman became sick after giving birth. Any extension of the minimal maternity leaves usually meant the ter-mination of the woman's job. Those workers with babies had to feed them during meal breaks, and very often this delayed their own meal time. In some factories, each worker was allowed to go to the wash-room twice a day — nine o'clock in the morning and three o'clock in the afternoon![92] This restriction of the workers' movements sometimes forced them to urinate at

Table 3.5
Holidays for Women Workers in Tianjin, 1927

Holidays	Number
Half a day in 7 days	74
One day in 7 days	3,880
One day in 10 days	600
One day in 14 days	1,170
Sporadic holidays in year	22
No holidays/year	118

Source: Gongdu: 'The Issue of Chinese Women Workers', *Women's Magazine,*
Vol.15, No.9, September 1929.

their workpoint or to give birth to babies in the hallways of the factories.[93]
In fact, due to the 'complications' attached to married women, factory
employers were usually reluctant to hire them, with the result that most
women workers were between 10 and 18 years old.[94]

As in other kinds of factories, the working conditions in the cotton textile
factories were far from satisfactory, especially in the medium or small factories.
They were usually poorly lit and ill-ventilated. The smells generated by the
machines and workers were nauseating. The temperature inside sometimes
went as high as 120 degrees Fahrenheit and many young and feeble women
workers fainted after working there for a few hours, especially during the
summer. Usually when someone fainted the supervisor (or 'Number One' as
the working-class women called them at that time) poured a bucket of cold
water on her and she was ordered back to work again immediately.[95]

Some workers, describing the unhygienic conditions of their factory, stated,
'This factory is poorly equipped: You will find that the lavatory is just a big
hole on the ground with a few pieces of wood piled across it. The urine and
faeces are usually gathered around the rim, and worms are crawling everywhere.
Going to the lavatory once requires one to spit several times. In the factory,
there is not even a spit-container, and there is so much cotton pollutant and
dust in the air, making it very easy to breathe it into our lungs and making
us cough. The spit that comes from coughing covers the whole ground . . . .'[96]
This dust was not only a general health hazard, with workers eating meals
covered in dirt,[97] but caused many women with allergies to leave. Women
who brought their babies to work had to feed them in these filthy conditions;
it was not uncommon to find dead babies within the factories. The following
newspaper item reveals the depressing conditions in the factories: 'A woman
worker fed her baby secretly during work. As the supervisor came in, she hid
the baby under the machine. When the supervisor left the work site a few
minutes later, [she] discovered that her baby was dead.'[98]

Not surprisingly, after working in these conditions for a while, many
workers suffered from illnesses such as tuberculosis, ulcers, eye-sight problems,

and so on. Yet, in order to keep their jobs, women went to work even when they were sick; and as they were poor and the companies did not provide medical care for them, they were unable to see a doctor. Consequently, the death rate in cotton textile factories was high. In the Yufeng Cotton Mill in Shanghai, 30% of the workers died within three years of starting work there and the majority of those who did not die were chronically sick.[99]

Table 3.6
Workers and their Illnesses in an Industrial Hospital in Shanghai in the early 1930s

	Number of Workers	% of Patients	Number of Patients with Industrial Diseases	% of Patients with Industrial Diseases among Total Number of Patients
Men	566	65	231	41
Children	164	18	43	26
Women	150	17	100	66
Total	880	100	374	42

Source: Guo Zhenyi, *The Issue of Women in China*, Shanghai: Shangwu Yinshuguan, 1937, p.191.

A study of 880 patients in an industrial hospital in Shanghai in the early 1930s showed that 66% of the woman patients were affected by industrial or occupational diseases. (Table 3.6 documents the over-representation of women with industrial diseases.) It should be noted that most of the patients (women) came from foreign-owned factories (cotton textile); there are no equivalent statistics for Chinese-owned factories, but since they were mostly small-scale enterprises, the figures would probably be larger. The same study also demonstrated that 44% of these women patients were permanently handicapped, mostly with eye damage from the machines. Among these women 15% had asthma, 14% had tuberculosis, 3% had beriberi, 4% had worms and 10% had chronic foot boils. All these complaints were related either to the poor working environment, including unsafe machinery and construction, or to nutritional deficiencies. (The figures on industrial accidents are given in Table 3.7.)

Some of these urban workers had not come to the city voluntarily or willingly; They had been 'commissioned' to middlemen by their poverty-stricken families. These middlemen came from the cities, claiming to be representatives of the cotton textile factories. (In Shanghai in 1937, there were roughly 70,000 to 80,000 'middlemen'.) In the villages poor peasants would pay them about Chinese $20 to 30 to take their daughters to the factories, usually for three years. 'Commission fees' were generally paid by instalment, but there must have been some form of downpayment. In return, the female workers were to be supplied with food and shelter while working in the factories, but all the wages received by the women workers were to be confiscated by the 'middlemen' , and the clothing and other provisions were totally inadequate.

There was another kind of arrangement in which women who applied for jobs in the factories were required to submit 'guarantee fees' as well as written or oral guarantees to obey unconditionally the regulations of the factory, to refuse to join any strikes or make complaints to their boss, and to refuse to join organizations of workers, etc. Once their applications were accepted, they had to live in the small and poorly constructed residences associated with the factories. Sometimes 30 workers crowded into an area as small as 84 square feet. Where these women had been introduced by middlemen, they were provided with thin blankets and in some cases four workers shared one blanket. Early in the morning, at roughly three or four o'clock, they were woken by alarm bells or by superintendents yelling 'wake up! wake up!' After a breakfast of thin porridge with a few pieces of salted vegetables, they were hurried to their workplace where they were lined up like prisoners and led inside by the superintendants well before the sun came up; 12 to 16 hours later, they were led back to their residence. It was not unusual for these workers not to see the sun for weeks or months.

Living in the residences and working in the factories under the agreement made with the middlemen was like being in a concentration camp. Women were not allowed to talk with any outsiders and could not correspond with their parents. Even if their parents came to visit them, they were not allowed to see them alone. These measures were used to prevent them from telling anyone about their inhumane treatment. If these workers were caught running away from the factories (which meant breaking the contract signed by their parents), they were given a severe beating.

Punishment for disobeying any regulations in the factories was especially harsh for these women, since they were contracted to work there for a number of years. In fact, beating and various forms of physical torture were very common: disobedient workers were ordered to put their hands and knees on the four legs of an upside-down chair and stay there for hours; ropes were fastened around them and they were hung from a beam and beaten; their hands were bound behind them and they were hung up on the wall. One particularly unpleasant punishment involved fastening their trousers at both ends, with a cat placed inside, and then beating them — the cat would scratch the body of the rebellious worker for three or more hours. There were cases in which workers were beaten until they lost consciousness or even died. There were also milder forms of torture, such as beating the palms of the hand, beating the knees and legs, twisting ears and squeezing eyelids, forcing women to stand for hours, or kneel for hours, etc.[100]

One woman worker recalled her days in a cotton mill before the Liberation: 'I worked in the spinning department taking off bobbins. When I didn't work well enough, I was beaten by the foreman — the Number One, as he was called — or beaten by other members of the staff. When I would come home and show the marks from my beatings my mother would weep and try to comfort me.'[101]

A song was written about the pitiful condition of the women workers at that time:

> Living in the countryside was full of hardship,
> Trying one's best still left the stomach empty,
> No other choices,
> Come all the way to find jobs,
> Letting people know that [we] can bear hardship, . . .
> There are more than ten hours of work everyday,
> Work until the head aches and the waist gets sore,
> Eyes become red and swollen,
> But dare not yawn,
> For the Number One's evil spirit is severe . . .[102]

Working in a foreign-owned firm was sometimes even worse. For example, when humiliating the Chinese workers, the Japanese factory employers required them to line up and carry the Japanese flags; workers had to bow to Japanese soldiers they met in the street. Women workers were not permitted to gather in groups of three or more persons in case they planned anti-Japanese activities and, in some cases, were harassed by the Japanese soldiers inside the factories or forced to dance with them. In the evening, the soldiers would climb over the walls of the women's residence, and rape them. Resisting these advances could result in being killed, burned, or buried alive. And it was not uncommon in the late 1930s to find dead bodies in wooden boxes or wrapped in mats lying in the streets.[103]

The factory owners' managers' distrust of their women workers led them to build special kinds of gates for checking against theft. Each worker had to pass through the gate as they left work, to be searched by guards in full view of passers-by. This intimidating form of checking was instituted in the late 19th Century and continued well into the first half of the 1900s. One woman described the search in the following way:

> Near the gate, there were a few strong and evil-looking old women, who barred the gate and searched the passengers. We were all searched from top to bottom without reason. I was quite angry, and asked a woman: 'I come to work, not to steal things, why did you search me like that!' After she heard it, she revealed her horrifying face, and said to me: 'This is the rule of the factory, if you don't like being searched, you don't have to come tomorrow, we did not send out an invitation card for you to come.' At that time, the policeman [standing] nearby, came forward with his hand on his club, he did not wait to find out the matter, but waived his club as if he was going to strike, saying: 'Go! Go!' This was alarmingly coercive . . . .[104]

When the Japanese invaded Hangzhou and took over the factories, they proved even more tyrannical in their search for workers. One woman, who was too poor to buy a pair of cotton shoes and hobbled around on frozen feet, used a few remnants of cotton from the factory to bind them up. When this was discovered during the search, she was beaten and burned, and, despite the winter weather, was stripped of her clothing and hung on a large tree near the factory. And this was not an isolated incident. In a similar case in Shanghai, a woman was found with a small bag of cotton in her pocket; most of her clothing was stripped off, and she was carried around the factory festooned with signs describing her 'crime' to demonstrate to the other workers that she was a thief. Her employer took several pictures of her 'disgrace'. When she went home that evening she committed suicide.[105]

But however appalling working conditions were, it was not as bad as being unemployed. The cotton textile industry had been declining since the 1930s, and many workers were forced to leave their jobs. Although there is some debate as to the exact number of unemployed at the beginning of the 1930s, the figures are high. One estimate shows that over 5,000,000 workers were unemployed in China in 1933. In Shanghai, for example, roughly 25% of the workers in the cotton textile industry were dismissed in 1934, most of them women.[106] When the Japanese formally attacked the country in 1937, the number of unemployed women increased drastically. In Wuhan, some factories dismissed over two-thirds of their employees in 1938.[107]

Conclusion

The larger economic and political changes in China could not fail to affect Chinese women. Military attacks and interventions completely disrupted the daily life of women, and they were harassed and raped. Economically, these wars led to female unemployment and its distresses. The declining handicraft industry forced women to give up their traditional skills and eliminated the key contribution they had made to the peasant economy.

As the peasants rapidly became poorer, Chinese peasant women became more and more peripheral to the family economy, and were, in ever-increasing numbers, sold to landlords as servants or child-wives. Their treatment in their new homes was rough at best, and very often they were tortured. Then famine certainly accelerated the deterioration in women's life-situations.

One way to escape from rural destitution was to migrate to the cities in search of a job. In many cases, peasant girls and women were 'sold' to factory owners to work for a number of years without pay. The poor working conditions, long hours of work, low or no wages, plus other means of exploitation and maltreatment, resulted in a sub-human form of existence. Staying in the countryside or migrating to the cities both involved exploitation and oppression, and physical and psychological pain. It was in this inhuman context that the women's movements aimed at resisting imperialism and revolution emerged in China.

The fact that resistance and revolution on the part of women arose within the context of specific determinations of their position does not necessarily imply that such rebellion can arise *only* in the context of poverty, exploitation and oppression. In fact, history has demonstrated that this is usually not the case. People suffering under severe poverty and agony do not usually have the time or confidence to rebel. But without poverty and oppression, peasant and proletariat resistance and revolution are meaningless and without purpose. The previous chapters have shown that, with the world-wide rise of imperialism and the collapse of China's sovereignty and economy, peasant and working-class women felt these structural changes in their daily existence. Whether or not women organize to resist and revolutionize depends to a great extent on their consciousness and enthusiasm. In China, two major forces were attempting to rectify the deteriorating conditions of China: the K.M.T. and the C.C.P. These two political parties, with their ideologies, mobilization strategies and organization, reflected two opposing directions in which China and in particular Chinese women could go – either to accept the *status quo* of imperialism and capitalism which had wrecked the country or to reject it and build a new society. These two conflicting tendencies were the consequences of the internal contradictions of capitalist development, not only in China but throughout the world. It was on the basis of their own life-experiences that Chinese women selected which force they would side with, for they could think, feel and act. It would be naive to say that the K.M.T. or the C.C.P. manipulated women into blindly following their doctrines. Their own experiences provided women with the determination and anger to rebel against imperialism and any forces which supported it.

References

1. Sir Robert Hart, 'The Tragedy of China's Defeat' in Franz Schurmann and Orville Schell, *Imperial China,* New York: Vintage Books, 1967, p.260.
2. Schurmann and Schell, op. cit., p.263.
3. These provinces are: Jiangsu, Zhejiang, Anhui, Jiangxi, Hubei, Hunan, Shandong, Shanxi, Henan, Fujian, Guangdong and Suiyuan.
4. Joseph Esherick, *Lost Chance in China,* New York: Vintage Books, 1974, pp.131-2.
5. Schurmann and Schell, op. cit., p.266.
6. Ibid., p.261.
7. John F. Schrecker, *Imperialism and Chinese Nationalism: Germany in Shantung,* Cambridge, Mass.: Harvard University East Asian Series, No. 58, 1971, pp.138-9.
8. *Jingzhong Ribao,* 3 November 1904, No. 252, p.4.
9. Schurmann and Schell, op. cit., pp.266-7.
10. *The North-China Herald,* 3 July 1901, p.27.
11. *The People's Wail,* 22 May 1909, p.4; 27 May 1909, p.5; *The Times*

(Shibao), 1 May 1919, section 3, p.5.

12. Zhujing, 'The Shanghai Women Workers are in Struggle', *Funu Shenghuo*, Vol. IX, No. iv, 16 October 1940, pp.20-21.

13. *Shibao*, 1 May 1919, section 3, p.5.

14. Pan'gu 'Guo-gong zhanzheng jishi' Bianxiezu, *The Great Transformation: Record of K.M.T.-C.C.P. Internal War, 1945-1949*, Xianggung: Pan'qu Chubanshe, 1975, p.13.

15. *Shibao*, 7 March 1937, p.1.

16. Hui, 'Another Bloody Account', *Funu Shenghuo*, Vol. VI, No. i, 5 May 1938, p.10.

17. Ibid.

18. Zhujing, op. cit., pp.20-1.

19. Hui, op. cit., p.10.

20. Meng Xianzhang, op. cit., pp.20-1.

21. Chen Biyun, 'The Sufferings of Women and Children of Shanghai under the Japanese Invasion', *Eastern Miscellany*, Vol. XXXV, No. 1, January 1938, pp.75-8.

22. Biyun, 'The Situation of Women in the Island', *Dongfang zazhi*, Vol. XXXV, No. xiii, July 1938, pp.52-6.

23. Albert R. O'Hara, *The Position of Women in Early China*, Xianggang: Orient Pub. Co., 1955, p.278.

24. Isaac Taylor Headland, 'The nu erh ching; or Classic for Girls: translated from the Chinese', *The Chinese Recorder*, Vol. XXVI, No. xii, December 1895, pp.554-60.

25. Lu Kun, *The House Rule of Women's Chambers*, Ming keben duplicate copy, 1927, Vol. 1, p.11.

26. Lin Xiaoqing, 'The Situation of Women of Meixian', *Funu zazhi*, Vol. XIV, No. 1, January 1928, pp.56-8.

27. Marion J. Levy, Jr., *The Family Revolution in Modern China*, New York: Octagon Books, 1971, pp.153-4.

28. Si Qi, 'The Women of Guizhou Panxian', *Shenbao Monthly*, Vol. IV, No. 4, April 1935, pp.236-7.

29. Zhen Li, 'Portrait of the Women's Life-styles in Western Jiangxi', *Shenbao Yuekan*, Vol. IV, No.7, July 1935, pp.207-8.

30. Peng I, 'The Rural Women of Yunnan', *Funu Shenghuo*, Vol. VIII, No. 2, October 1939, pp.8-9.

31. Shanghai Tongshe, *Materials for the Research on Shanghai: Supplement*, Taibei: Zhongguo chubanshe, 1973, pp.601-4.

32. Jianyue, 'Xingning Women', *New Women*, Vol. III, No. vii, July 1928, pp.805-23; Lin, op. cit., pp.56-8; Li Aizhen, 'The Situation of Women of Songgou', *Funu zazhi*, Vol. XIV, No. i, January 1928, pp.63-6; Hui, 'The Women of Xinhui', *Family Weekly*, Vol. I, No. xlvii, October 1946, p.350.

33. Luo Shuhe, 'The Situation of Women of Tianpu', *Funu zazhi*, Vol. I, No. vii, July 1955, p.4.

34. Levy, op. cit., pp.153-4.

35. Yixing, Changshu and Tongshan of Jiangsu; Wuyi of Zhejiang; Chengdu and Wenjiang of Sichuan; Yulin of Guangxi; and Beitang (Jinjing) and Baodi of Hebei.

36. Yan Zhongpin et al., *Selection of the Statistical Materials on the History*

of Modern China, Beijing: Kexhe chubanshe, 1955, p.311.

37. As quoted in Jack Belden, 'Stone Wall Village' in Schurmann and Schell, *Republican China,* op. cit., pp.317-18.

38. Lou Yiwen, 'Speaking for Peasant Women', *Women's Monthly,* Vol.III, No. i, July 1943, p.10.

39. Meng Xianzhang, *Teaching Materials for the History of Chinese Modern Economy (Zhonqquo jindai jingi shi,* Shanghai: Zonghua Shudian, 1951, p.338.

40. Ibid., pp.174-5.

41. *Time,* Vol. CXII, No. 1, 3 July 1978, pp.32-3.

42. As quoted in Arthur H. Smith, *Village Life in China,* London: Oliphant, Anderson and Ferrier, 1900, pp.308-9.

43. Fu Baoshen, 'The Facts on the Situation of Peasant Women in our Country and the Duties of the Y.W.C.A.', *Young Women,* Vol. IX, No. ix, November 1930, pp.1-14.

44. Li Changnian, 'Female Infanticide and the Issue of Unequal Ratios of the Sexes in China', *Dongfang zazhi,* Vol. XXXII, No. xi, June 1935, pp.97-101.

45. Xuejian, 'The Situation of Haifeng Women and their Movement', *Funu zazhi,* Vol. XIV, No. xii, December 1928, pp.1-4; Lou, op. cit., p.7.

46. Meng, op. cit., p.333.

47. Walter H. Mallory, 'China, Land of Famine', in Schurmann and Schell, *Imperial China,* op. cit., 1967, p.264.

48. Guo Zhenyi, *The Issue of Women in China,* Shanghai: Shangwu Yinshuguan, 1937, pp.152-5.

49. Wang Yi, 'The Situation of Childwives', *Dongfang zazhi,* Vol. XXXII, No. xv, August 1935, pp.119-22.

50. Xuejian, op. cit., pp.1-4.

51. Liu Quiying, 'The Sufferings of Child-wives', *Jiangxi Women,* Vol. I, No. i, March 1937, pp.40-1.

52. Liying, 'The Situation of Child-wives of Min-Nam', *Funu shenghuo,* Vol. III, No. iii, August 1936.

53. Guo, op. cit., pp.142-3.

54. Fu, op. cit., pp.1-14.

55. Lou, op. cit., p.9.

56. As quoted in Dymphna Cusack, *Chinese Women Speak,* Sydney: Halstead Press, 1959, pp.52-63.

57. Smith, op. cit., p.309.

58. Feuerwerker, *The Chinese Economy, ca. 1870-1911,* Ann Arbor: Center for Chinese Studies, University of Michigan, 1969, p.19.

59. As quoted in Lucinda P. Boggs, *Chinese Womanhood,* Cincinnati: Jennings and Graham, 1913, pp.17-18.

60. R.H. Van Gulik, *Sexual Life in Ancient China: A Preliminary Survey of Chinese Sex and Society from ca. 1500 B.C. till 1644 A.D.,* Leiden: E.J. Brill, 1961, p.100.

61. As quoted in Xie Kang, 'The Traditional Views on Women's Education in Chinese Families', *Journal of Zhongshan Academy and Culture,* Vol. VI, November 1970, pp.497-530.

62. As quoted in Headland, op. cit., pp.554-60.

63. O'Hara, op. cit., p.278.

64. Yan Zhongping, 'Examples of the Provincial Official Encouragement of Textile Industry in the Ming and Qing Dynasties', *Dongfang zazhi,* Vol. XL, No. viii, April 1946, pp.20-6.

65. Peng Zeyi, *Materials on the Modern Chinese Handicraft Industry, 1840-1949 (Zhon qquo jindai shouqonqye ziliao),* Beijing: Zanlian Shuju, 1957, Vol. 1, p.224.

66. Florence Ayscough, *Chinese Women,* Boston: Houghton Mifflin, 1938, pp.18-20.

67. Liu Gu, 'The Maid Servants of Guizhou' *(Guizhou de nubi), Women's Weekly,* Vol. XIX, No. 5, February 1935, pp.60-2; Wang Yi, op. cit., pp.119-22.

68. Peng, op. cit., Vol. 2, pp.217-20.

69. Ding Fengjia, 'From What I Observed on the Life-styles of Women in this Place', *Women's Magazine (Funu zazhi),* Vol. I, No. 9, September 1915, pp.1-10.

70. Ibid., pp.1-10.

71. Luo Qiong, 'The Rural Working Women in Northern Jiangsu', *Dongfang zazhi,* Vol. XXXII, No. xiv, July 1935, pp.107-9.

72. Ding, op. cit., pp.1-10.

73. Ibid., p.3.

74. Luo, op. cit., pp.107-9.

75. Chow Tse-tung, *The May Fourth Movement,* Cambridge, Mass.: Harvard University Press, 1960, pp.381-3.

76. Peng, op. cit., Vol. 2, pp.233-5.

77. Ibid., pp.258-60.

78. *Chinese Economic Journal,* Vol. I, No. 6, June 1927, pp.564-78.

79. Guo, op. cit., pp.87-100.

80. Chen Chongguang, 'The Changing Status of Women in the Early Republic', Taiwan: Sili Zhongguo wenhua xueyuan shixue yanjiusuo, M.A. Thesis, 1972, pp.65-9.

81. Ibid.

82. Li-Wang Limeng, *The Chinese Women's Movements,* Shanghai: Shangwu Yinshuguan, 1934, p.60; Guo Zhenyi, 'The Greater Shanghai Plan Should Note a Few Issues on Women', *Dongfang zazhi,* Vol. XXXI, No. v, March, 1934, section on 'women' *(fu),* pp.1-4; Gu Bingyuan, 'The Issues of Shanghai Women Workers', *Nugingnian,* Vol. VIII, No. v, May 1929, pp.4-10; Biyun, 'The Misfortunes of Contemporary Career Women', *Dongfang zazhi,* Vol. XXXIII, No. xv, August 1936, pp.112-17.

83. Zi, 'The Present Stage of Working Women', *Women's Voice of Xianggang* Vol. I, No. i, May 1947, pp.4-5.

84. Huang Junlue, 'The Wage System of China', *Dongfang zazhi,* Vol. XXIV, No. xviii, September 1927, p.44.

85. Shi Jingxing, 'The Deduction of Wages' in Li Yuqing, *The Calamity of Old China,* Xianggang: Zhaoyang Chubanshe, 1971, p.42.

86. Xiuling, 'I Am Also a Woman Worker', *Women's Circle,* Vol. VIII, No. ix, March 1941, p.23.

87. Shanghai Renmin Chubanshe, *The Sinful Old Society,* Shanghai: Renmin chubanshe, 1966, Vol. 5, pp.26, 28. 30.

88. Jieyu, 'The Women of the Slum in Nanchang City', *Jiangxi Women,* Vol. I, No. i, January 1937, pp.36-9.

89. Gongdu, 'The Issue of Chinese Women Workers', *Funu zazhi*, Vol. XV, No. ix, September 1929.
90. Ibid.
91. *Nugingnian*, Vol. X, No. ii, February 1931, p.56.
92. Guo, op. cit., pp.170-1.
93. Zi, op. cit., pp.4-5.
94. Hefa, 'The Labour Legislation and the Protection of Women', *Nugingnian*, Vol. IX, No. viii, October 1930, pp.14-23.
95. Shi Jingxiang, 'Indentured Workers', *(Baoshen gong)* in Li, op. cit., pp.22-8.
96. Zhang Shen, 'The Voices of Women Workers', *Funu Shenghuo*, Vol. VII, No. vi, 1 May 1939, p.10.
97. Chen Huili, 'Apprentice', in Li, op. cit., pp.14-21.
98. Biyun, 'An Examination of the Contemporary Women's Labour Issues', *Dongfang zazhi*, Vol. XXXIII, No. xxiii, December 1936, pp.101-6.
99. Shi, op. cit., pp.22-8.
100. Ibid.; Wang Xusheng, 'Textile Women Workers Talked of the Past and Present', *Chinese Women*, January 1963, pp.14-17; Chen, op. cit., pp.14-21.
101. Dymphna Cusack, *Chinese Women Speak*, Sydney: Halstead Press, 1959, p.105.
102. Jihong, 'An Account of the Visit to the Labour School of the Y.W.C.A.', *Funu Shenghuo*, Vol. IV, No. vi, 1 April 1937, pp.38-42.
103. Hu Ziying, 'Industrial Women Workers of Chongqing', *Funu Shenghuo*, Vol. VIII, No. x, 20 February 1940, pp.7-9.
104. Huachen, 'The Narrative of a Woman Worker ', *Funu zazhi*, Vol. XVII, No. vi, June 1931, pp.80-4.
105. Zhang Chuanhong, 'The Body-search System', in Li, op. cit., pp.36-41.
106. Guo, op. cit., pp.194-6.
107. Zeng Wan, 'The Improvement of Women's Situation during the War', *Dongfang zazhi*, Vol. XXXV, No. xiii, July 1938, pp.49-52.

4. Women's Ideas of Resistance

Before we deal with the resistance activities which working-class and peasant women engaged in, it is important to look at the *ideological* components of the women's resistance. This will enable us to understand (1) how women related to the changing political and economic context which we have described in the previous chapters, and (2) what suggested directions these ideas gave to women's movements. But this does *not* mean that the ideas of women dictated their actions. We have seen in Chapter Three the objective conditions and human experiences of women, and it was precisely these conditions and experiences which compelled peasant and working-class women to act. The explicitly formulated ideas of women's resistance therefore represent one moment of the crystallization of women's experience.

In this chapter, we will study the ideas of resistance expounded in the 'women's literature' — the publications (magazines, newspapers, books, etc.) written by women and for women, as well as a few articles pertinent to the issue of women's resistance found in other sorts of periodicals.

It was estimated that at least 159 women's journals were published between 1900 and 1949: the 54 which were openly anti-imperialist in content were mostly published during the Sino-Japanese War, and were affiliated with the K.M.T.'s Women's Guidance Committee of the New Life Movement *(Xinyun Funu Zhidao Weiyuanhui).*[1] But because of the K.M.T. policy of institutionalization it is very difficult to determine which of the publications on women (or by women) published before 1937 were affiliated with the K.M.T. However, it is doubtful that all women's literature was under their influence. The C.C.P., on the other hand, believing that 'class' was more important than 'gender',[2] tended to promote its views on women through a variety of publications other than women's literature as such. Thus, articles on women appeared in journals addressed to issues related to the working class or to peasants in general, and this meant that much more women's literature was published under the K.M.T. than the C.C.P.

In any case, one suspects that the circulation of 'women's literature' was small and mainly urban, since 98 to 99% of Chinese women in the 1930s and 1940s were illiterate. (Women's magazines, for example, would only sell hundreds or thousands of copies.) Thus, the ideas found in the women's literature, almost by definition, represented the opinions of an elite of literate women (whether they were affiliated to the K.M.T., C.C.P., or independent women's organizations). While this literate elite may not have constituted the actual leadership of the women's resistance, it articulated and justified the viewpoints of its members and other women involved in the resistance.

Themes and Rationales

Three general themes persisted in women's literature throughout the first half of this century: (1) women should engage in resistance work; (2) women of all countries should unite to oppose the spread of fascism and imperialism; and (3) men and women must unite to defend China.

Women Should Engage in Resistance Work

Although there had been a brief period of concern with resisting the economic effects of imperialism in the 1900s, when the U.S. tried to renew its treaty with China governing the 'import' of 'Chinese coolies', this concern declined until the 1930s. However, resistance could be directed against non-economic forms. For instance, the C.C.P. was quite sceptical of the influence of missionaries on the status of women in China. In some of its publications, such as *Pioneer (Xiangu)* and *Special Issue on Anti-Christianity (Fei Jidujiao Tekan)*, it strongly attacked the portrait of sexual inequality in Christianity, and viewed Christianity as a mechanism for oppressing women.[3]

In its literature of the 1920s, the C.C.P. also urged women to fight against capitalism and feudalism as well as against different forms of imperialism. It emphasized the eradication of the private property system as a condition for liberating women. As one article in the *Pearl River Review (Zhujiang Pinglun)* stated in 1922: 'Only when the proletariat comes to hold political power can the masses of women then be liberated.'[4] This association of women's oppression with the private property system made an appearance in the 1920s, and persisted well into the 1940s.[5]

Although China was going through a capitalist phase and was subjected to surveillance and constraint by imperialist powers during the first half of this century, there is no doubt that feudal relations still persisted, with their institutionalization of 'male chauvinism' and the 'traditional value system' (that is Confucianism). The C.C.P. argued that Chinese women should rise up in a militant manner to shatter these 'chains of oppression'.[6] The C.C.P. also called for the participation of women in anti-imperialist activities. It saw women as an integral part of the revolutionary process, argued that 'women's liberation cannot be devoid of politics' and said that women should 'engage in national revolution so as to liberate themselves'. This was the message in the 1920s.[7]

With the intensification of the Japanese invasion, the C.C.P. position of involving women in anti-imperialist activities became more and more explicit. In one of her articles, Deng Yingchao wrote: 'Only in the active participation of Chinese women in the war of resistance to gain the victory of national

liberation can the victory of women be attained.'[8] Here we note the association of resistance, revolution and women's liberation which, for the C.C.P.,
was the ultimate formula for women's liberation.

Before the consolidation of power, the K.M.T., while paying little attention
to anti-imperialist work, nevertheless glorified itself as a revolutionary party,
thus connecting the idea of women's liberation with revolution. In a leaflet
entitled 'March 8th Is International Women's Day' *(San Yue Ba Ri Wei Guoji
Funu Ri),* issued by the Central Executive Committee of the K.M.T., it
proclaimed that: 'All women should unite; if [they] want to attain women's
liberation, it can only be achieved in the society after the struggle of a revolutionary party. Therefore, the acknowledgement of Women's Day is very
important in China. This is because [the K.M.T.] can use it to raise the
consciousness of the masses of women, so that [they] understand the goals of
the revolutionary movement sponsored by the Chinese K.M.T.'[9]

What the K.M.T. actually meant by 'revolutionary' movement was the
'citizens' revolution' launched by the K.M.T. to oust the warlords in its
Northern Expedition. There was no real intention of angering the imperialist
powers in China. Nevertheless, the K.M.T. did pay lip service to kicking out
imperialism, as witnessed in a memorandum sent to the women's organizations in Guangdong (Canton) on 5 March 1924. It declared: 'March 8th is the
International Women's Day . . . . [The K.M.T.] wishes all women's organizations in Guangdong to organize on that day, so as to promote [the consciousness of women] . . . . Please follow the slogans listed below for making
placards and leaflets for the demonstrations on that day . . .: (1) Down with
foreign imperialism; (2) Liberate China from its semi-colonial status; . . .'[10]

In the 1930s and 1940s, as the Japanese invasion intensified (especially
after 1937), the mobilization of women in the war of resistance became the
central theme in the K.M.T. literature. Women were urged 'to work hard in
patriotic work', 'to boycott Japanese goods' and 'to sacrifice oneself for the
benefit of the country'.[11] It was claimed that 'the anti-war and anti-fascist
struggles and the struggle for women's rights are inseparable'.[12] It was only
at this point that the K.M.T. associated women's liberation with anti-fascism
and came just short of anti-imperialism.

Apart from a few outcries of anti-Americanism in the 1900s, the women's
literature itself manifests an increasing concern with women's resistance in the
1930s. Examples of foreign invasion and its human consequences are
increasingly quoted in order to forge a sense of urgency among the readers.[13]
As Jin Er wrote: 'China was under invasion by Japanese imperialists for many
years! [They] occupy large pieces of land, send in large troops of soldiers
[in the Chinese territories, and] severely oppress our people; should these
phenomena remain unconquered, we can never turn over a new leaf.'[14] This
sense of urgency is further articulated in articles addressed directly to educated women or schoolgirls. Ji Hong, for example, warned: 'Time does not
allow us to lock our doors and study, we should . . . exert our efforts for the
liberation of the nation, and fight for world peace.'[15]

Thus, to many writers, the task of fighting against imperialism could not

101

be delayed. Two quotations illustrate this sense of urgency: 'We cannot tolerate any more the multiple slaughters of imperialism and the increasing brutality, exploitation, and oppression imposed upon us. We can no longer sheepishly and quietly allow them to slaughter [us]. We can only unite and struggle in the name of freedom and equality, and earnestly fight back all evil power under the banner of life-fulfilment and women's liberation.'[16]

> Look, the iron hoofs of imperialism have pounded our soil; . . .
> Come quickly, come quickly, come quickly and get rid of all these
>   tigers and foxes, and sweep away all obstacles.
> We, we, we are the free masters of our country, and not born slaves . . . .
> Come, come dear sisters,
> And unite together as one heart,
> The last victory belongs to us.
> Work hard,
> Struggle,
> Resist,
> The last victory belongs to us.[17]

Although the women's literature called for the general mobilization of all women for resistance, there was little attempt to speak for peasant women (or working-class women for that matter). Only one quotation could be found which indicated concern for peasant women: 'We have many urgent tasks to do . . . but we have a task which requires our extra effort, and that is the mobilization of masses of peasant women, so that they may rise and join the resistance.'[18]

Men and Women Should Unite to Defend China

Based on the assumptions that revolution is a gigantic task which requires maximum (wo)manpower to tackle, and, secondly, that the oppression of women is more severe than that of men, the C.C.P. argued that men and women should join forces in national liberation and revolution. The declaration of the *Youth Weekly (Qingnian Zhoukan)*, issued in 1922, clearly said that: 'We believe that men alone cannot launch the social revolution; if women who constitute half of the population still remain apathetic, then it is impossible to have social reconstruction. . . .'[19]

This message of male-female unity was again repeated in the midst of the Sino-Japanese War. In 1939, the C.C.P. sent a telegram to the Women's Guidance Committee of the Chongqing New Life Movement Main Office and to all women's organizations in China maintaining that 'We enthusiastically wish all our women compatriots to co-operate with all our men in supporting the war of resistance so as to attain the final victory.'[20]

With respect to the peasantry, the C.C.P. had become more explicit between 1946 and 1949, arguing that both men and women in the countryside were oppressed by feudalism: 'In fact, the basic needs of both peasant men and women are the same. Although peasant men are under the influence of the landlords' backward feudalistic ideas, after being liberated from being trampled under the feet of the landlords and having [their] livelihood improved, [their] backward ideas will be changed! Don't the women themselves also have many backward feudalistic ideas? . . .'[21]

This theme was also prevalent in the women's literature in the 1930s and 1940s. Tao Fen argued that 'the combined efforts of the male and female compatriots throughout the country' are necessary for the defence of China.[22] Wang Minyi maintained that 'we women should not antagonize men . . . [but] should unite with those men whose consciousness has been raised.'[23] Baishuang, in repeating the slogans of the K.M.T. — 'Make Every Effort to Fight Against the Japanese' and 'National Interests Are Superior to All Others' — urged women to 'work closely with male comrades to resist [the Japanese]'.[24] 'The Marching Song of Women' *(Funu Jinxingqu)* epitomizes the essence of this male-female unity:

With men, we walk hand in hand, shoulder to shoulder,
We walk to the front and join the war,
We are the housewives of the war,
We are the women of the war,
Get up, we 200 million women,
And carry our flag of war, and move to the front.
We demand,
Demand tomorrow's liberation.
With men, we walk hand in hand, shoulder to shoulder.
We walk to the front to join the war.[25]

Women of All Countries Must Unite to Oppose Fascism and Imperialism

In the middle of the Sino-Japanese War, when China formally supported the Allies in containing the expansion of Germany and Japan, Song Qingling urged 'the Chinese women and women of other [anti-fascist] countries' to stand together in defeating fascism.[26] Chinese women were asked to 'work as closely as possible with the women of those democratic countries within the anti-aggression nexus',[27] and to 'establish an international women's anti-fascist front'.[28]

But why should Chinese women fight against imperialism and unite with men and women of other countries? Three arguments (justifications) were presented in the women's literature: (1) women are citizens and they should take on their responsibility as citizens; (2) women are human beings, and they should take on their responsibilities as human beings; and (3) women's liberation follows the victory of anti-imperialism.

Argument 1: Women as Citizens: Like men, women are members of a country and should fulfill their duties as citizens.[29] These responsibilities include the protection and defence of the country in times of crises and foreign invasion; and the building of the society in times of peace.[30]

Argument 2: Women as Human Beings: Women are 'human beings', and they 'should take up their responsibilities as "human beings"'. Besides demanding

103

self-liberation, [they] should demand national liberation.'[31] Although the concept 'human beings' was used, it was never clear why 'human beings' should be patriotic and work for the liberation of the country. Daiming presented her argument in the following manner: 'The war . . . has started, we should quickly prepare ourselves, radically clear our thinking, and recognize our position as "human beings" and the duties of "human beings": to train our bodies to be iron-strong, to efficiently use our brains, and to work hard and persistently . . . so that the half-paralyzed body of China can be resurrected; that is [what we call] "the salvation of the country by women".'[32]

Argument 3: Women's Liberation Lies in Anti-Imperialism: Along with warlordism and feudalism, imperialism was seen as an obstacle in the path of women's liberation. 'Only when the nation is liberated can the women who belong to the nation be liberated.'[33] Lin Hao argued strongly for this position: 'Women should take up the present duties, and become the vanguard of the time, unite with the proletariat in a strong alliance to fight on the anti-imperialist and anti-feudalist front. Work hard together and demand real human freedom and equality! Then, [we] can talk about the radical liberation of women.'[34]

This position, as one might expect, was strongly favoured by the C.C.P., which had been consistently urging women to demand 'human rights' and 'citizens' rights' before asking for 'women's rights' since the 1920s.[35] For the C.C.P., the elimination of imperialism and the consolidation of the socialist revolution are the pre-requisites of women's liberation. Similarly, national liberation is incomplete without the liberation of women. 'The members of the C.C.P. believe that, in order to liberate Chinese people, it must simultaneously liberate the Chinese women; [this is] because Chinese women not only constitute half of the population, but are also more oppressed than men, [and therefore] suffer more.'[36]

In the women's literature, some articles specifically addressed the topic of the relationship of working-class and peasant women to national liberation. For instance, it was argued that only after the liberation of the whole nation could 'the issue of women's livelihood be dealt with'. According to Gao Yufen, 'We should first of all overthrow the domination of imperialist power in China, secondly, [we] can concentrate on the liberation of working-class and peasant women.'[37]

But this position of national liberation first, and women's liberation later must be distinguished from the following argument, which insists that national liberation is itself an integral part of women's liberation: 'Since the sacred national resistance began, the Chinese women's movement is moving to yet another new level. For adapting to the objective condition of the resistance, the women's liberation movement is adjusting to the objective needs of the resistance. We believe that without the victory of the national liberation, the victory of women's liberation is not attainable. . . .'[38]

Although both positions give priority to the issue of national liberation (resistance), the former position views national liberation and women's liberation as separate issues; while the latter maintains the inseparability of the two concerned issues, to such an extent that national liberation is used as a means to attain the liberation of women.

Thus, it appears that both the C.C.P. and the K.M.T., as well as the women's literature, agreed on the three themes of the role of women in resistance, the united front with men on the issue of national liberation and the international struggle against fascism and imperialism. In terms of the justifications for these positions, K.M.T. and the women's literature seem to emphasize women as citizens and human beings, while the C.C.P. was convinced of the inseparability of women's liberation and anti-imperialism. These themes and rationales of women's resistance were most predominant in the 1930s, although the preceding and succeeding decades also saw discussion along these lines. The 1930s saw the intensification of the Japanese invasion, which increased the urgency of persuading women to join the resistance movement. However, the C.C.P. had been concerned with mobilizing women for resistance work in the 1920s.

Proposed Strategies

Four basic types of strategies are suggested in the women's literature: economic, educational, familial and legislative. These strategies were concerned with mobilizing women for resistance purposes and improving the welfare of women.

Economic Strategies
The involvement of women in economic production for the benefit of the country was proposed towards the end of the Qing Dynasty.[39] This was picked up as a theme by some women's magazines in the early days of the Republic (ca. 1912). Some women argued that the temperament of women (their kindness, wisdom, tolerance, honesty, etc.) best equipped women to sew, take care of silk worms, and so on.[40] Some women thought that the involvement of women in handicraft work (such as embroidery and spinning, in cultivating cotton, mulberry trees and tea plants, would not only enhance the position of women and their rights, but also help to improve the Chinese economy.[41]

Towards the end of the 1920s, some women shifted the argument by claiming that it was important for women's own sake to learn skills which would allow them to be employed, and thus take a step towards economic independence and liberation. There was, however, some debate as to how intensive their training should be.[42]

In 1933, one woman writer stressed the significance of production for the salvation of the country. She suggested that in order to expand national capitalism (instead of imperialist-dominated capitalism), Chinese women and men should 'overthrow the domination of imperialism in China', 'eradicate the unequal treaties', 'maintain tariff autonomy', 'correct the unreasonable feudalistic landownership system', etc. Although this proposal was part of a polemical engagement with the advocates of educational and military changes, it nevertheless represented a breakthrough in the women's literature, because for a long time women had been talking about improving the status of women without relating it to imperialism.[43]

As the Sino-Japanese War began, concern for the development of the Chinese economy deepened. Most immediately, the supply of army clothing had to be maintained and, according to Tang Guozhen, this was to be solved by mobilizing women to establish 'women's factories' to produce army uniforms 'in support of a prolonged war'.[44] It was also proposed that women be mobilized to do all sorts of war work, such as transportation, construction, nursing, food-processing and laundry work.[45] A third suggestion was for the creation of thousands and thousands of 'industrial co-operatives'.[46]

Not all groups of women would be equally affected, and thus it was considered important that women be involved in this war-time production work, because, as Yinqiu put it, 'Working women are the most oppressed under imperialism, they are the ones who suffer most under the direct influence of imperialism'.[47] Further, lack of manpower in production behind-the-front (as men went to war) and the need for women to be self-sufficient during war time[48] were also put forward.

Peasant women were discussed similarly to working-class women in the literature written in the early period of the Republic. One woman suggested that women 'should not be ashamed to work in agriculture', and should be involved in farm work such as mulberry tree cultivation, tea plantations, fruit orchards, and raising chickens and bees.[49]

There was nothing written on peasant women before the Sino-Japanese (1937-45) War, with the exception of one article in 1927 which contained a radical discussion of the equalization of landownership according to the sexes. It traced the history of landownership in China, and noted that the lack of landownership by women was a recent phenomenon. The writer argued that 'in order to overthrow the patriarchal society', it is important to equalize landownership by sex.[50] The writer did not, however, demand the redistribution of land by class, in order that the hired farm labourers or small peasants might share the land of big landlords.

As the war intensified, women's literature began to show great concern with the declining peasant economy: the disintegration of the handicraft industry and of agricultural production. Women were encouraged to work in uninhabited areas so as to cultivate farmlands and to escalate agricultural production. At one point, the Soviet model of collectivization was proposed so as to increase production.[51] Peasant women were also encouraged to renew their work in embroidery, spinning, weaving, sewing, etc. Some writers suggested that small-scale handicraft workshops and co-operatives be established in villages and that peasant women be recruited to work in them.[52] In the middle of the war, some writers suggested that it might be feasible to introduce an incentive system to encourage women to farm or to organize 'women farming teams' or 'model farming women'.[53] The drive to have women working in agricultural production was not limited to the women's literature or the K.M.T.; the C.C.P. was also eager to improve agricultural production by women.[54]

In the middle of this drive, there were two 'deviant' voices in the women's literature which called for different kinds of measures. One was expressed in the form of a letter to the editor of *Women's Life (Funu Shenghuo)*: Lu Lin argued that unless the K.M.T. Government raised the standard of living of the peasantry and solved their 'survival' problems in the villages, it was impossible to mobilize peasant women.[55] The other argued that peasant women should demand an independent right to land use not restricted by the present system of landownership, in which land was controlled by the gentry-landlord class or by the peasant women's husbands.[56]

In sum, with only a few exceptions, the overall position in the women's literature was to involve women in both agricultural and industrial production mainly for the benefit of the country, and only secondarily to improve the status of women. Although there were a few independent voices urging women to be more productive in the 1910s and 1920s, it was not until the 1930s that we witness a deepening concern for working-class and peasant women. However, land redistribution, which was the key strategy of the C.C.P., was seldom mentioned. In fact, considering the vast number of articles written on the issue of women, relatively few of them referred to working-class and peasant women.

Educational Strategies

The idea of educating working-class women was not suggested until the late 1920s and early 1930s when some women began to note that the current women's movement was too middle class and that learning skills was essential for women's economic independence.[57] This theme was dropped until the beginning of the Sino-Japanese War, when Jiang Yixiao reminded women that, 'Henceforth, the women's movement should not be [only] a middle-class movement, but [should] know how to educate [and] to awake those working-class and peasant women who are most oppressed.'[58]

However, if one investigates the women's literature during the war, it is quite obvious that what educating working-class women in factories actually meant was raising their awareness of the war-time economy and teaching them productive skills for war-time production. There was a certain concern with raising the literacy rate of women.[59] At one point, when the idea of constructing 'productive co-operatives' was tossed around, there was some suggestion that women should learn the managerial skills needed to administer the co-operatives, so that in the process of doing so they might become 'well-cultured' and patriotic.[60]

As in the case of working-class women, interest in educating peasant women was not much in evidence in the late 1920s.[61] It was only revived at the beginning of the Sino-Japanese War, again with the purpose of publicizing war-time events, inducing patriotic sentiment and raising the literacy rate of women. This was to be done through the formation of literacy classes, drama-playing, cartoons, posters, etc.[62] But, as early as 1940, the women's literature reported on the difficulty of finding students in the villages.[63]

In addition to the economic and educational strategies the women's literature proposed two others, which, in terms of the coverage they had in the literature, remained minor and secondary. These were familial and legislative strategies.

Family-based Strategies

There is only one article in our survey of women's literature which called for familial changes in working-class families. Bolin argued that one of the reasons why women's wages were lower than men's was the familial constraints on women, and urged the creation of a public child-care system.[64]

Again, the call for familial changes in peasant families was limited to only two articles. One argued for the abolition of the 'kinship system',[65] the other called for the formation of temporary child-care centres for peasant women, especially during the seeding and harvest seasons.[66]

On the whole, the women's literature seldom suggested familial changes as a strategy for mobilizing women for resistance work. And it must be remembered that familial (especially marriage) reforms were among the key mechanisms which the C.C.P. was to use in recruiting peasant women in the countryside (see Chapter Six).

Legislative Strategies

Another ignored area in women's literature is the call for legislative changes which might affect the livelihood of working-class women and peasant women. There were only a few articles in our survey which mentioned this possibility. One called for the right of association for working-class women.[67] Others advocated changes in labour law to eliminate the exploitation of working-class women by equalizing wages between men and women, instituting maternity leave with pay, limiting working hours and night shifts and bettering working conditions.[68]

Only one article in the entire survey dealt with legislative changes affecting peasant women. The writer called for changes in legislation on landownership, inheritance, property and freedom of movement, so that women could inherit land and properties and attain the freedom that men had.[69] For the most part, however, the literature concentrated on the demand for 'woman suffrage', either because middle-class feminists were simply ignorant of the wider legislative changes that were necessary for peasant and working-class women or because they mistakenly believed that the vote in itself would automatically bring other changes in its wake.

Proposed Tactics

In this section, we will examine the organizational and the recruitment tactics suggested in the women's literature. Both of these tactics will be of concern when we examine the policies and approaches of the C.C.P. and the K.M.T.

in Chapter Six, and it is important to find out the extent to which they were discussed in the women's literature.

Organizational Tactics

Only a few articles in the women's literature deal specifically with the organizational tactics of working-class women. They all deal not with developing structures for recruiting working-class women, but with the formation of alliances between middle-class and working-class women, women and the working class, men and women of the working class, as well as strengthening working-class organization.[70] Judging from these few articles, working-class organizations were to be used to form alliances and to absorb women. As Quanshao said, 'We wish to unite the Chinese labour movement [so as] to unite our working women; to organize the national unified democratic headquarter [so as] to mobilize our working women to involve them in wartime efforts in a systematic and coordinated manner and on a massive scale.'[71]

Similarly, the women's literature gives little indication of how to organize peasant women. There were two suggestions: one was to organize them through the established channels (such as K.M.T. party branches, departments of public work or the education system) and mobilize them for education or skill training;[72] along the same lines, during the war the C.C.P. suggested recruiting women through existing defence committees, solicitation teams, consolation groups, etc.[73]

The other suggestion was to create and strengthen any 'women's organizations' in the villages. If there was no women's organization in the village, a 'village women's productive co-operative' could be formed which, in turn, would be linked to a 'town women's productive co-operative'. The latter would be co-ordinated by a 'provincial women's organization'. It appears that this bureaucratic set-up was suggested by the K.M.T.[74] It should be noted that while the first proposal does not view 'women' as an entity separate from other groups, the second one treats 'women' as a distinct group for organization.

After the Sino-Japanese War, the C.C.P. began to talk of the 'peasantry' as the friend of women's liberation. It assumed that the needs of peasant women and men were the same, and that they could co-operate.[75] However, the C.C.P. felt that in mobilizing peasant women, one had to consider the different strata of peasant women. It was suggested that in land reform one must begin with the poor (as opposed to middle or upper) peasant women.[76]

Recruitment Tactics

The women's literature suggested two ways of approaching working-class and peasant women: mass line and elitist. In both cases, the coverage was limited.

The working-class women's basic concerns were 'survival' issues such as food, clothing and shelter. In addition, there were anxieties about pregnancy, sexuality, footbinding, familial relationships and so on. Thus, according to one writer, 'In order to expand the working-class women's movement, we must begin with their basic needs first; in other words, we must begin with solving their poverty, sadness, bitterness and anxiety. . . .'[77] The same writer maintained that one must proceed with honesty, passion and patience to teach these women. Such emphases may be considered a 'mass line' tactic.

The elitist tactic called for educated women to set an example for working-class women and/or educate them. There was little regard for working-class women's basic needs or concerns, and it was assumed that it was ignorance which kept poor working women from greater involvement in resistance efforts.[78]

Mass line tactics were also suggested for the mobilization of peasant women. Women cadres were urged to 'go to the countryside and mix with the villagers as well as to get intimate with the countryside environment'.[79] One had to know the 'life-styles' of peasant women as well as their 'bitterness'.[80] As Deng Yingchao said, one had to note specifically 'their status in the family and society, their most . . . urgent demands'. Furthermore, in teaching them, one should avoid using abstract languages and 'draw from their daily existence examples and questions' and link them to war-time situations.[81]

The mass line tactics for mobilizing peasant women are succinctly portrayed in the following message:

> Indeed, the task of raising the consciousness of peasant women is not easy. Under the condition of strong traditional values, it is rare to have village women coming out to listen to speeches and watch dramas . . . [If] you want to wake them, [you] must blend with them completely and not let them see you as people coming from another class. If you act like a lecturer speaking on stage, they may suspect that you are selling medical herbs or auctioning; in that case, in spite of your hard work, it will be ineffective. Therefore, going to the countryside is not a self-glorifying thing, but [a task] demanding that you use your knowledge to cultivate the minds of peasant women within the context of their experience. As for the pre-requisites, [they include] simple clothing, a warm personality, clearly expressed speeches, and local language and slang, all these are your working tools . . . .[82]

The elitist approach to peasant women is indicated by one writer's suggestion that before women cadres went to the countryside to mobilize peasant women, they should contact local governments or administrators.[83] These women cadres usually had a brief training in cities or towns and were assigned to work in the countryside. They were asked to set up literacy classes and seminar groups without really understanding the local customs and economic conditions.[84]

However, these proposed organizational tactics (non-women-specific and women-specific) and recruitment (mass line and elitist) had only minimal coverage in the women's literature, which, while urging women to be unified and join the resistance and suggesting different tasks that women could do for the resistance, actually failed to provide guidelines and methods for the organization and recruitment of working-class and peasant women. The few articles which did discuss strategies and tactics of mobilization very often failed to be concrete and specific.

Although some of the suggested organizational structures and recruitment tactics bore some relation to actual practice, the mass line tactics remained speculative. First of all, although urban-educated women had been urged to mobilize working-class and peasant women through understanding and living with them, our examination of the actual practice of women cadres in the non-C.C.P. areas (see Chapter Six) contradicts this: Women cadres, even where they worked in the factories or in the countryside, tended to employ elitist tactics of mobilization.

Conclusion

We have classified the ideas of resistance expounded in the women's literature (supplemented by other publications) during the period 1900-49 under four headings: themes, rationales, strategies and tactics. Although there was some discussion of resistance in the 1920s (especially by the C.C.P. on Christianity, feudalism, the private property system and imperialism), the question of resistance was not really raised until the 1930s, especially during the early stage of the Sino-Japanese War. In general, there were only a limited number of articles on working-class and peasant women.

The three themes were: (1) women should join the resistance movement; (2) men and women should unite in resistance; and (3) there should be a global unity of women in fighting against fascism and imperialism. Of all these themes, the first one seemed to be the most predominant in the literature.

Persuading women to join the resistance effort required definite arguments. Three rationales were put forward: (1) women are citizens; (2) women are human beings; and (3) women's liberation lies in anti-imperialist activities. The C.C.P. emphasized the last one, and, indeed, it was generally the most prevalent in the literature.

Women writers proposed two major and two minor strategies for mobilizing women for resistance. The major ones were economic and educational changes — the involvement of women in production (handicraft and agriculture) and various formal and informal means of educating women. Although there were brief discussions on the positive effects of production on women's liberation, the key objective of economic changes was pragmatic, that is to say, the improvement of the declining Chinese economy and the maintenance of the army's war-time needs. This was especially the case with the women's literature affiliated with the K.M.T. Educating women meant the indoctrination of women with regard to war-time events, patriotism and general government propaganda. Most of these proposals were made in the 1930s.

The minor strategies proposed were familial and legislative changes — the institution of child-care centres for women and the changes in legislation on labour and the inheritance of property.

To carry out these strategies, women writers suggested two kinds of tactics, organizational and recruitment, but not very much was written about either. Two kinds of organizational formats were proposed: (1) mobilizing women through the existing non-women-specific organizations; and (2) absorbing women by creating specific women's organizations. As for methods of recruiting women, the literature suggested two key ways: (1) a mass line approach — working with women on the grass-roots community level; and (2) an elitist approach — organizing women from the top down with little concern for their daily situation and basic needs.

Without getting entangled in statistical data on the frequencies of the occurrence of these themes, rationales, strategies and tactics, one gets the impression that, prior to 1937, these themes and rationales occurred frequently; and that more definite strategies and tactics were proposed mainly after 1937. Such a pattern suggests that the idea of women participating in anti-imperialist activities was not yet generally accepted and that women's journals were launching a campaign promoting the involvement of women. The Sino-Japanese War made the participation of women (working-class and peasant women) a necessity, and the focus of the articles shifted to a discussion of strategies and tactics for mobilizing women. It now appeared to be generally accepted that women should become involved in the fight against imperialism, and the question 'why' was replaced by 'how' in the general movement to build women's resistance. In other words, a connection can be made between the ideas of resistance and the changing political situation in China.

As we have seen in the 19th Century, imperialism had an impact on the Chinese political, economic and social systems. After her defeat in the Opium War (1839-42), China signed numerous treaties with Western countries including Japan, treaties which resulted in a situation of permanent debt, lost territories and a general erosion of self-determination. The payment of indemnities, the opening of treaty ports, the leasing of territories, the admission of missionaries and the loss of the right to determine tariff-rates, postal services, financial affairs and judicial matters — all these weakened China's independence.

From the perspective of the imperialist powers, a *weak* China was more profitable than a *dead* one, because its weakness permitted imperialist manipulation and exploitation. (This view was especially popular after 1860.) British policy has been described as an attempt 'to perform the delicate operation of snuffing without extinguishing' the Chinese Government and to deliver a blow to the head that would not injure the body. This ensured that China remained weak enough to be manipulated and lacked the political and economic strength to compete on the world market. By 1900, foreign countries had established claims in 13 out of 18 provinces of China.[85]

During the first half of this century, imperialist intervention and domination continued. Economically, there was a continuous outflow of capital because of foreign control of markets, transportation, mining, manufacturing industries and financial institutions. Politically, there were signs of increasing attempts at domination by Japanese imperialism as witnessed in the

Twenty-One Demands put forward by the Japanese in the 1910s.[86]

Military invasion may be singled out as a particularly provocative form of imperialism, and we will show its links with the ideas of resistance found in women's periodicals. It is well known that, beginning with the Opium War, 19th-Century China was beset by one military invasion after another. In the 20th Century, imperialist intervention included the occupation by the Allies in Beijing (Peking) (1900), the entry of the Russian forces into Manchuria during the Boxer Uprising (1900), the outbreak of the Russo-Japanese War in northern China (1904-05), the intrusion of the Japanese navy and army in Fuzhou (1919), armed intervention in various parts of China by foreign countries (1920s), the 'September 19th Incident' (1931) and, finally, the Sino-Japanese War (1937-45). The most significant difference between the military invasions in the 19th Century and those in the 20th Century was that where European countries such as Britain, France and Germany dominated the former, Japan was dominant in the latter.

It was in the context of these military invasions that the ideas of women's resistance (anti-imperialism) emerged in the women's periodicals. Yet 'women's resistance' as a system of ideas did not really emerge until the 1920s, and became popular only in the 1930s and 1940s. The question that must be asked is 'why'?

The absence of women's anti-imperialism in the 19th Century and in the first two decades of this century was certainly not due to a lack of imperialist invasions. This phenomenon must be explained by other factors, such as the educational level of women. Schooling for women came late in the 19th Century, beginning with missionary schools, and later Chinese-sponsored women's schools. These schools were concentrated in the coastal cities, especially in Shanghai and Guangzhou (Canton), and most of them were elementary schools. Thus, throughout the first half of this century, only a small minority in the urban areas had the chance to go to school. As late as 1929-33, the illiteracy rate of women was very high: 99.1% women in northern China, and 98.3% in southern China.[87] This lack of educational opportunity prevented many women from either expressing their own thoughts in writing or increasing their knowledge through reading newspapers, periodicals or books.

Another factor which may explain the lack of women's anti-imperialism in the 19th Century is the absence of any communication network among women for mutual knowledge or support. In the 1900s, such a network began to emerge in the form of women's schools, student associations and political organizations. These were essential elements in the formation of women's organizations and publication of women's journals. However, even in the 1900s, there was little trace of women's anti-imperialism in women's journals, and the explanation lies in ideological factors.

The ideologies of the revolutionary and constitutionalist movements in the 1900s maintained that the weakness of China lay not in imperialist intervention, but in the backwardness of indigenous political and economic processes. Influenced by this ideology, women tended to blame the weak Manchu regime rather than demand the expulsion of imperialist powers. All their efforts were therefore geared towards the abolition of the dynastic system.

In the 1910s, this way of thinking began to lose support because the new republican regime did not prove to be any better than the old Manchu one. More specifically, the K.M.T. did not keep its promise of sexual equality, and the repressive character of the regime soon disenchanted women activists.

Meanwhile, China joined the Allies in the First World War, only to be greatly disappointed by the Paris Conference of 1919 where their demands were largely ignored. The Conference made some Chinese men and women realize the close ties among imperialist powers and the true nature of imperialism. It was no longer possible to maintain the old ideology of indigenous structural weaknesses, rather than imperialist manipulation, as the reason for China's problems. The sending of troops by the imperialist powers to 'protect' their factories and properties in the 1920s and 1930s reinforced this new awareness, and ideas of resistance became much more prevalent among women. As the Sino-Japanese conflicts escalated to a total war in 1937-45, 'anti-imperialism' became the dominant topic in women's literature.

Although 'resistance' had become the dominant theme in women's literature in the late 1930s, our survey indicated that there was not much written on working-class and peasant women. Women's literature was written and read mainly by educated women living in the cities. These privileged women did not work in factories or in the countryside; when they spoke of 'women', they actually meant educated women. The position of working-class and peasant women was peripheral in their eyes, and even when the Sino-Japanese conflicts intensified in the 1930s, the coverage of working-class and peasant women remained minimal. Since educated women had little contact with their underprivileged counterparts, they had difficulty articulating their experiences, and although they may have recognized the importance of mobilizing these women, they did not know how to do it. It is no wonder that the discussion of mobilizing working-class and peasant women was so limited in the women's literature.

References

1. Almost three-quarters of these were published between July 1938 and 1949, mostly in Shanghai before 1938, and after that in many places in China, such as Zhejiang, Hunan and Guangdong.
2. An issue which will be elaborated in Chapter Six.
3. The C.C.P. Central Committee's Editorial and Translation Department Research Branch translation of the writings of Marx, Engels, Lenin and Stalin, *The Introduction of the Periodicals of the May Fourth Era*, Beijing: Renmin chubanshe, 1958, Vol. 2, pp.12, 620-6; Vol. 3, pp. 68-9.
4. Ibid., Vol. 3, pp.6-7.
5. Wu Yuzhang, 'The Chinese Women have been on the Path of Independent

Liberation during the May Fourth Movement' in *Documents on the Women's Movements (Funu yundong wenxian)*, Xianggang: Xin Minzhu chubanshe, 1949, pp.65-73.

6. Zhong Tiemou, *The Peasant Movement of Hailufeng*, Guangdong: Renmin chubanshe, 1957, pp.47-8.

7. The C.C.P. Central Committee's Editorial and Translation Department Research Branch, op. cit., Vol. 3, pp.17-18.

8. Deng Yingchao, 'Anti-Japanese Invasion and Chinese Women' *(Fandue rikou qinlue yu Zhongguo funu)* in Baishui, *Zhou Enlai and Deng Yingchao*, Hankou: Yixing Shuju, 1938, pp.909-98.

9. *Huazi Ribao*, 6 March, 1924, p.3.

10. Ibid.

11. 'A Letter to Women from [Shanghai] City Women's Association', *Dagong Bao*, 8 March 1937, p.7; 'The Speech of Chairperson Shao of the Central Party Propaganda Department', *United Voices of Women (Funu Gongming)*, Vol. VII, No. iii, 20 February 1938, p.4; Shanghai Women's Modesty Movement Committee, 'A Letter to All Women in the Country', *Shenbao*, 8 March 1940, section 3, p.9.

12. Song Qingling, 'Concerning the Call for Assisting Guerrilla Fighters – the speech made in the international day meeting in Xianggang', *The Collected Works of Song Qingling*, Xianggang: Zhonghui shuju, 1967, pp.137-41.

13. Jin Zhonghua, 'Talking National Affairs with Women', *Funu Zazhi*, Vol. XVII, No. xii, December 1931, pp.2-12.

14. Jin Er, 'A Letter to [my mother]' *(Gei muqin de xin)*, *Funu Shenghuo*, Vol. III, No. iii, 16 August 1936, p.51.

15. Jiehong, 'How to do Extracurricular Work [?]', *Funu Shenghuo*, Vol. III, No. 4, 1 September 1936, pp.12-13.

16. Zhang Xiuxia, 'Awake! Dear Women Compatriots!', *Nuzi Yuekan*, Vol. I, No. viii, 15 October 1933, pp.12-13.

17. Zhuang Ming, 'The Marching Song of Women', p.34.

18. Wenna, ' "March 8th" Day and Village Work', *Funu Gongming*, Vol. VIII, No. iv, 5 March 1938, p.7.

19. The C.C.P. Central Committee's Editorial and Translation Department Research Branch, op. cit., Vol. 2, pp.51, 531-2.

20. *Liberation Weekly*, Vol. LXVII, 20 March 1939, p.40.

21. Li Baoguang, 'Women Should Enthusiastically Join the Liberation Movement', *Shidai Funu*, Vol. I, No. ii, August 1946, pp.1-3.

22. Tao Fen, 'The Women's Question and Men', *Funu Shenghuo*, Vol. III, No. iii, 16 August 1936, pp.10-12.

23. Wang Minyi, 'Celebrating "March 8th Day" ', *Jiangxi Funu*, Vol. I, No. i, 8 March 1937, pp.14-15.

24. Baishuang, 'Sincerely Unite, Express Democratic Spirit', *Funu Shenghuo*, Vol. VI, No. viii, 20 August 1938, pp.7-8.

25. Yao Lan, 'The Marching Song of Women', *Funu Shenghuo*, Vol. VI, No. xi, 1 January 1939, p.6.

26. Song Qingling, 'The Chinese Women Demand Freedom of Struggle', *The Collected Works of Song Qingling*, pp.154-65.

27. Jian Pu, 'The Goal and Direction of the Contemporary Chinese Women's Movement', *Guangxi Funu*, Vol. XXI, 15 January 1942, pp.12-14.

28. Ge Qin, 'The Women's Liberation Movement in the Anti-fascist War', *Guangxi Funu*, Vol. XXI, 15 January 1942, p.19.

29. Baishuang, 'Sincerely Unite . . .', op. cit., pp.7-8.

30. Shang Mu, 'The Foci of Women's Liberation', *Funu zazhi*, Vol. XIII, No. v, May 1927, pp.2-6; Chen Ying, 'Women in the Four Years of Resistance', *Guangdong Funu*, Vol. XXI, No. xi-xii, 15 July 1941, pp.17-18.

31. Ye Chusheng, ' A Short History of "March 8th" ', *Jiangxi Funu*, Vol. I, No. i, 8 March 1937, pp.10-12.

32. Daiming, 'The Women that are Mostly Needed in Contemporary China', *Nuzi Yuekan*, Vol. I, No. i, 22 February 1933, pp.3-6.

33. Si Ding, 'The Liberation of Women and the Revival of Nation', *Zhongguo Funu*, Vol. II, No. i, December 1940, pp.24-25.

34. Lin Hao, 'The Chinese Women's Liberation Movement', *Nuzi Yuekan*, Vol. I, No.8, 15 October 1933, pp.14-17.

35. Jingyu, 'The Future of Chinese Women's Citizen Revolutionary Movement', *Funu Zazhi*, Vol. I, No. x, January 1914, pp.28-32.

36. Cheng Fangwu, 'The C.C.P. and the Liberation of Chinese Women', *Shidai Funu*, Vol. I, No. i, 1946, pp.4-5.

37. Gao Yufen, 'How to Liberate the Peasant and Working Class Women in China [?]', *Nuzi Yuekan*, Vol. I, No. ii, 1933, pp.15-17.

38. Guixiu, 'How to Go About with the Education of Peasant Women's Education during Wartime', *Funu Shenghuo*, Vol. VI, No. iii, 5 June 1938, pp.11-12.

39. *The People's Grief*, 19 October 1909, p.3.

40. He-Zhang Yazhen, 'Women and Industry', *Women's Times (Funu Shibao)*, Vol. IX, 25 February 1913, pp.1-5.

41. Fu Menglan, 'On the Necessity of Speedy Improvement Plans of Women's Industries', *Funu Shibao*, Vol. X, 25 May 1913, pp.3-6; Lin Yilun, 'Women's Handicrafts Should not Ignore Embroidery', *Funu Zazhi*, Vol. I, No. iv, April 1915, pp.11-12.

42. De'en, 'Elementary Education and Training and Women of our Country', *Funu Zazhi*, Vol. XV, No. i, January 1929, pp.19-23; Liu Chengfu, 'Elementary Education and Training and Women's Occupation', *Funu Zazhi*, Vol. XV, No. i, January 1929, pp.26-9.

43. Chen Yubai, 'Production for the Salvation of the Country', *Nuzi Yuekan*, Vol. I, No. ii, 1933, pp.5-7.

44. Tang Guozhen, 'How to Help Women and Children during the War', *Funu Gongming*, Vol. VII, No. i, 20 January 1938, pp.5-7.

45. Ye Yuying, 'May 1st Labour Day and the Future of the Issue of Women's Labour', *Funu Gongming*, Vol. VII, No. vii, 20 April 1938, pp.11-12.

46. Huang Suxin, 'How to Carry on the Tasks of Women's Movement in the War Districts through the Industrial Cooperative Movement to Proceed the Tasks of Women's Movement', *Funu Gongming*, Vol. VIII, Nos. v-vi, 15 October 1938, pp.4-5, 8.

47. Yinqiu, 'Working Women Should Stand on the Front Line of National Defence', *Funu Gongming*, Vol. VII, No. vii, 20 April 1938, pp.9-10.

48. Hu Ziying, 'The Mobilization of Women for Production during the War', *Funu Shenghuo*, Vol. VI, No. ix, 1 December 1938, pp.8-9; Wangli, 'Women and Production Cooperative', *Funu Shenghuo*, Vol. IX, No. iii,

16 September 1940, pp.4-6.
49. Zhou Jingchu, 'Women and Agriculture', *Funu Shibao*, Vol. XI, 20 October 1913, pp.5-7.
50. Chen Zonglic, 'The Sexual Equalization of Landownership', *New Women*, Vol. I, No. ii, 1927, pp.7-14.
51. Wang Pingling, 'The Labour-Training of Women during the War', *Funu Gongming*, Vol. VII, No. vii, 20 April 1938, pp.7-8; Yinqiu, 'What Can Peasant Women Do?', *Funu Gongming*, Vol. VII, No. vi, 5 April 1938, p.9; Zi, 'Let Us Use Indigenous Cloth', *Funu Shenghuo*, Vol. V, No. xii, 16 April 1938, p.2; Qin Liufang, 'How to Carry Out the Textile Handicraft Industry of Peasant Women', *Funu Shenghuo*, Vol. VI, No. v, 5 July 1938, pp.8-9.
52. Zuo Songfen, 'The Two Key Issues of the Work among Rural Women', *Funu Shenghuo*, Vol. VIII, No. viii, 20 January 1940, pp.3-4.
53. Ying, 'The Issue of Women's Farming in the Fields', *Funu Gongming*, Vol. X, No. v, July 1941, p.5; Liu Hengjing, 'War and Women', *Funu Gongming*, Vol. XI, No. i, March 1942, pp.7-10.
54. Deng Yingchao, 'Land Reform and the New Tasks of Women's Work', *Documents of the Women's Movement*, Xianggang: Xin minzhu chubanshe, 1947, pp.40-6.
55. *Funu Shenghuo*, Vol. VIII, No. i, 16 September 1939, p.29.
56. Lou, 'Speaking for the Peasant Women', op. cit., pp.5-11.
57. De'en, 'Elementary Education . . .', op. cit., pp.19-23; Liu, 'Elementary Education . . .', op. cit., pp.26-29; Zhu Yingmei, 'The Ways to Improve the Livelihood of Peasant Women', *Funu Zazhi*, Vol. XVII, No. xi, January 1931, pp.9-12
58. Jihong, 'An Interview with Jiang Yixiao, a Woman Reporter', *Funu Zazhi*, Vol. IV, No. ii, 1 February 1937, pp.37-43.
59. Meng Qingshu, 'Concerning the Opinions on the Wuhan Working Class Women's Movement', *Funu Shenghuo*, Vol. VI, No. i, 5 May 1938, pp.5-6; Luo Shuzhang, 'Dedicated to those Working Comrades who Relocate Women Workers', *Funu Shenghuo*, Vol. VI, No. viii, 20 August 1938, p.8; Huang, 'How to Carry on the Tasks of Women's Movement . . .', op. cit., pp.4-5, 8; Shuying, 'Several Views on the Publicity and Organization of Peasant and Working Class Women', *Funu Gongming*, Vol. X, No. v, July 1941, pp.18-19.
60. Wangli, 'Women and Production Cooperative', op. cit., pp.4-6.
61. Xu Yasheng, 'Peasant Women's Elementary Education and Training', *Funu Zazhi*, Vol. XV, No. i, January 1929, pp.5-12.
62. Deng Yingchao, 'How to Organize Peasant Women [?]', *Funu Shenghuo*, Vol. V, No. xii, 16 April 1938, pp.9-10; Guan Meirong, 'How to Organize Peasant Women [?]', *Funu Shenghuo*, Vol. V, No. xii, 16 April 1938, pp.5-8; Liang Ying, 'Visits and Publicity in the Countryside', *Funu Gongming*, Vol. VII, No. vi, 5 April 1938, pp.11-13; Guixiu, 'How to go about with the education of . . .', op. cit., pp.11-12.
63. Zuo, 'The Two Key Issues of the Work . . .', op. cit., pp.3-4.
64. Bolin, 'The Issue of Women Labour from the Medical Perspectives', in Mei Sheng, *A Collection of Discussion Papers on the Issue of Chinese Women*, Shanghai: Xinwenhua Shushe, Vol. 1, 1929, pp.41-58.
65. Chen, 'The Sexual Equalization of Landownership', op. cit., pp.7-14.

66. Hu Ziying, 'Several Methods of Mobilizing Women to Participate in Production', *Funu Shenghuo*, Vol. VI, No. x, 16 December 1938, pp.9-10.

67. Zhang Peifan, *The Issue of Women*, Shanghai: Shangwu Yinshuguan, 1922, pp.88-102.

68. Cheng Wanzhen, 'Research on New Industries I', *Funu Zazhi*, Vol. VIII, No. viii, August 1922, p.125; Luxing, 'The Women Labour Legislation in Labour Legislation', in Mei, op. cit., Vol. 1, pp.58-62; Bolin, 'The issue of women labour . . .', op. cit., pp.41-58; Miaoran, 'The Issue of Women Labour', in Mei, op. cit., Vol. 1, pp.34-41; Zhu Yingmei, 'The Ways to Improve the Livelihood . . .', op. cit., pp.9-12; 'The Popularization of Treating Women with Maternal Leaves', *Funu Shanghuo*, Vol. VIII, No. ix, 5 February 1940, pp.5-6.

69. Chen, 'The sexual equalization of landownership', op. cit., pp.7-14.

70. Selu, 'The International Women Labour Union and the Chinese Women', *Funu Zazhi*, Vol. VII, No. xi, November 1921, pp.1-5; Zang, *The Issue of Women*, op. cit., pp.88-102; Jihong, 'The Path of the Liberation of Chinese Working Class Women', *Funu Shenghuo*, Vol. VII, No. vi, 1 May 1939, pp.3-4.

71. Qianshao, 'The Tasks of the Chinese Working Class Women's Celebration of May 1st Day', *Funu Shenghuo*, Vol. VI, No. i, 5 May 1938, pp.3-4.

72. Xu, 'Peasant Women's Elementary Education and Training', op. cit., pp.5-12.

73. Zhennong, 'Organize the Large Masses to the Anti-Japanese Front Line', *Jiefang Zhoukan*, Vol. I, No. xii, 15 August, 1937, p.29.

74. Guixiu, 'How to Go About with the Education of Peasant Women's Education . . .', op. cit., pp.11-12; Gao Nengcheng, 'The theory and Practice of Organizing Women's Production Cooperatives', *Funu Gongming*, Vol. X, No. v, July 1941, pp.15-17.

75. Li Baoguang, 'Women should Enthusiastically Join . . .', op. cit., pp.1-3.

76. Deng, 'Land Reform and the New Tasks . . .', op. cit., pp.40-6.

77. Yuan, 'How to Expand the Working Class Women's Movement?', *Funu Gongming*, Vol. VII, No. vii, 20 April 1938, pp.9-10.

78. Jihong, 'An Interview with Jiang Yixiao . . .', op. cit., pp.37-43; Yinqiu, 'Working Women should Stand on . . .', op. cit., pp.9-10; Jihong, 'The Path of Liberation . . .', op. cit., pp.3-4.

79. Shijin, 'Wish this Assocaition Can Pay More Attention to Peasant Women', *Jiangxi Funu*, Vol. I, No. i, 8 March 1937, pp.3-4.

80. Wenna, ' "March 8th" Day and Village Work', op. cit., p.7.

81. Deng, 'How to Organize Peasant Women [?]', op. cit., pp.9-10.

82. Jin Qihua, 'How to Call upon the Women in the Countryside[?]', *Funu Gongming*, Vol. VII, No. vi, 5 April 1938, p.10.

83. Huang Suxin, 'Expanding the Wartime Women's Work into the Villages', *Funu Gongming*, Vol. VII, No. vi, 5 April 1938, pp.7-8.

84. Lu Yunzhang, 'How to Organize Peasant Women's Movement [?]', *Funu Gongming*, Vol. XI, No. iii, May 1942, pp.21-22.

85. W. Woodruff, *Impact of Western Man*, New York: St. Martin's Press, 1967, p.32; G. and J. Stokes, *The Extreme East*, London: Longman, 1971, pp.213-14.

86. Joseph Esherick, 'Harvard on China: the Apologetics of Imperialism', *Bulletin of Concerned Asian Scholars*, Vol. IV, No. 4, 1972, pp.9-16.

87. J.L. Buck, *Land Utilization in China,* New York: Council on Economic and Cultural Affairs, 1956, pp.373-9.

5. Struggling Together: Women, Peasants and Labourers

The Major Peasant and Labour Movements

The effects of imperialism — military, political, economic and cultural — coupled with the effects of internal capitalist development, the remnants of feudalism and mismanagement by the K.M.T., created immense human suffering for many people in China, particularly for the working class and peasantry. However, this victimization was not passively tolerated.

Peasant Uprisings

In the 19th Century, before the Opium War, there were several rebellions and revolts, especially among the non-Han minority groups. After the Opium War, when the effects of imperialism began to be felt in both the coastal regions and the interior, peasant rebellions became much more widespread; some were nation-wide. These rebellions were usually anti-Manchu (government), sometimes anti-imperialist and anti-landlord, and very often involved stealing food and looting. In some cases, secret societies fomented peasant unrest,[1] while some of these rebellions were millenarian movements.[2]

Anti-government and anti-gentry protests constituted an important part of peasant history. One form of protest found in some regions was the peasants' refusal to pay their rent or taxes.[3] The Taiping Rebellion of 1850-64 was the most widespread peasant movement in the 19th Century, an anti-Manchu movement sweeping over the heart of China in Hubei, Hunan, Anhui, Jiangxi, Jiangsu and Zhejiang provinces. The Taiping rebels would refer to the 'Manchu demons' with their 'stinking odour'. They believed that 'the empire belongs to the Chinese and not to the Manchu. Clothes and food are provided by the Chinese, not by the Manchus. Sons and daughters and other people living here are subjects of the Chinese, not of the Manchus. Why should we Chinese humble ourselves to be their servants and slaves?'[4] However, judging from the rebels' cultural arrogance towards Westerners, there was also a certain element of anti-imperialism. As Karl Marx observed, the rebellion may be attributed to the decline of the indigenous handicraft industry in the countryside as a result of the influx of foreign goods.[5]

Another anti-Manchu movement emerged after the Taiping Rebellion was smashed in 1864. It was the Boxer Uprising in the 1890s. Explicitly anti-Manchu in its initial stage, towards the end it became predominantly anti-imperialist, and in this was probably *supported* by the Manchus. By 1899 its slogan was: 'Support the Qing; Destroy the Foreigners.'[6] Thus the focus of the two largest 19th Century peasant uprisings was mainly anti-government and anti-imperialist, while withholding government taxes was one of its major manifestations, as witnessed, for instance, by the action of tens of thousands of peasants in Guangdong (Kwangtung) and Guangxi in 1906-7.[7]

Prior to this, anti-foreigner feelings were already germinating at different social levels during the Opium War, when a popular milita was organized among local gentry, who refused to open Quangzhou (Canton) city to the British residents in the 1840s.[8] After the Opium War, there was an increase in hostility to missionaries; local elites sometimes led groups of peasants in attacking missionaries and Chinese Christians. Such incidents were especially common in the last quarter of the 19th Century.[9]

In the Boxer Uprising, which, as previously mentioned, took the form of anti-imperialist struggle, the rebels looted and burned churches. This continued from 1900 to 1910, with peasants burning churches and the homes of missionaries and Christians, as well as Christian schools. In this period peasants often resisted the government census for fear that the government might then betray them to the foreigners.[10]

Although specifically anti-missionary sentiments were on the decline in the 20th Century,[11] anti-imperialist feeling remained strong. In his book, *These from the Land of Sinim* (1901), Sir Robert Hart commented, 'It is all but incredible that we [British] have so long been living on the flanks of a volcano; and yet it is apparently beyond dispute that, however friendly individuals may have appeared or been, general intercourse has all along been simply tolerated and never welcomed. . . .'[12]

In the first decade of this century, anti-imperialism was manifested again in 1904-05 and 1908-09.[13] There were also incidents in which peasants were driven to rob food-stores, noodle-factories, grain-boats and even rich people's homes. In some cases, food-stores were burned, and incidents became more violent when the local gentry tried to suppress such activities. Sometimes peasants tried to stop grain-boats from moving their grains, especially in the first decade of the 20th Century, just before the collapse of the Manchu dynasty.[14]

The participation of peasants in the Revolution of 1911 brought the peasant movement to another level. Before this, it had been quite localized (with the exception of the Taiping Rebellion) and sporadic. After that year, the peasant movement in China took on a more organized and nation-wide character. Of course, there were still localized and sporadic peasant riots – refusing to pay taxes, destroying the houses of rent collectors – such as those in Sichuan in 1933. Between 1922 and 1931, at least 197 riots were reported in two Shanghai newspapers,[15] some organized by secret societies, such as the Red Spear Movement in Shandong, Henan, Shaanxi and Shanxi around 1925-30. In addition, banditry – looting and smuggling – among the peasantry was rampant in the 1920s and 1930s.[16]

The formation of the C.C.P. contributed to some extent to the organization of peasant movements. Already in the 1920s there were some weak links between the C.C.P. and the peasants, as witnessed in the establishment of a school for peasant cadres in Guangzhou (Canton) in 1925 and the development of a peasant association in Hunan in 1926-27, and especially in the formation of peasant associations in Haifeng and Lufeng between 1922 and 1927.

Although these peasant uprisings suffered a temporary setback during the White Terror in 1927, peasant resistance was far from dead. Between 1928 and 1930, the C.C.P. set up 11 main insurgent rural bases, mainly in southern China; and between 1931 and 1934, it formed a Jiangxi Soviet Republic which, in effect, signified the beginning of the peasant-based revolution. But suppression by the K.M.T. forced the peasant rebels to make the Long March of 1934-35 to avoid complete liquidation of their movement.

In spite of great hardship, the C.C.P. recovered during the Sino-Japanese War of 1937-45 and established peasant guerrilla bases in northern China, especially in the Shaanxi-Gansu-Ningxi regions. Here, the peasants organized themselves into militia, guerrilla troops, production teams, etc. to strengthen their bases. They pursued a policy of rent and interest reduction as well as anti-imperialism. By the end of the war (1945), the liberated areas consisted of some 950,000 square kilometres and a population of nearly a million; and the C.C.P.'s strength was spreading.[18] By 1949, the peasants, along with workers in the cities, were able to change the agrarian movement into a socialist revolution.

The Labour Movement

In addition to the peasant movement, there was the labour movement. As early as 1885, the dock-workers in Xianggang (Hong Kong) had gone on strike, when the French warship which had attacked Taiwan came into port for repairs.[19] It was the first workers' strike in China. Towards the end of the 19th Century, there were also anti-taxation protests from the workers, as witnessed in the strike of rickshaw pullers in the treaty port of Shanghai in 1897.[20]

However, these were fairly isolated incidents; before the 1920s strikes in China were quite sporadic.[21] The forerunners of the Chinese labour movement were the workers' clubs, which were mostly founded between 1919 and 1921 for educational, welfare, co-operative and protective purposes.[22] In 1919, 26 'unions' were reported. However, between 1920 and 1925, labour unions organized by Communists began to grow.[23] By 1922, there were 91 unions with 150,000 members.[24] The K.M.T. by contrast, showed little interest in organizing workers.[25]

Before 1926, unions tended to cluster in big cities, but then local unions on the town and village levels emerged in Hunan and Hubei.[26] There were three types of labour unions in this period: (1) 'red' unions (underground but influential); (2) 'grey' unions (refusing the directions of both the K.M.T. and the C.C.P.); and (3) 'yellow' unions (fascist organizations run by the K.M.T.).[2]

After 1918, the total number of strikes appeared to be increasing. While there were only 25 strikes in 1918, the number reached 535 in 1926. The total number of strikes during this period was 1,232. Most of these occurred in the textile industry, especially in the foreign-owned factories (such as the Nagai Cotton Mills in Shanghai) and were sparked off by allegations of the employers' ill-treatment of the workers.[28]

The Xianggang (Hong Kong) seamen's strike in January 1922 started the first big wave of the labour movement, reaching its climax in 1923. This wave involved a hundred large and small strikes with more than 300,000 workers taking part. Most of them were successful.[29]

After the suppression of the railway strikes in February 1923, the labour movement went underground for more than two years. (Even so, labour activities in Hunan, led by Mao Zedong (Mao Tse-tung), were comparatively active during this period.[30]) Judging from the nature of the workers' demands before 1925, these strikes were largely economic — they demanded higher wages.[31] But from 1924 onwards, more and more strikes took on a political and patriotic tone.[32]

The next wave of the labour movement began in 1925 and ended with the White Terror of 1927. During 1925, there were 318 strikes throughout China, mostly in Shanghai.[33] Several hundred strikes occurred in 1926-27, especially in south and central China.[34]

Between 1927 and 1937, the labour movement was largely suppressed by the K.M.T., and many of its leaders were beheaded.[35] Those radicals, if lucky enough to save their heads, joined the C.C.P.'s first Peasants' and Workers' Red Army in 1927. During the initial stage of suppression one heroic act stands out: the Gaungzhou (Canton) Commune uprising on 11 December 1927, when the workers occupied the city for three days.[36]

Even the repressive measures of the K.M.T. could not prevent strikes, at least not in Shanghai, where 517 strikes were reported between 1928 and 1932. Most of them were concerned with wages, the dismissal of workers and violations of collective agreements.[37] The C.C.P. maintained 114,525 members in the 'red' unions, half of them in K.M.T. regions and the rest in the soviet areas.[38] But its influence in the city was severely restricted in this period.

According to Helen Snow, the labour movement was far from organized between 1931 and 1945, except in the C.C.P. areas where peasants and workers were forming themselves around a set of political demands.[39] The few labour activities in urban areas mostly shifted from fighting for wage increases or better working conditions to a rearguard action of defending what had been won in the past decade. This was due to the worsening economic conditions as well as to the repressive measures of the K.M.T. Although the K.M.T. claimed that there were 872 unions in China in 1936 (with 743,764 members), these were not unions in the usual sense, since they were K.M.T. controlled organizations.[40] In 1934, the C.C.P. claimed that there were 300,000 men and 10,000 women in their trade unions in the central soviet districts.[41]

With the onset of the Sino-Japanese War, the K.M.T. used their 'unions' to mobilize workers for resistance against the Japanese, and by 1942, it had made union membership in the K.M.T. areas compulsory, while declaring strikes and picketing illegal.[42] Strikes still occurred, but as a rule they were much more low key and used only as a last resort. For example, in 1941, there were only 57 strikes and 81 cases of unrest.[43] By 1942, the K.M.T. Government reported that there were 4,033 labour 'unions' with just over one million workers.[44]

The new Labour Union Code of 1943 forced workers to join these 'unions'. This Code was, of course, formulated to serve political motives, intended to stablize wages, enforce conscription, 'educate' workers for political purposes, prevent labour unrest and control workers' self-mobiliz-ation.[45]

By contrast, a strong network of workers-turned-guerrilla-fighters existed in the C.C.P. areas after 1941.[46] The Communists claimed a membership of one million workers in their labour unions. In 1943, the North China Feder-ation of Trade Unions was formed to organize workers.[47] After the Sino-Japanese War, the workers became active once more, even in the K.M.T. areas. For example, in 1947, workers in Shanghai organized boycotts of American goods and fought for higher wages to keep up with galloping inflation rates.[48]

Thus, throughout the 19th Century and the first half of the 20th Century, there were strong underlying currents of discontent and struggle among both peasants and workers. These struggles were sometimes anti-government and anti-feudalism; sometimes anti-imperialist and, especially among the workers, anti-capitalist. They shifted from sporadic fights in a few isolated locations to systematic organized movements on a national scale. It was in the context of this massive struggle against feudalism, capitalism and imperialism that the women's resistance movement occurred. Women's anti-imperialist efforts and attempts to bring about revolution can be seen as continuous with and supplementary to the larger struggles.

The Rise of the Women's Resistance Movement, 1902-12

Chinese women's first independent attempt to fight against imperialism in an organized manner occurred among educated women (not among working-class or peasant women) in Japan (not in China). With the exception of a few female members of the gentry, education had been closed to women and, of course, both the men and women who belonged to the working poor or peasantry had little education. In the 19th Century, the missionaries, who came *en masse* to 'Christianize' and 'civilize', saw schools as an instrument for 'improving' the Chinese. Missionary schools for women were introduced to reduce the illiteracy rate among women and, by 1902, 4,373 were studying in these schools.[49]

In response to the imperialist threat, on the one hand, and to the growing pressure from Chinese officials/intellectuals interested in bringing about reform, on the other, the Manchu Government reluctantly established women's schools. The first was being built in Shanghai in 1898, and more were established in the 1900s. To compensate for their slow start in women's education and to make it appear that they were eager for reform, the Manchu Government also sent a few Chinese women abroad to study. Since Japan appeared to be strong and modern (as witnessed in the Sino-Japanese War of 1894-95), and was close by, the government sent most of its students there. Between 1902 and 1906, roughly 70 Chinese women studied in Japan, mostly in Tokyo.[50] An even smaller number went to study in the U.S.

For the first time in Chinese history, women studied in schools similar to those for men. Although small in number, women's schools offered a place for women to congregate, allowing them to talk about their views and exchange experiences. As more Chinese came to study in Japan in the early 1900s, they formed various social, 'provincial' and political clubs to promote friendship and common interests. The Foreign Students' Centre, established in 1902, was especially important in bringing together all the Chinese students, male and female, in Tokyo. The Chinese women who came to Japan usually joined these clubs.

As the political situation in China worsened (as described in Chapter Two), and student clubs merged with revolutionary groups in Japan, Chinese women students became more politicized. Some of the student clubs were, indeed, originally formed for political purposes, such as the Organization for the Autonomy of Guangdong *(Guangdong Duli Xiehui)* (1901) and the Association of Military Citizens' Education *(Junguomen Jiaoyuhui)* 1903.

Meanwhile, the students and political activists made some attempts to mobilize the Chinese in Japan. For example, the Organization for the Autonomy of Guangdong (Kwangtung) invited Sun Yixian (Sun Yatsen) to become a member in 1902; students were invited to attend the Commemoration of the 242nd Anniversary of the Manchu Conquest of China, which was organized by the Patriotic Education Society *(Aiguo Xueshe)* and sponsored by Sun Yixian in 1902. Sun Yixian attended the Welcome Party for the Foreign Students just before the formation of the *Tong menghui* in 1905. He invited students in Japan to join.

The radicalizing effect of this organization network can be seen in the life of Qiujin (Ch'iu Chin), claimed by some to be the first Chinese feminist. She left her husband, and went to study in Japan, participated in socialist and feminist politics and was later executed by the Manchu government. On her arrival in Tokyo in 1903, Qiujin joined the Hunanese and Zhejiangese students' clubs. Later, she studied the Japanese language in the Foreign Students' Centre for three months. She revived and reorganized the Humanitarian Society *(Gang'aihui)* in 1904, and then joined the Tongmenghui in 1905.[51] The Humanitarian Society was the first independent women's organization in Tokyo, founded in 1902 — for the purpose of raising the consciousness of Chinese women about their rights, especially their educational rights, and their relationship to the Manchu Government. It had a very small membership, roughly 20, when it began, and a short life-span — less than one year. When the news of the Russian 'invasion' reached Tokyo in 1903, its members quickly organized nursing teams to serve in the front,[52] and sent telegrams to women's schools in Shanghai urging the students there to join the Red Cross Societies and help the Anti-Russian Courageous Troop *(Ju-E Yiyongjun).*[53]

Meanwhile, the women students also organized themselves into anti-Russian groups, for example, the Anti-Russian Association of Women Comrades *(Dui'e Tongzhi Nuhui),* an organization parallelling the male Anti-Russian Association of Comrades *(Dui'e Tongzhi Hui).* This organization was formed in Shanghai in 1904 and was quite small with approximately 30 members in the beginning. Some anti-Russian women troops were formed in 1903;[54] and women participated in anti-Russian public meetings.[55] The reaction of the Manchu Government to this was negative: it advised the Japanese Government to prohibit anti-Russian activities in Japan,[56] and tried to discourage such activities in China proper.

Meanwhile, in China itself, women were becoming involved in various protests. Towards the end of 1904, the U.S. Government wished to renew a treaty with China concerning the migration of Chinese workers, and suggested modifying the treaty in such a way as to allow further discrimination against and exploitation of the Chinese in the U.S. This request angered Chinese women as much as men; women participated in a series of protests and boycotts of American goods. The Manchu Government's response was an order to stop these activities.[57]

In 1907, the Manchu Government announced its intention of borrowing loans from foreign countries to build railways. Had this been done, it would have put even more Chinese economic assets in the hands of the imperialist powers. At least two women's organizations were formed to protect the interests of Chinese merchants on this issue. Some women raised funds for the merchants, and it was reported that prostitutes delivered pamphlets and encouraged people to buy shares for the railways.[58]

In the same year, a debate occurred on the apparently imminent granting to foreign powers of the right of search and arrest in the area of Xijiang in Guangdong (Kwangtung). Several hundred women living in the area held a public meeting and recommended that foreign powers be denied the right to search and arrest Chinese.[59] A 'National Shame Meeting', called in the following year, was attended by over 1,000 women.[60] The Manchu Government, afraid that such protest would spread, issued an order prohibiting students from assembling or engaging in public speeches. Soldiers were sent to the National Shame Meeting.[61]

Two incidents in 1909 brought forth protest from women: one was the discovery that Japanese ships were smuggling gunpowder into China, and the other was the hiring of foreign hydraulic engineers by Guangdong provincial government. Students and teachers at women's schools called for demonstrations and public meetings to protest.[62]

In 1911, the Manchu Government re-announcement of its policy of nationalizing the railways, on the basis of loans from the U.S., Germany,

Britain and France, created so much anger not only among women, but also among the rest of the people, that the regime was brought down.

Throughout the first decade of this century, there were protests, demonstrations and other forms of resistance by Chinese women, sometimes autonomously and at other times along with men. It is important to note, however, that *it was between 1900 and 1910 that Chinese women first organized independently for anti-imperialist purposes.* Their organizations were small in membership and very often had only a brief existence, but at least it was a beginning.

Judging from the nature of these protests and the components of the membership (and leadership) of these women's organizations, it appears that these were largely made up of educated women from well-off families of gentry/intellectual official origin. At this stage working-class women in the cities were still a minority, and little, if any, organization existed among the working class in general. Consequently, working-class women had not yet emerged as an anti-imperialist force.

Peasant women, on the other hand, appear to have been organized, at least locally. But their protests were different in nature from those of the educated women and tended to be concerned with the starvation and poverty imposed upon them by the mixture of feudalism and imperialism. As explained in Chapter Three, peasant women's economic situation was actually worsening and becoming more insecure. A group of women, for example, had been reported 'pillaging the private granaries of certain well-to-do farmers' in the market town of Suzhou in 1907.[63] In 1909, over 100 women of Anqing organized a march and a picket to protest at the fact that their children had been maltreated and their houses wrecked as a reprisal for their withholding fees to pay for dykes.[64] In both cases, these women were dispersed by military force and threats of coercion from the local governments. Unlike their well-to-do counterparts in the cities, the peasant women appear to have been much less well-organized and their protests were more random and localized – they did not direct their anger and frustration at the imperialist powers *per se.*

During this period, both local and national governments were uneasy about the protests by women, and threatened prohibitive legislation and military force in order to intimidate them. Given the lack of systematic organization among peasant women, this intimidation was largely successful and their protests were usually suppressed, whereas the well-organized educated women survived the repressive episodes.

The Movement Subdued: 1913-18

In this period, the nascent women's anti-imperialist movement suffered a severe set-back. Yuan Shikai, the new Republican president, passed a series of laws restricting the freedom of the press, free speech, association and assembly, etc. Women were not allowed to join any political groups or attend any political meetings.[65] The newly-formed K.M.T. was dissolved. These measures were meant to prohibit any revolutionary activities which could jeopardize the regime. Women's activities were closely scrutinized. Nor did the death of Yuan Shikai in 1916 end the repressive controls: in 1907, an order was issued by the Department of Education prohibiting students from joining any political groups.[66] In these circumstances, women's resistance efforts were forced to go underground, which meant that even the acceptance of the Twenty-One Demands of the Japanese (1915) and the signing of the 'Military Agreement of Sino-Japanese Mutual Defence' (1918), both obviously to the advantage of foreign powers, failed to elicit any anti-imperialist protests by women.

However, the maltreatment and lower pay of women workers did produce some protests. For example, ten women workers in a cotton mill in Shanghai, angered by the surveillance system in the factory, attacked and wounded their employer on 15 August 1917.[67] But these incidents were sporadic and far from systematic.

The Movement Regains its Strength: 1919-27

The Paris Peace Conference of 1919 re-ignited women's activism, insofar as the resolution of the Conference openly demonstrated the collaboration of imperialist powers at the expense of Chinese sovereignty. At least 14 patriotic anti-imperialist organizations of women were founded during this period, of which the most powerful were the Alliance of Women's Rights Movement of Beijing *(Beijing Nuquan Yundong Tongmenghui)* and Alliance for Women's Rights Movement of Shanghai *(Shanghai Nuquan Yundong Tongmenghui)*, both formed in 1922. Besides anti-imperialism, they dealt with a variety of issues, such as educational and legal rights for women. There were also some women's organizations whose concern was predominantly anti-imperialist, such as the Women's Association of Salvation *(Funu Jiuwanghui)*, founded in 1919 in Beijing.

Most of these organizations were formed in large cities, such as Shanghai, and consisted mainly of educated women. There was quite a variation in the number of members in these organizations; one of the larger ones, the Alliance for Women's Rights Movement of Beijing, was reported to have over 300 members in 1922.

Strong nationalist sentiments prevailed among these educated women. In 1919, many 'national shame' meetings were organized in women's schools in Shanghai; patriotic lectures and boycotts of Japanese goods were also set up.[68] Throughout 1919, women protested the decision of the Paris Peace Conference, by organizing strikes, demonstrations, petitions and telegrams, and opposed the Japanese and the support given them by the Beijing warlord government.[69]

Military intervention by Japan and the landing of Japanese soldiers in Fuzhou were further spurs to women's anger. The Federation of All-Shanghai

Women *(Shanghai Gejie Funu Lianhehui)* immediately sent protests to the Fujian Government.[70] Along with their male counterparts, women students demanded the abolition of the Military Agreement for Sino-Japanese Mutual Defence (signed in 1918) and freedom of association, assembly and publication.[71] These demands were followed up by mass demonstration in Beijing in which over 10,000 male and female students participated.[72]

The close collaboration of the Beijing Government and the Japanese called for military intervention by the K.M.T. and in 1924-25 the women of various provinces, especially Guangdong, Sichuan and Hebei formed their own 'Northern Expedition Armies', as well as soliciting funds for the K.M.T.[73]

Throughout the 1920s, the imperialist powers, such as Japan and Britain, continued to repress strikes in their Chinese factories by military means, usually resulting in casualties among the workers. Women students formed an alliance with workers on these issues and organized petitions, telegrams and demonstrations. There was a sense of solidarity between students and workers, especially when foreign powers were involved in these strikes. For both students and workers, the exploitation of Chinese workers by foreign employers was seen as an illegitimate infringement of Chinese sovereignty, but not for exactly the same reasons.

While educated women were motivated by a strong sense of nationalism, working-class women were driven by a desire to better their working conditions, wages and job security, and to eradicate the maltreatment of women. The first women workers' strike illustrates this point: between 8 and 15 February 1919, the women workers of the Shanghai Sino-Japanese Cotton Mill stopped work, demanding a better wage structure, job security, dismissal of supervisors and better treatment of child labour.[74]

In the 1920s, there were a number of strikes by women workers in both Chinese and Sino-Japanese factories, most of them around the issues of wages and job security. The most spectacular one occurred in mid-June, when more than 4,000 workers refused to go to work in the Shanghai Textile Company. According to one source, the workers broke some glass windows and more than a thousand light-bulbs in the factory.[75] During the next year, there were many strikes by women workers. In addition to the usual demands (higher wages, better working conditions, etc.), made in concert with the male workers, they demanded political power. This is witnessed in the demonstration organized by the Wuhan Textile Mills Union *(Wuhan Shachang Gonghui),* when tens of thousands of workers participated in a show of strength. They carried flags bearing the slogans: 'Workers Unite' and 'Power Comes From Unity', and yelled slogans such as 'Raise the Political Status of Workers' and 'Improve Workers' Lives'. This march, while surprisingly peaceful, illustrated the growing consciousness of workers' solidarity and rights. Instead of the general economic demands, women workers began to be aware of their political mission.[76]

A systematic organization of women workers spearheaded by Xiang Jingyu, a member of the C.C.P. was begun in 1922. Xiang dedicated her energy to the political education of women workers, especially textile workers.[77]

She maintained that the women's movement should unite with the Chinese revolution, and that working-class women are the vanguard of women's liberation.[78]

According to Helen Snow, more than 100 strikes took place in 1922, and many women participated in most of them.[79] One of the most impressive women' strikes involved more than 20,000 women workers in 44 (some say 24) silk filatures (silk-reeling factories). They demanded higher wages, shorter working hours and the rights to unionize, and others.[80]

Two years later, the women workers of the silk filatures went on strike claiming that, 'unless our daily wages return to 45 cents, we will not work; unless our daily working hours return to ten hours, we will not work; unless the captured workers are returned, we will not work; and unless our unions are acknowledged to protect our interests, we will not work.'[81] Their determination encouraged other workers; 14 other silk filatures in Shanghai became involved, making a total of 140,000 workers on strike. Although the only demand they secured was the right to associate, the strike clearly indicated that the women working in factories had begun to see strength in solidarity. A central demand of the many strikes by women workers in 1924 was for better treatment of women in the workplace. Working-class women strongly condemned the maltreatment of women and the brutality of their supervisors.[82]

In summary, between 1919 and 1924 striking women workers were concerned with higher wages, better working conditions and better treatment of workers in factories. Beginning in 1921-22, workers began to demand political rights and unions, and women became more organized. The extensive participation of women in some of the strikes indicates their growing awareness of the need to be united and organized.

Beginning in 1925, women's demands began to take on an anti-imperialist tone, struggling against the human consequences of imperialism. Women workers began to fight back, and demand the ousting of imperialist powers from the country. After the 'May 30th Incident' (1925) which involved the killing of many student demonstrators shouting slogans such as 'Down with Imperialism' and 'All Chinese Unite', the workers of the Japanese Yuda Cotton Mill *(Riben Yuda Shachang)* staged a sympathetic strike. Sympathetic strikes were also organized in Beijing and Guangdong.[83] More and more people joined the students and workers and a general strike was called in various parts of China, notably in Beijing, Gaungzhou, Nanjing and Fuzhou. Tens of thousands of workers, students, businessmen and others took to the streets in various cities to protest.

In 1925 and 1926, in the midst of these anti-imperialist struggles, women workers continued to strike for higher wages, better treatment and improved working conditions. Most of these strikes occurred in the textile industry. Although there were some strikes in 1927, they were not significant for reasons which will be elaborated on later. According to one report in Shanghai, there were 59 fewer strikes than in 1926.[84]

Throughout the period 1919-27, it was obvious that the women's labour movement was on the offensive. It moved from sporadic skirmishes to cohesive strikes and organizations. While, for the most part, the K.M.T. ignored women workers, it made a minimal effort to mobilize educated women, especially during the Northern Expedition when women were organized as spies, nurses, transportation service workers, etc. The C.C.P. on the other hand, consciously organized working women. Xiang Jingyu's efforts to mobilize working-class women in the early 1920s constituted a short but pioneering effort. After that beginning the C.C.P. had been working with women's organizations, such as the Organization of Chinese Women *(Zhongguo Funu Xiehui)* in Shanghai to organize women workers and demand special rights for women workers.[85] During the Gaungzhou Commune (Canton Commune) of December 1927 — which lasted three days — women workers were mobilized by the C.C.P.[86]

Although peasant women were not quite as well organized as men, certain incidents indicate that they were beginning to feel the need to organize to overcome their economic difficulties. In Gaungdong (Kwangtung), for example, approximately 30 peasant women formed a petition group and marched to see President Sun Yixian. Their complaint was that when a member of their local gentry had failed to obtain taxes from the villagers, he robbed them of all their property in revenge. They were now without food or shelter. During the trip, these 30 women dressed in rags and went barefoot, some of them carrying babies on their backs. They covered their faces and heads with old face towels and cried all the way to the provincial government treasurer, insisting that, although they were innocent, they were being punished. They passed out leaflets to the passersby on the way.[87]

Increasing hardship due to the decline of the peasant economy in the 1920s hit the poorest peasants first. As in the previous decades, there were incidents of rice-robberies; for example, hundreds of peasant women, especially older women, took rice from several stores in Jiangsu.[88]

Consistent with its policy of ignoring working-class women, the K.M.T. made little attempt to mobilize peasant women. The C.C.P. did try to organize them, but was unsuccessful until the mid-1920s, when the peasants of Haifeng and Lufeng in Guangdong rose up, and a few women peasants were in the Red Army there. In the Hailufeng Soviet *(Hailufeng Suweiai)* in 1927-28, tens of thousands of peasant women joined the Congress of Armed Peasant Women and were organized into teams known as the 'Pink Rifle Teams' *(Fenqiang Tuan);* every woman was armed. But, apart from this short-lived soviet, most of the peasant women in China remained unorganized.

Thus, after several years of inactivity in the 1910s, the Chinese-educated women and women workers rose up to fight against the forces of imperialism and to demand workers' rights; towards the end of 1927, peasant women, alongside peasant men, were able to establish a soviet for a short period under the directorship of the C.C.P. How did the governments in power respond to these struggles?

Generally, the warlord government of Beijing countered these protests by imposing severe military repressions and prohibitive orders. However, these measures were not carried out consistently, especially in 1919 and the early 1920s. In response to the anti-imperialist activities of educated women, the Beijing Government sent police and troops to beat up students and arrest them. Tight police patrols were used at every public protest meeting. (In some cases, the government was forced to give in to public pressure to release the arrested students.) In addition, the government issued orders to restrict and suppress student activities and stated that students had no right to interefere in government policies.[89] The government then prohibited marches, public speeches and pamphlet distribution, and dissolved student organizations.

More than 1,000 students were arrested in 1919 between 1 and 3 June as part of the effort to contain the spread of radicalism; when women representatives came to Beijing to petition and demand an end to boycotts of Japanese goods campaigns they too were arrested.[90] When women organized rallies, or public meetings, policemen were usually found among the crowd.[91] In the 1920s, it became illegal for women to attend political meetings or join political groups. The imperialist powers did *not* remain neutral in these incidents; the U.S.-British representatives issued orders forbidding marching in the streets and sent troops to tear down all the protest (anti-imperialist) posters on the walls in Shanghai.[92]

While the warlord governments confined themselves to expressions of disapproval of the protests and demonstrations by educated women, they used outright brutality in their treatment of working-class women. The arrest of strikers, especially the leaders, was a common practice used to intimidate women workers. For example, in 1922, a strike of the silk filatures workers in Shanghai was called off because the women workers were afraid that the five arrested leaders would actually be executed if the strike continued.[93] In some cases, executions did occur: two leaders arrested during the strike of Huashi Cotton Mill *(Huashi Shachang)* in 1922 were executed within two hours of their arrest.[94]

Military troops and policemen were often sent to the scene of strikes, not just to 'keep order', but to kill striking workers. During a strike by textile workers in Shanghai in 1922, policemen came into the factories with armoured vehicles, throwing tear bombs and shooting. More than 200 women were arrested at gunpoint. In this case, it was alleged that the police department actually used 'provocateurs' to create violence to justify police use of firearms. More than 160 provocateurs threw stones at the workers, sprayed them with water, and even rolled burning oil tanks at them.

It appears that as time went on the policemen became even more cold-blooded. In 1925, when the workers of Dakang Cotton Mill *(Dakang Shachang)* in Qingdao went on strike, the police force was sent in by the provincial government and eight workers were killed and ten wounded.[95] And when the women workers of the Japanese Yuda Cotton Mill were on strike, soldiers were sent in to deal with the crises. On one occasion, when 6,000 workers protested in front of a factory, 5,000 soldiers were sent in to contain the crowd; 20 persons were killed and 60 drowned when they jumped into the river trying to escape.[96] Similar incidents happened in 1926 and 1927.[97] Since many industrial workers lived in company dormitories, police intervention in strikes sometimes took the form of sieges, cutting off food supplies and communication links with the outside. Such sieges would be kept up even to the point of starving workers to death.[98]

As the K.M.T. began to consolidate its power in 1927 during its Northern Expedition, it decided it was time to smash the C.C.P. Any political activities not under the co-ordination of the K.M.T. were suspect. Several women's organizations in Shanghai and Guangzhou were scrutinized and searched.[99] By the end of 1927, orders were issued prohibiting the public from assembling, associating or marching, especially in Jiangsu. The Jiangsu Government also prohibited the public from forming teams to search people for Japanese goods in the streets and placed restrictions on organizations and associations.[100]

Besides prohibitive legislation, the K.M.T. used strong coercive measures. By April 1927, many unions had been closed down and dissolved. Just before the onslaught of terror, the C.C.P. adopted the policy that union members should give up their arms; this rendered the workers defenceless. Then came the White Terror: gangsters were employed to destroy unions and police and military soldiers broke up picket lines; workers on strike were dismissed or forced to pay huge fines and many people were imprisoned without a trial. Consequently, in 1927 alone, it has been claimed that 32,316 persons were sent to jail and 37,985 were executed, '25,000 died in open struggle, and 13,000 were "executed barbarously" '.[101]

This policy of wiping out the Communists also hurt the women's movements. The Central Executive Committee directed the Women's Bureau 'to purge Communist members or those with Communist connections from the Central Women's Bureau'.[102]

After the K.M.T. army smashed the Guangzhou Commune, 200 to 300 women were reported murdered because they had bobbed their hair — a symbol of liberation. In 1927 alone, over 1,000 women leaders were killed by the K.M.T., many of them not Communists at all, although they had been active in the women's movements. Women were sometimes tortured before they were executed: their breasts cut off, their bodies were wrapped with cotton and burned with oil; and in some cases, their bodies were stripped naked and hung in public places with pieces of wood stuck in their vaginas.[103]

Two things ought to be remembered: first, during the 1920s, the K.M.T. tried to incorporate the women's movements, as will be elaborated in Chapter Six. Competition from the C.C.P. had forced the K.M.T. to recruit women, but, even so, it succeeded only in mobilizing educated women, not working-class and peasant women. Once the K.M.T. had consolidated its power in 1927, they then turned on the women's movement and crushed it, showing that the K.M.T.'s concern for women's causes had been purely instrumental. Second, both the K.M.T. and the warlord government had used repressive measures to discourage, control and eliminate women's anti-imperialist efforts or anti-capitalist activities throughout this period; the women's movement suffered setbacks under those attacks, but nevertheless recovered itself each time. In fact, there was growing militancy and mobilization among the educated and working-class women in the 1920s as repression escalated. Even the formerly unorganized peasant women rose up under the leadership of the C.C.P. whose efforts to mobilize working women in the cities had been curtailed and re-directed at peasant women. However, of the repression that women experienced in the 1920s, the White Terror of 1927 was the most severe blow, and it took a number of years for women to recover.

Protest Despite Repression: 1928-37

Women continued their anti-imperialist activities, but now their efforts were increasingly dictated by the K.M.T. As will be discussed in Chapter Six, the K.M.T. was in the process of institutionalizing the women's movements in the urban regions. Increasingly, educated women helped the K.M.T. Government defend the country by providing nursing services to the soldiers, collecting food, clothes and funds for the armies at the front, and helping the refugees. Some even attempted to join the armies.[104]

There were, however, some activities that the K.M.T. Government frowned upon. For example, anti-imperialist protest speeches, demonstrations and petitions;[105] boycotts of the Japanese goods, the burning of Japanese stores and storage space;[106] the forming of alliances among anti-imperialist organizations, such as the Great Alliance of Patriotic Women of Shanghai in 1931; and the merger of other non-women organizations with women's organizations in resistance in 1932.[107]

An upsurge in the number of women's organizations occurred in this period in response to the growing crisis. Between 1928 and 1937, at least 26 organizations were founded to carry out a variety of tasks, including: the Philanthropic Association of Shanghai Women *(Shanghaishi Funu Jiujihui)* (1913?), the Patriotic and Courageous Anti-Japanese Team of Nanjing Women *(Nanjing Funu Kangrijiuguo Yiyongtuan)* (1931), the Women's Nursing Team *(Nuzi Jiuhudui)* (1931), the Organization of Chinese Women for Consolation *(Zhongguo Funu Weilaojiangshi Hui)* (1931), the Association of Women in the Capital for the Promotion of National Products *(Shoudu Funu Tichangguohuo Hui)* (1931), the Organization of Guangzhou Women for the Care of Refugees *(Guangzhou Funu Jiujianmin Hui)* (1932) and the Guangxi Women's Military Troop *(Guangxi Funu Zhandoudui)* (1937?).

During this period, as part of their policy of institutionalization, the K.M.T. created two important national women's organizations to co-ordinate activities: the Women's Work Committee of the New Life Movement *(Xinshenghuo Yundong Funugongzuo Weiyuanhui)* in Nanchang (1934) and the Headquarters of Chinese Women for the Consolation of Self-defence and Resistance Soldiers *(Zhongguo Funu Weilao Zaiwei Kangzhan Jiangshi Zonghui)* in Chongqing (1937). The first was created to promote traditional moral values among women, but later became the national co-ordinator of women's resistance work. The second was formed in response to increasing

Japanese attacks.

It appears that the organizations created in this period had a larger member-ship than previous ones. For example, even the non-governmental Patriotic Federation of Shanghai Women *(Shanghai Funujie Jiuguo Laihehui)* (1935) claimed to have over 1,000 members. The forerunner of the Headquarters for Chinese Women for the Consolation of Self-Defence and Resistance Soldiers formed by the K.M.T. in 1931 had 42 branches (including branches abroad) and 54 sub-branches.

As we have already noted, the labour movement was on the decline after the 1927 massacre; the total number of strikers dropped from 230,256 in 1927 to 69,613 in 1929. Women workers, being an integral part of the move-ment, were also affected by the suppression. The number of women partici-pants in strikes dropped from 195,200 in 1927 to 31,263 in 1929.[108] There was also a shift of concern from higher wages and anti-imperialism to job security, largely due to the economic recession China had to confront in the 1930s, when factories were closed and workers laid off.

There were a few militant strikes in this period; for example, during a strike at a cotton mill in Shanghai in 1929, more than 400 women workers rushed into the factories and smashed many windows.[109] In another strike, the workers sabotaged the machinery in the factories.[110] The most spec-tacular strike in this period took place in 1932 and involved more than 13,000 women in the silk filatures in Shanghai. In 1936, 15,000 workers of mainly Japanese-owned cotton mills in Shanghai (many of them women) went on strike demanding higher wages and better treatment of workers.[111] These were not the only strikes involving thousands of workers.

During this period, women workers also held public meetings for education-al purposes;[112] formed teams of women to seek out Japanese goods as part of a campaign to boycott Japanese goods;[113] and organized family service teams to investigate the welfare of women workers, provide women with basic knowledge of hygiene and teach them how to care for their children.[114]

There is some evidence that the C.C.P. was involved with the mobiliz-ation of working-class women at this time, especially for the anti-Japanese front. For example, the Great Alliance of Patriotic Women of Shanghai *(Shanghai Funu Jiuguo Tatongmenghui)* was directed by the C.C.P. It had six branches and actively mobilized women, including working-class women, to work as nurses on the front.[115]

As the economic situation of China deteriorated in the 1930s, especially in the few years just before the Sino-Japanese War, the situation of peasant women steadily worsened. The familiar food robberies continued — there were incidents of groups of women robbing pre-harvest crops for food in Guangdong[116] and in northern China[117] — and women in groups of three to five knocked at doors begging for rice.[118]

As well as these sporadic acts, peasant women began to organize them-selves under the leadership of the C.C.P. They were especially active militarily in the Jiangxi Soviet in 1931-34, with thousands joining the Women Guards. This was a local defence force, consisting of women of 16 years of age and over who were of poor and middle peasant origin. In the soviet, women's aid corps were organized to nurse the wounded and to transport supplies to the front. Some women served with the combat troops, while others engaged in spying or guerrilla activities.[119] The C.C.P. also organized women's propaganda teams to encourage their husbands, and brothers to join the Red Army.[120]

After the Long March, when the C.C.P. began to consolidate its power in the border regions, women were mobilized into political and military work as well as production work, such as agricultural field work and spinning, weaving and sewing for the soldiers. In northern Shaanxi in 1937, for example, there were 130,000 women engaged in productive work, and 7,000 active members of the C.C.P.[121]

The K.M.T. Government's reaction to women's anti-Japanese resistance efforts varied, depending on whether they were undertaken by educated, working-class or peasant women. Basically its policy was to promote the activities of the educated women which it could control, and to smash the efforts of working-class women and peasant women. Chapter Six will discuss K.M.T. co-ordination of women's activities, so here we will consider only techniques for controlling or repressing women's resistance.

First of all, in the 1930s, the 'New Life Movement' under the leadership of the K.M.T., set out to discipline 'modern women' who cut their hair, used cosmetics, danced or wore short sleeves and trousers. For example, in 1936, the provincial government of Shandong arrested 450 'modern women' for violating the regulations of the New Life Movement.[122] These regulations affected educated women more than their working-class or peasant counterparts.

The K.M.T. also regulated the types of assemblies and associations which could be held in the provinces, seeking to eliminate Communist gatherings. Students were prohibited from petitioning or forming patriotic armies to defend the country from the Japanese.[123] When more than 8,000 male and female students petitioned in Beijing urging the government to fight against Japanese imperialism, the government sent armed police to assault and arrest the students; more than 200 students were wounded in that incident.[124]

Although the K.M.T. Government had been issuing orders since 1927, warning workers to be wary of 'trouble-makers', they were to resort to even dirtier methods.[125] Using Hitler's secret police as a model, the K.M.T. squads engaged in systematic terrorization of workers. Besides controlling unions, the K.M.T. sent spies and provocateurs into the labour movement, and used gang leaders as the 'arbiters' of labour disputes or strikes.[126] These gangsters, hired by the gang leaders, not only blackmailed the workers, but also co-operated with the police department in framing labour leaders , or in kidnapping or killing them. Leaders were also arrested and charged with communism, usually on the basis of false evidence. Armed soldiers or police with sub-machine guns were used to contain the strikes.[127]

As a result of these K.M.T. tactics, more than 100,000 workers and peasants were reported killed in the first eight months of 1928. In October of the same year, it was claimed that 17,200 were in jails.[128] Brutality and killing were a very common part of the strike scene. For example, when the Shanghai Yong'an Cotton Mill *(Shanghai Yong'an Shachang)* locked the workers out in 1932, more than 6,000 workers (men and women) broke through the gate of the factory only to find policemen waiting for them. In short, the period 1928-37 saw the continued but controlled activity of educated women, while working-class women's labour struggles posed a constant threat, and brought down the full weight of the K.M.T.'s repressive apparatus. Peasant women, on the other hand, under the mobilization of the C.C.P. engaged in an offensive struggle and were well organized; despite severe blows from the K.M.T. after 1927, the C.C.P. was able to continue its mobilization in the countryside.

The Great Mobilization: 1938-45

The total number of women's anti-imperialist organizations after 1938 cannot be assessed conclusively, but estimates range from 313 to 358 K.M.T. women's anti-imperialist organizations in 1940.[129]

In response to an intensification of the Japanese attacks between 1937 and 1945, the K.M.T. Government designated the Women's Guidance Committee of the New Life Movement as the chief co-ordinator of women's anti-imperialist activities on 1 July 1938. Its organizational structure consisted of an administrative department, a training department, a department of cultural affairs, a life guidance department, a group of counsellors, a production affairs department (which included four experimental industrial sites), a consolation department (including nine teams), a department of child-care, a department of rural services, a co-ordination committee, 12 provincial women's guidance committees of the New Life Movement, an external women's guidance committee of the New Life Movement and 34 New Life Movement women's working teams.

The C.C.P. also founded at least four umbrella women's anti-imperialist organizations before July 1938, such as the Patriotic Federation of Shanghai Women *(Shanghair Funujie Jingue Lianhehui)* (1935), the Patriotic Federation of Jiaodong Women *(Jiaodong Funu Jiuguo Lianhehui)* (1937), the Federation of All-Women *(Gejie Funu Lianhehui)* (1938), and the Federation of All-Northern-Shaanxi Women *(Shanbei Gejie Funu Lianhehui)* (1938). There were 21 women's organizations formed by the C.C.P., such as the Association of Women Comrades for Resistance *(Funu Kangdi Tongzhihui)* and Women's Self-Defence Teams *(Nu Ziweidui)* (1940). It is difficult to guess the precise number: first of all, we are not sure how many of these C.C.P. women's organizations were counted in the survey made by the K.M.T. Second, some of the C.C.P. women's organizations had branches and sub-branches and their exact number is not known. It was estimated in 1939 that in northern China more than 8,000 locations had women's anti-Japanese patriotic associations.[130] By the end of 1945, within the liberated areas of the C.C.P., there were 34,061 branches of the Federation of All-Women with

137

a membership equalling 88% of all women villagers.[131]

During this period, there was a tremendous increase in the number of Chinese women participating in these women's organizations. Most of them had a membership in the thousands. One of the largest ones was the Organization of Chinese Women for the Consolation of Soldiers (formed in 1931), whose membership reached over one million in 1941. Membership in the various C.C.P. organizations was also in the thousands. The largest was the Women's Patriotic Headquarters of Southern Hebei (formed in 1939), which had roughly 400,000 members. Membership increased through time: in 1937 there were 130,000 women in the women's organizations in the C.C.P. areas; by June 1943, the figure had risen to 2,532,208.[132]

In this period, the women's resistance efforts were largely incorporated into the two parties, the K.M.T. and the C.C.P. This, of course, was the continuation of the developments of the early 1930s.

With respect to the K.M.T., the structuring of activities of the Women's Guidance Committee can be taken as a guide:

(1) Officer-training: From July 1938 to December 1943, 1,111 women graduated from the training programme and 1,256 were still in the process of training; most of these women were trained in 1939. Women were prepared for work in the countryside, to serve the disabled soldiers and young children, to assist in production, educational, political and medical tasks. Most of the graduates worked in the countryside and for the handicapped soldiers.[133]

(2) 'Life Guidance': This involved providing educational services, entertainments, etc. for women as a whole. The K.M.T. selected six factories within which to implement this service, but it found that not many working-class women were interested or enthusiastic about it. The Committee also engaged in war-time publicity and solicited funds.[134]

(3) Consolation of Soldiers: Services for the wounded and disabled soldiers were provided, and women wrote letters and cleaned the clothes of these soldiers; they also tried to educate and entertain them.[135]

(4) Child Welfare: Children, especially the children of refugees, were entertained, fed and educated by women; but due to economic reasons, only one day-care centre and roughly 15 children's groups were formed to help the Wartime Childcare Headquarters.[136]

(5) Cultural Affairs: Six women's periodicals and a variety of pamphlets and books for the general public and children were published. The *Funu Xinyun* published 6,000 copies each month, most of which were circulated in Sichuan. Owing to the illiteracy of the working-class and peasant women, this service was not of much benefit to them.[137]

(6) Surveys and Statistics: Data on the activities of the branches, teams and bureaux of the Women's Guidance Committee, as well as other women's organizations, were compiled to determine the amount of work which had already been done and which lay ahead.[138]

(7) Rural Services: Between Autumn 1938 and Autumn 1939, the K.M.T. focused its attention on the war districts in Hubei and Hunan. Then, it shifted to Sichuan, and in 1942-43, Baxian of Sichuan was selected as the

district for experimentation in rural services. In 1944, Jiangbei of Sichuan was also selected. There were four types of rural services: (a) publicity through notices, posters, speeches, dramas and home-visiting; (b) officer-training; (c) organizations of women's teams; and (d) activities in recreation, education, production, hygiene, soliciting of funds, consolation of soldiers and helping soldiers' families.[139]

Although these services concentrated on the education of peasant women, it failed to touch most of them, as can be seen in the following statistics: during the period between July 1938 and December 1943, only 242,883 women out of a female population of roughly 300 million became literate, 414,819 persons were trained and 1,326,393 gathered at the publicity meetings. One of the reasons for this failure lay in the feudal relationships between men and women in the countryside. Husbands and mothers-in-law hated to see their wives and daughters-in-law going to school and 'wasting' their time doing schoolwork; it was not uncommon for women to be dragged from the class-rooms by their husbands. Nor were the other methods of education — dramas, story-telling, singing songs, putting up posters, etc.[140] — any more successful in mobilizing peasant women.

The training of officers or service workers was undertaken in the country-side. The rural service provided in the war district of Hubei between the autumn of 1938 and 1939 illustrates the range of tasks involved. Forty-seven new graduates in rural services went to the war district, carrying with them some simple medical equipment, cartoons and books. It was claimed that, within 50 days, they had trained 200 men, 160 women and 200 children. Nursing teams, women's consolation teams and child consolation teams were formed, providing moral support for soldiers and carried out the emergency evacuation of refugee children. Forms of engagement with the soldiers and local population included: family-visiting, dramas, women's training classes, workers' training classes and literacy classes for wounded soldiers. Most of the rural service workers stayed in an area from 50 days to three months.[141]

(8) Production Work: To increase the production of textile goods, handicrafts and silk, the Women's Guidance Committee mobilized 52,282 women — peasants, refugees, soldiers' families and workers.[142] Several kinds of production work were promoted: (a) production co-operatives were created and low-interest short-term loan services were provided to stimulate production. These co-operatives engaged in sewing, spinning, weaving, poultry, sheep-rearing, etc. In 1942, only three counties in Sichuan had such co-operatives;[143] (b) handicraft-skill-training classes were formed to train women to spin, weave and sew. These classes usually lasted for three months and were attended by women whose brothers or husbands were at the front; (c) factories were established to produce towels, clothing, rugs, socks, etc.; and (d) farming teams of men and women were organized for working on the farms belonging to soldiers' families.[144] The K.M.T. Government, as late as 1943, experimented with an agricultural project in Hunan which involved farming, industrial sites, and accommodation for honoured soldiers' families.[145]

139

Apart from these feeble attempts to mobilize peasant women, the K.M.T. also tried to mobilize working-class women for resistance purposes. The extent to which the K.M.T. actually recruited factory women for resistance is difficult to judge. It was claimed that some factory women managed to organize 'wartime staff members' service teams' in factories, which washed the clothes and bed-sheets of soldiers in hospitals, organized choirs and sing-songs for the wounded and donated money for resistance. However, the factory women were not as enthusiastic as some people claimed: only 11 workers from three cotton mills attended the panel for working-class women organized by the Association of *Funu Shenghuo* in Wuchang in 1938.[146] Literacy classes for factory women were established. The classes usually lasted two hours, during which introductory talks were given on the war and resistance efforts.[147] Women's service work at the front included conducting surveys, propaganda, consolation and saving refugees, spying and organizing literacy classes for women.[148]

In 1939, some women formed their own armies in Guangdong, Guangxi and Fujian.[149] Towards the end of the war, the K.M.T. initiated a campaign to recruit young female intellectuals into the armies, and thousands of them registered as soldiers.[150] However, these armies of women dealt mainly with nursing, cultural activities, communication and managerial services.[151]

In addition to encouraging service work, the K.M.T. tried to promote production among the working-class women to overcome the war-time shortage of products, especially textile goods. A factory for making bandages, trousers, shirts, etc. was created for the refugee women in Changsha; it included class rooms for literacy classes in the evenings and accommodation for workers. Unfortunately, there were no day-care centres for the working mothers.[152] In some districts, due to lack of funding, factories could not be formed. In such cases, women were encouraged to learn textile handicraft production which could be undertaken at home.[153] Where funding was available, classes were set up to train women how to spin and weave and sew—tasks considered very important by the K.M.T.[154] In Guangdong (Kwangtung), where some of these classes lasted for three months, co-operatives were also set up to help women in the production of textile handicraft goods, shoe-making, etc.[155]

Like the K.M.T., the C.C.P. mobilized women, especially peasant women, for resistance. According to one claim, in central Hebei, 80% of women worked for the liberation army, mostly as nurses in hospitals. Of workers in the hospitals behind the front 80 to 90% were women; and even in the hospitals at the front, roughly 30% were women. These nurses prepared blankets, pillows, etc. for emergency situations and learned to work in difficult cond-itions. They were taught how to walk over a single log bridge, jump over streams and trenches, and so on.[156]

Women also participated in self-defence armies. In an inconclusive study made in 1940, it was stated that, of the 70 million women in the liberated areas, 1,386,780 joined the self-defence armies [157] which were organized to trace traitors and robbers, and protect the regions. At least 3,000 women foot soldiers participated in the liberation army and worked as guerrilla fighters, especially in southern China.[158]

As part of their war effort, the C.C.P. mobilized women to solicit food and weapons for the soldiers. A patriotic food and weapon donation campaign was launched in the countryside. These items were sent to the front. In addition, many women prepared gift packages, usually containing towels, books, needles, etc., suitable for the soldiers at the front. Behind the front, women cultivated the farms, washed the clothes, prepared food and generally took care of the concerns of the soldiers' families, especially those with elderly persons or babies.

Of all the tasks that women engaged in, agricultural production and textile handicraft work were considered the two key ones in the liberated areas. Due to the K.M.T. blockade, and general war-time conditions, the liberated areas had great difficulty in providing enough food and basic commodities for the population.

To alleviate this situation, the C.C.P. launched a land reform movement to provide men and women with their own land. They strongly recommended that women work in the fields, for many men had left to join the armies and if the fields were left unploughed and uncultivated, the people left behind might starve to death. The participation of women in farming was of great benefit to women themselves. Since, in northern China, they were not used to working on the farms, the C.C.P. encouraged the men who were not fighting to teach them how to plough, sow seeds, etc. In the beginning, households were grouped together to help each other out, and, where household work and child-care were obstacles to the participation of women in **outside** work, a certain division of labour was designed: mothers-in-law were encouraged to stay at home and do the housework and child-care, while their daughters-in-law worked in the fields; or there was a rotational division of labour in which women alternated between work at home and work outside. Income based on production was shared among them. For the first time, women earned a living that could support the whole family.

'Self-sufficiency' became very important in the liberated areas and, in addition to agricultural work, women learned how to work in handicraft industries. At first, this was difficult; not only did many women in northern China not know how to spin, weave or sew, but also there were not enough spinning wheels or weaving looms to allow for the massive participation of women. However, the men who knew these skills taught the women and some simple technologies of spinning and weaving were set up. Once again, whatever women earned was shared among all family members, so mothers-in-law did not object to taking care of the domestic work while their daughters-in-law did handicraft work.

During this period, the K.M.T.'s desire to wipe out the Communists remained strong. Although the government was busy fighting the Japanese, it kept an eye on the movements of radical women. For example, in the capital of Guizhou, the K.M.T. accused the Y.M.C.A., and even the local women's New Life Movement, of being Communist. It broke up a Y.W.C.A. meeting on 'What Is Democracy?' and prohibited any further meetings of this kind unless they were approved by the K.M.T., with a K.M.T. member acting as chairperson.[159] Women's magazines were scrutinized. For example, issues of the *Contemporary Women (Xiandai Funu)* had to be sent to K.M.T. inspectors before they could be published and distributed. Articles were often censored. Even March 8th celebration meetings were suspected. In 1945, one of these meetings in the K.M.T. area was disturbed by K.M.T. officials who cut off the microphones.[160] In the countryside, there had been clashes between K.M.T. and C.C.P. troops since 1941. After 1941, the liberated areas of northern China were blockaded by the K.M.T. troops. All this illustrates the extent to which the K.M.T. intended to smash the Communists.[161]

It is ironic that the K.M.T., which had tried so hard to stamp out peasant and working-class women's struggles and to contain and incorporate women's movements, was overthrown at the end of the Sino-Japanese War when the resistance effort of these women specifically turned to revolutionary acts.

Resistance Turns to Revolution: 1946-49

After the war, the K.M.T. Women's Guidance Committee continued to co-ordinate women's activities. In 1946, there were 351 women's organizations,[162] but the K.M.T. had relaxed its effort to bring about the liberation of women. Instead, as noted, it launched a campaign to push women back to the home. The tasks of the Women's Guidance Committee were reduced to cultural affairs, child welfare, social welfare and, to a much lesser extent, production.

Meanwhile, in the cities, women turned to anti-U.S. activities. The assault of a female student by an American soldier in 1947 sparked off a series of anti-American campaigns, led mainly by students. When more than 3,000 male and female students protested in Hangzhou, it was suspected that they had been organized by the C.C.P.[163]

The number of strikes, which had been few during the war, increased again, in the context of the economic crises exacerbated by K.M.T. mismanagement of wages and the illtreatment of workers which became the two key issues in labour disputes. Galloping inflation in the postwar period created extra hardship for working-class women, and striking was one common way to bargain. As usual, the K.M.T. resorted to intimidation and arrest to control the masses.[164]

But the main drive for revolution came from the C.C.P.-led peasants, both men and women, in the countryside. The anti-imperialist movement shifted to a fight against the K.M.T. Government (which was pro-landlord and pro-U.S.).[165] Continuing its policy of concentrating on production as a supplement to warfare against the K.M.T., the C.C.P. utilized the land reform and rent-and-tax-reduction movements to mobilize peasant women to help eradicate landlords and the feudalistic relationships between men and women. 'Speak-bitterness' meetings of women helped to raise the consciousness of women. In Hebei, for example, 84% of the women aged 17 and over attended these meetings in Dingxian in 1947-48. Moreover, in the whole country, the majority of women joined peasant unions or women's committees. In fact, women formed the core of the land reform movement.

In this movement, every woman obtained a piece of land. They pulled out weeds, grew crops, ploughed, fertilized, etc. Not only poor women, but also middle-level and rich peasant women worked in the fields, providing them with incomes for their families. Many people now said, 'This year women accomplished a lot; it would have been impossible without women.'

Women also participated in industrial production, especially in the textile handicraft industry. This was merely continuing work they had done during the war. After the war, more women worked in areas which had been traditional male preserves, such as construction work. Between 1946 and 1949, many women in Jiaodong carried stones, moved lumber and mended roads, etc. Women also continued to work as nurses, transportation service workers and spies for the armies, now fighting against the K.M.T. Government, and to do the washing.

The C.C.P. policy on the issue of organizing women remained basically unchanged in 1948: the participation of rural women in production continued to be the focus of its concern. However, it now decided to unite women's organizations in the liberated areas with women in the K.M.T. areas who were against U.S. imperialism. In April 1949, C.C.P. attention shifted to urban women. It decided that, 'On the condition that our work among rural women not be jeopardized, our present work with women should focus on the urban women's movement.'[166]

In towns, such as Zhangjiakou, street production groups and street representative groups were formed to mobilize women for a variety of purposes, but mainly to produce — to make insoles, socks, hats, shoes, cut lumber and so on. Other tasks included education, re-forestation and hygienic work.

These grass-roots women's organizations were quite useful in linking the central body of the C.C.P. with the women in local districts. They also ensured the production of sufficient food for the peasants and soldiers, and united women. Moreover, they were the driving force behind the land reform movement, as well as other political movements aimed at eliminating landlord-tenant relationships in the countryside and townships. These campaigns to make the villages and townships self-sufficient and to demolish feudal relationships were so successful that the C.C.P. was seen by many Chinese as a political party capable of overthrowing the corrupted and fragile K.M.T. Government.

Conclusion

The history of Chinese women's resistance shows that although educated women established the pioneer organizations, it was the C.C.P. which mobilized working-class and peasant women and which was the vanguard of women's resistance. Although the K.M.T. geared up its mobilization work during the Sino-Japanese War, it managed only to mobilize a few educated women. Throughout this period, working-class women were largely ignored, since the C.C.P. had been 'exiled' from the urban areas.

Obviously, women had different interests according to their class back-grounds. The educated women were interested in kicking out the Manchus in the early 20th Century and in promoting nationalism during the Sino-Japanese War. Those progressive elements within this group of women were concerned with imperialism and the capitalist exploitation of workers in the cities; but they were severely suppressed by the K.M.T. The K.M.T. was interested in promoting women's rights only to the extent that it benefited the party and its affiliated capitalist ventures. It used repressive measures to stamp out all radical women's activities in the late 1920s and 1930s, as well as in the last few years of the 1940s.

Working-class women were interested in upgrading workers' conditions: better wages, working conditions, and treatment and job security. Their anti-imperialist activities in the 1920s and 1930s demonstrated their ability to link capitalist exploitation with imperialism. With the exception of the period before 1927, working-class women were not organized, partly because the C.C.P. had been ousted from the industrial regions, and partly because the industries in which women participated were usually consumer goods industries. The latter did not play as important a role in industrialization as the producer-goods industries, and workers in the consumer goods industries had less bargaining power. The K.M.T. repressive apparatus certainly played an important part in fragmenting the labour movement in China.

Peasant women were the vanguard of women's resistance activities. Although at first quite sporadic and localized, their movement gradually developed into full-blown systematic effort led by the C.C.P. Along with men, they established a number of soviets in the late 1920s and early 1930s. Although these were smashed, they did provide, among other things, valuable lessons in organization. The Japanese invasion did not stop harassment by the K.M.T., but it did provide a great stimulus for them to unite. In contrast with educated women and working-class women, peasant women were concerned with land and production. The C.C.P. land reform movement was greeted favourably since it was aimed at providing them with land and food. With the blockade by the K.M.T., they had to create a 'self-sufficient' economy in the liberated areas. Even without the mobilization of the C.C.P., peasant women might have learnt to produce food crops for themselves, since otherwise they could well have starved to death.

In the final analysis, the K.M.T. Government's mismanagement and corruption brought about its own downfall. Even though the Japanese had been defeated and the K.M.T. Government had 'won' the war, the hardship that had been imposed upon peasant and working-class women would not be forgotten. The economy in the post-war period was far from satisfactory: food prices rose at a tremendous rate and unemployment was rampant; furthermore, the K.M.T. showed no sign of being able to cure the sick economy. The C.C.P., by contrast, had provided the peasants with a variety of ways to better themselves during the war, and there was no reason why it would not be able to do even more in the postwar period. As a political party, the C.C.P. was well liked by the people, not because of its contribution to eliminating the Japanese, nor because the war had forced the peasants to work for it (as Chalmers Johnsons has argued), but because the C.C.P. stood for hope for many people in the liberated areas. The peasant and, to a lesser extent, working-class women had learnt through their resistance efforts how to fight against yet another enemy — namely the K.M.T., which supported the hated landlords and capitalists. Indeed, the K.M.T. Government officials were, in some cases, themselves landlords and capitalists. Peasant and working-class women worked to bring about an overthrow of the government. The 1949 revolution brought a victory for these women and the liberation of the country as a whole.

References

1. A. Feuerwerker, *Rebellion in the Nineteenth Century,* Ann Arbor: Centre for Chinese Studies, University of Michigan, 1975, pp.8, 38-45, 69.
2. Frederick Wakeman, 'Rebellion and Revolution: the Study of Popular Movements in China', *Journal of Asian Studies,* Vol. XXXVI, No.2, 1977, p.208.
3. Feuerwerker, op. cit., p.75.
4. Ibid., p.18.
5. Ibid., pp.32, 54.
6. Ibid., pp.38-45.
7. Pin Xin, *The History of the Chinese Democratic Constitution Movement,* Shanghai: Jinbu Shuju, 1946, p.68.
8. Wakeman, op. cit., p.219; Feuerwerker, op. cit., p.55.
9. Feuerwerker, op. cit., p.60.
10. Hubei Federation of Philosophy and Social Sciences Learned Societies, *A Collection of Papers Celebrating the 50th Anniversary of the 1911 Revolution,* Beijing: Zhonghua shuju, Vol. 2, 1962, p.680.
11. Feuerwerker, *The Foreign Establishment in China in the Early Twentieth Century,* Ann Arbor: Center for Chinese Studies, University of Michigan, 1976, p.49.
12. Sir Robert Hart, 'The Boxers: 1900' in Franz Schurmann and Orville Schell, *Imperial China,* New York: Vintage Books, 1967, pp.199-200.
13. Feuerwerker, op. cit., 1976, pp.92-3.
14. Wu Yuzhang, *On the 1911 Revolution (Lun Xin-Hai Geming),* Beijing: Renmin chubanshe, 1972, p.7; Hubei Federation of Philosophy and Social Sciences Learned Societies, op. cit., p.68; Zhang Hui and Bao Cun, *The Revolutionary History of Shanghai in the Last Hundred Years,* Shanghai: Renmin chubanshe, 1963, p.83; *Dongfang Zazhi,* Vol. VII, No. iv, 2 June 1910, pp.56-7, 63.
15. Jean Chesneaux, *Peasant Revolts in China, 1840-1949,* London: Thames and Hudson, 1973, pp.68, 84.

16. Ibid., p.86.
17. Ibid., p.94.
18. Ibid., pp.139-40.
19. Jean Chesneaux, *Secret Societies in China in the Nineteenth and Twentieth Centuries*, Xianggang: Heinemann Educational, 1971, p.126.
20. Zhang and Bao, op. cit., pp.52-9.
21. He Ganzhi, *The Contemporary Revolutionary History of China*, Beijing: Gaodeng jiaoyu chubanshe, 1956, p.12.
22. Helen Snow, *The Chinese Labour Movement*, New York: John Day, 1945, pp.20-1.
23. Ibid., p.42.
24. Ibid., p.173.
25. Ibid., p.24.
26. Ibid., p.48.
27. Ibid., pp.68-9.
28. Ibid., pp.169-70.
29. Ibid., p.169.
30. Ho Kan-chih, 'Rise of the Chinese Working-Class Movement: The Working-Class Movement in Hunan, the Big Political Strike of the Peking-Hankow Railway Workers' in Schurmann and Schell, *Republican China*, New York: Vintage Books, 1967, p.118.
31. Snow, op. cit., p.40.
32. Ibid., p.171.
33. Ibid., pp.46-7.
34. Ibid., pp.47, 49.
35. Ibid., p.65.
36. Ibid., pp.63, 76.
37. Ibid., p.172.
38. Ibid., p.178.
39. Ibid., p.66.
40. Ibid., p.69.
41. Ibid., p.77.
42. Ibid., pp.112, 122.
43. Ibid., p.85.
44. Ibid., p.185.
45. Ibid., p.118.
46. Ibid., pp.88-9.
47. Ibid., pp.90-1.
48. Meng Xianzhang, *Teaching Materials for the History of Chinese Modern Economy*, Shanghai: Zhonghua Shudian, 1951, pp.324-6; Zhang and Bao, op. cit., pp.190, 195-6.
49. Meng Ru, 'The Illiteracy of Chinese Women', *Dongfang Zazhi*, Vol. XXXI, No. i, January 1934, section on 'women' *(fu)*, p.2.
50. *Alarming Bell Daily News*, 13 June 1904, p.3.
51. M.B. Rankin, 'The Emergence of Women at the End of the Ching: The Case of Ch'iu Chin' in M. Wolf and R. Witke, *Women in Chinese Society*, California: Stanford University Press, 1975, p.51.
52. Bao Jialin, 'The Trend of Women's Thought during the Period of 1911's Revolution, 1898-1911', *Zhonghua Xuebao*, Vol. I, No.i, January 1974, pp.1-22.

53. *Jiangsu,* Vol. II, 1 May 1903, p.149.
54. *Subao,* 9 May 1903, p.1.
55. *China's Newspaper,* 24 April 1904, p.2.
56. Bao, op. cit., pp.13-14.
57. Zhang and Bao, op. cit., pp.72-8.
58. Bao, op. cit., pp.1-2; *China's Newspaper,* 16 January 1908, p.3 and 24 October 1907; Rankin, op. cit., p.54.
59. *China's Newspaper,* 22 October 1907.
60. *Huazi Ribao,* 6 April 1908, p.2.
61. Ibid., 8 April 1908, p.2.
62. Mary C. Wright, 'Introduction: The Rising Tide of Change' in *China in Revolution: The First Phase, 1900-1913,* New Haven: Yale University Press, 1968, p.33; *Huazi Ribao,* 1 September 1909, p.2.
63. *The North-China Herald,* Vol. LXXXII, No. 2068, 28 March 1907, p.679.
64. *Minhu Ribao,* 6 July 1909, p.3.
65. Chow, *The May Fourth Movement,* p.43.
66. *Zhonghua Xinbao,* 12 February 1917, p.3.
67. Ibid., 15 August 1917, p.3.
68. *Shibao,* 10 May 1919, section 3, p.3.
69. Ibid., 2 July 1919, section 3, p.3; 10 August 1919, section 3, p.5; 3 September 1919, section 3, p.5.
70. Ibid., 7 December 1919, section 3, p.3.
71. *Zhongguo Funu,* Vol. X, 1959, p.3.
72. *Shibao,* 1 February 1920, section 1, p.2.
73. *Huazi Ribao,* 1 July 1921, section 3, p.4; 8 January 1925, section 2, p.4.
74. Ma Chaojun et al., *The History of Labour Movement in China,* Taibei: Zhongguo laogong Fuli chubanshe, Vol. 1, 1959, pp.129-31.
75. Ibid., pp.141-2.
76. Bobby Siu, *Fifty Years of Struggle,* Xianggang: Revomen, 1975, p.82.
77. Julia Kristeva, *About Chinese Women,* London: Marion Boyars, 1977, p.116.
78. *Zhongguo Funu,* Vol. V, 1958, pp.16-17.
79. Suzette Leith, 'Chinese Women in the Early Communist Movement' in M.B. Young, *Women in China,* Ann Arbor: Center for Chinese Studies, University of Michigan, 1973, p.58.
80. Laurie Landy, *Women in the Chinese Revolution,* Highland Park: International Socialist, 1974, p.15.
81. Ma, op. cit., Vol. 2, pp.298-9.
82. *Funu Zhoubao,* Vol. XXXVII, 7 May 1924, p.6; Vol. XXXVIII, 14 May 1924, p.4.
83. Siu, op. cit., pp.88-9.
84. Landy, op. cit., p.17.
85. *Shibao,* 3 January 1927, p.4.
86. Wu Naiyin, 'In Memory of Martyr Chen Tiejun' *(Ji Chen Tiejun lieshi),* *Zhongguo Funu,* Vol. X, No. 16, 1962.
87. *Huazi Ribao,* 4 November 1921, section 3, p.4.
88. *Shibao,* 1-3 July 1926, section 2, p.3.
89. Chow, op. cit., pp.134-7.
90. *Zhongguo Funu,* Vol. X, 1954, p.9.

91. *Shibao,* 3 May 1920, section 2, p.4.
92. Yin Falu, 'The Direct Destruction of Imperialism on the May Fourth Movement', in Central China's Technical College Materials Room on Marxism and Leninism, *Collected work on May Fourth Movement,* Wuhan: Renmin chubanshe, 1957, p.27.
93. Landy, op. cit. p.15.
94. Siu, op. cit., pp.86-7.
95. Ma, op. cit., Vol. 2, pp.397-8.
96. Ibid.
97. Guo, *The Issue of Women in China,* Shanghai: Shangwu yinshugan, 1937, p.211.
98. Ma, op. cit., Vol. 1, pp.196-7.
99. *Huazi Ribao,* 6 May 1927, section 2, p.2; *Shibao,* 7 May 1927, p.7.
100. *Jiangsu Civil Administration Bureau Gazette,* Vol. CXXXIII, 1 December 1927, p.1; Vol. CCIXIX, 20 May 1928, p.1; Vol. LCXXXII, 14 January 1929, p.5; Vol. CMLXXXIII, 4 May 1930, pp.1-2.
101. Snow, op. cit., pp.56, 182.
102. Leslie E. Collins, 'The New Women: A Psycho-historical Study of the Chinese Feminist Movement from 1900 to the Present', unpublished dissertation, Yale University, 1976, p.620.
103. Ibid.; Landy, op. cit., p.16; Zhong, *The Peasant Movement of Hailufeng,* Guangdong: Renmin chubanshe, 1957, p.73.
104. *Shibao,* 2 December 1931, section 2, p.6; 1 February 1932, section 2, p.7; 9 March 1936, section 2, p.5; 3 December 1936, section 2, p.8; *Huazi Ribao,* 6 June 1936, section 3, p.3.
105. *Shibao,* 9 May 1929, p.6; 5 November 1931, section 2, p.6.
106. *Shibao,* 10 May 1928, p.2; 1 January 1934, p.4; *Funu Shenghuo,* Vol. VII, No. vi, 1 May 1935, p.24.
107. *Shibao,* 6 December 1931, section 1, p.4; 5 May 1932, section 2, p.8; *Huazi Ribao,* 9 March 1937, section 2, p.2.
108; Landy, op. cit., pp.17-18.
109. *Shibao,* 1 February 1929, p.2.
110. Ma, op. cit., Vol. 3, pp.1066-7.
111. Ibid., pp.1110-12, 1269-74.
112. *Shibao,* 10 March 1928, p.5.
113. *Shibao,* 8 September 1928, p.6.
114. Zijiu, 'Concerning visits of labour families', *Funu Shenghuo,* Vol. IV, No. iii, 16 February 1937, pp.14–15.
115. Zeng and Bao, op. cit., p.165.
116. *Shibao,* 4 July 1935, p.4.
117. Guo, op. cit., pp.144-5.
118. *Huazi Riboa,* 3 June 1936, section 3, p.3.
119. Delia Davin, 'Women in the Liberated Areas', in M.B. Young, *Women in China,* Ann Arbor: Center for Chinese Studies, University of Michigan, 1973, p.75.
120. Jiangsu Federation of Women, *The Stories of Jiangxi Women's Revolutionary Struggle,* Beijing: Zhongguo Funu Zazhishe, 1963, pp.3-4.
121. Delia Davin, *Woman-Work,* Oxford: Clarendon, 1976, pp.35-6.
122. Landy, op. cit., p.19.
123. *Shibao,* 6 April 1932, 'Special'.

124. Pin, *The History of the Chinese Democratic Constitution Movement,*
     Shanghai: Jinbu shuju, 1946, pp.320-1.
125. *Guangdong Government Gazette,* Vol. II, 4 July 1929, pp.2, 19-20;
     Jiangsu Civil Administration Bureau Gazette (Jiangsu Sheng Minz-
     henting Gongbao), Vol. CMLXIV, 15 April 1930, pp.3-6.
126. Snow, op. cit. p.76.
127. Ibid., p.73.
128. Ibid., p.72.
129. Shiliang, 'My Opinion on the Present National Organization of Women',
     Funu Shenghuo, Vol. VIII, No. x, 20 February 1940, pp.4-6; Xia
     Yingzhe, 'The Pioneer Call for the Investigation of the Women's Work
     on the National Level'*Funu Shenghuo,* Vol. IX, No. iii, 16 September
     1940, pp.7-8, 22.
130. *Huazi Ribao,* 1 January 1939, section 3, p.2.
131. Li Baoguang, 'Move One Step Forward', *Shidai Funu,* Vol. I, No. i,
     July 1946, pp.6-9.
132. Helen Snow, *Women in Modern China,* The Hague; Mouton, 1967, p.225.
133. *Women's New Life Movement,* Vol. VI, No. vii, July 1944, pp.19-44.
134. *Funu Xinyun,* Vol. VI, No. vii, July 1944, pp.19-44; *Funu Shenghuo,*
     Vol. VI, No. viii, 20 August 1938, pp.23-4.
135. Ibid.
136. *Funu Xinyun,* Vol. VI, No. vii, July 1944, pp.19-44.
137. Ibid.
138. Ibid.
139. Ibid.; New Life Movement Women's Directing Committee, *Women's*
     Rural Services, Chongqing: Xin Yun Funu Zhidao Weiyuanhui, 1944,
     pp.5-73.
140. Ma Jin, 'In the Villages', *Funu Shenghuo,* Vol. VI, No. 1, 5 May 1938,
     pp.24-5.
141. New Life Movement Women's Directing Committee, *Women's Rural*
     Services, Congqing: Xin yun funu zhidao wenyuanhui, 1944, pp.6-8.
142. *Funu Xinyun,* Vol. VI, No. vii, July 1944, pp.19-44; *Guangdong Funu,*
     Vol. II, No. vii-viii, 8 March 1941, pp.31-5; Vol. III, No. viii, 25 April, pp.24-5.
143. *Funu Gongming,* Vol. XI, No. iii, May 1942, p.51.
144. New Life Movement Women's Directing Committee, *Women's Rural*
     Services, op. cit., p.22.
145. Luo Heng, 'The Creation Process of Rong District and its Afterthought',
     Funu Xinyun, Vol. VI, No. x, December 1944, pp.10-12.
146. Jihong, 'The Wuhan Women's Workers in the Wartime', *Funu Shenghuo,*
     Vol. VI, No. i, 5 May 1938, pp.7-10.
147. Qiufang, 'The Obstacles in Work', *Funu Shenghuo,* Vol. VI, No. ii,
     30 May 1938, p.21.
148. Jihong, 'Interviewing Madam Hu Lan'gui – Two Years [of history] of
     the Working Class Women's War-zone Service Teams', *Funu Shenghuo,*
     Vol. VII, No. xi-xii, 1 September 1939, pp.24-5.
149. *Huazi Ribao,* 7 January 1939, section 2, p.2; 8 May 1939, section 1, p.1.
150. *Funu Yuekan,* Vol. IV, No.i, October 1944, p.71; Vol. IV, No. ii,
     December 1944, p.44.
151. *Funu Yuekan,* Vol. IV, No. iv, June 1945, p.7.
152. Luo Shuzhuo, 'The Materialization of an Ideal Refugee Women's

Factory' *Funu Shenghuo,* Vol. VI, No.v, 5 July 1938.

153. Jihong, 'The Women's Textile Handicraft Industry Is Expanding in Bishan of Sichuan', *Funu Shenghuo,* Vol. IX, No. i, 1 July 1940, pp.27-8.

154. Shi Renru, 'The Training Situation of Spinning-Research Classes', *Guangdong Funu,* Vol. II, No. xi-xii, 15 July 1941, p.40.

155. *Guangdong Funu,* Vol. III, No. ix, 25 May 1942, p.29.

156. Luo Qiong, 'The Basic Rules of the Development of the Chinese Women's Movements', *New Chinese Women (Xin Zhongguo Funu),* December 1952, pp.26-8.

157. Luo, op. cit., p.26-8.

158. Yan'an Research Society of Current Affairs, *Chinese Wartime Politics,* Yan'an: Jiefangshe, 1940, p.385.

159. Landy, op. cit. p.20.

160. Cao Mengjun, 'Secure the Obtained Democratic Rights', *Zhongguo Funu,* September 1957, p.12.

161. Snow, op. cit., 1945, p.80.

162. Fu Xuewen, *Contemporary Women,* Shanghai: Shangwu Yinshuguan, 1946, p.21.

163. Situ Yan, 'The Student Unrest in the University of Zhejiang', *Xiandai Funu,* Vol. IX, No. iii, June 1947, p.12.

164. *Shenbao,* 4 February 1948, section 1, p.4.

165. Qi Yun, Ji Qian, 'Women of Jiaodong Enthusiastically Support the People's Liberation War'; All-women Democratic Federation, *Women's Movement for Participation in War in the Liberated areas of China,* Xianggang: Xin minzhu chubanshe, 1949, pp.26-31.

166. All-China Democratic Women's Federation, *Concerning the Urban-Rural Women Representatives Conference,* Beijing: Zhongguo Quan'guo Minzhu Funu Lianhehui, 1950, p.1.

6. Policies and Tactics of Mobilizing Women

Between 1900 and 1949, the C.C.P. was actively engaged in leading and mobilizing peasant and working-class women in anti-imperialist work and in revolution. By contrast, the K.M.T. failed miserably in mobilizing women, with the exception of groups of educated women. Why? In this chapter, we will examine the policies followed by these two political parties in mobilizing peasant and working-class women, and the tactics they used, and attempt to explain the final victory of the C.C.P.

Policies of Mobilization

1912-27

Even before the formation of the C.C.P., Mao Zedong showed an interest in mobilizing women for the cause of socialism. In one of his letters to Xiang Jingyu while she was studying in France, Mao said, '[I] wish you could recruit more women comrades: recruiting one person means saving one person.' This sentiment was also shared by the members of the New People's Educational Association *(Xinmin Xuehui)* — the prototype of the C.C.P. organized by Mao Zedong — who appeared to be concerned with training women cadres, for they believed that 'the best of women cadres are quite reliable.'[1]

At its establishment in 1921, the C.C.P. adopted a policy of mobilizing peasant and working-class women. It took the position that the liberation of women lay in national liberation from imperialism, capitalism and feudalism, and was very critical of the bourgeois women who fought for individual liberation during the May Fourth period.[2] Xiang Jingyu, a C.C.P. member for example, criticized feminist groups in general for being individualistic and for being co-opted by the bourgeois political structure.[3] In 1922, the C.C.P. declared: 'the Chinese Communist Party believes that the liberation of women will be assisted through the general liberation of the proletariat. When the proletariat gains political power, [women] will be liberated . . . . The Chinese Communist Party proclaimed to all women . . . our movement is the key step to the goal [of women's liberation]. Within the system of private property, the real liberation of women is impossible.'[4]

In line with this declaration, the C.C.P. incorporated several policies on women into its programme in the same year. For example, it acknowledged the right of peasant and working-class women to vote, assemble, associate and strike, as well as the right to freedom of speech and publication. The C.C.P. also maintained sexual equality in law, politics and economy, as well as drafting legislation to protect working-class women.[5]

Although recognizing the existence of class distinctions among women, the C.C.P.'s 1926 Central Committee passed a resolution maintaining a strategy of working with all women: educated women, working-class women and peasant women. This resolution stressed the strategy of a 'united front' involving the avoidance of unnecessary conflicts within and between women's organizations, and respecting the viewpoints of other groups. In 1926, the C.C.P. recognized that, although educated women are co-opted by the bourgeois system, they nevertheless are one 'instrument' of the women's movement. Still, in the opinion of the C.C.P., working-class women remained the back-bone of the movement, and it also planned to train women cadres in mobilizing women in the countryside, especially in the areas of Guangdong (Kwangtung) and Hunan.[6]

In contrast to the C.C.P., the K.M.T. did not show any interest in mobilizing women until 1925. In fact, when the K.M.T. came to power in 1912, it immediately abolished the clause of sexual equality from its political programme,[7] and it was not until 1924 that such a clause was re-instated.[8] A year later, the Women's Bureau of the K.M.T. (formed in 1923) advised women members of the party to work for the women's movement.[9] No indication was made as to which groups of women the K.M.T. intended to work with. The rationale behind such drastic changes in the K.M.T.'s policy towards women was hinted at in 1926, when it published 'The Organization, Development, Rights and Freedom of the Women's Movement: '(1) To expand the influence of the party; (2) to prevent the female population from being used by reactionaries; and (3) to act as a first step in political propagandizing.'[10] It is easy to speculate as to who these 'reactionaries' were, if we remember the resolution of the C.C.P. and the purge of the Communists and progressives in 1927.

This document, which illustrates that K.M.T. incorporation of women's movements had begun as early as 1926, suggested that the women's bureaux of the K.M.T. should observe the development of various women's organizations already in existence and encouraged women party members to participate in these organizations as well as training women for further women's actions.[11] Again, no special reference was made regarding which groups the K.M.T. was to mobilize. However, judging from K.M.T. activity between 1925 and 1927, it was primarily concerned with controlling the activities of *educated* women (female students and career women). As we have seen in the last chapter, the K.M.T. actively co-operated with the existing educated women's organizations in the cities and recruited female students.[12]

The K.M.T. did pass a resolution in 1926 for improving the treatment of female hired labourers in the countryside,[13] but in general, it appears to have neglected the mobilization of working-class women. Nor is it clear that the K.M.T. had any genuine interest in promoting women's rights or even in mobilizing women for their liberation, since they scrutinized many women's activities and women's organizations in Shanghai and Guangzhou.[14]

1927-37

The purge of 1927 drove the Communists into the countryside, and from that time onwards the C.C.P. focused its attention on the mobilization of peasant women. In his 'Report on An Investigation into the Peasant Movement of Hunan' (1927), Mao Zedong condemned the 'three rules of conduct' of Confucianism (the lord guides his minister, the father guides his son and the husband guides his wife). He argued that women were especially oppressed: in addition to political authority, the clan authority and religious authority, women had to overthrow the masculine authority of the husbands.[15] But Mao also recognized the difficulty of abolishing the old sexual morality in peasant society, without at the same time destroying peasant relationships and creating hostility and fragmentation among them.[16] In the light of this, the C.C.P. formulated policies on *marriage* and *land reform*.

With respect to land redistribution, the Land Laws of Jinganshan (December 1928) and Xinguo County (April 1929), as well as those promulgated by the Chinese Military Revolutionary Council (1930) and the Chinese Soviet Republic (November 1931), advocated sexual equality in land allotments, so that peasant women could become economically independent.

A pragmatic reason for the land reforms was the need for women to work in the fields in order to free men to join the Red Army of the C.C.P.[17] Although the C.C.P. policy on women was based on the socialist principle 'to destroy the legal norms of the old society, to oppose the exploitative relationships of the feudal family, etc. . . . to guarantee women's equality with men and permit them to acquire civil rights',[18] the 'liberation' of peasant women in the early 1930s actually meant the mobilization of peasant women in the resistance against the K.M.T. This was evident in the First Women's Meeting in Xinguo County (in Jiangxi) in 1933, in which the first topic on the agenda was 'enlarging the Red Army', 'aid to the Red Army' and 'looking after the dependants of Red Army soldiers'. These could be achieved, it was suggested by the C.C.P., by learning to plough, selling women's jewellery and buying government bonds, etc.[19] The 1933 resolution of the Jiangxi Provincial Committee of the Women Representatives' Congress clearly stated that sending off new recruits and caring for army dependants were 'the core of woman-work.'[20]

As for marriage reform, the two Marriage Laws of the Jiangxi Soviet (1931 and 1934) established freedom of choice in marriage and divorce, and the abolition of the custom of 'child-wives'. However, as Delia Davin has observed,[21] it appears that these laws were not thoroughly implemented by the soviets due to the immense difficulties in changing ideas on marriage.

Due to the 1927 purge and to continuous harassment and observation by the K.M.T. in the city, it was difficult for the C.C.P. to use any overt methods to recruit working-class women. However, it remained strong in its desire to mobilize them. K.M.T. raids on C.C.P. branches or cells usually revealed documents urging members to 'recruit the masses of working-class women', to absorb young women and to strengthen women's work in general.[22] This policy conformed to the general principle announced by the C.C.P. on 11 June 1930:

> Young people and women are a significant force in revolutionary struggle, we must be determined in opposing the tendency of neglecting youth movements and women's movements, because this is a severe political mistake. At present, any struggle [should] recognize the positive functions of youths and women, the party should be more active in absorbing them into the revolutionary route; the party should, from different directions, help to change youth work, [and] oppose the tendency of pure talk [which is popular] in the country.[23]

In line with its concern with working-class women, the C.C.P. passed a resolution in December 1927 which proposed a limit on the number of hours that women could work in the factories, improvements in hygiene and working conditions; wages equal to those of men; better treatment; better benefits for maternity leave; and the right to assemble, and to freedom of speech and of the press, etc.[24]

During the Long March, peasant women played a supportive role. The few women who participated in the Long March generally remained in the rear, working in production, communications, transportation and public health.[25] Women were trained as guerrillas only in those villages where men were largely absent. As late as 1934, Mao Zedong still maintained that peasant women should be encouraged to 'do farm work' and not to fight at the front.[26] As Janet Salaff and J. Merkle have noted, women in the People's Liberation Army 'remained in the rear, producing for the revolution, not fighting for it . . . . They never gain control of the means of coercion.'[27]

With the general relaxation of the Comintern's grasp in 1935, the C.C.P. became more autonomous, and Mao Zedong was able to assert his insistence on a *peasant* revolution. But, the mobilization of women for supportive tasks for the larger economic and military revolution still remained the central line of the C.C.P.[28]

However, due to the intensification of the Japanese attacks, the C.C.P. after the Seventh World Congress of the Communist International decisions in August 1935, adopted the Popular Front line, which required it to co-operate with the K.M.T. in the fight against the Japanese; as a result, compromises were made by the C.C.P. with regard to mobilizing women.[29] It discarded some of its principles regarding marriage reform and land redistribution and stressed that the key role of women in the anti-Japanese effort was participation in production. The slogans 'Abolition of Feudal Family' and 'Freedom of Divorce' were abandoned.[30] This emphasis on the productive role of women was apparent in the C.C.P.'s 1936 order:

To mobilize women . . . to participate in spring planting, and cultivation, each according to [her] ability to carry on either a principal or an auxiliary task in the labour process of production. For example, 'large feet' [women with natural feet] and young women should be mobilized to organize production-teaching corps, and tasks of agricultural production itself. 'Small feet' [women with bound feet] . . . must be mobilized to help in weed-pulling, collecting dung and for other auxilliary tasks.[31]

Between 1927 and 1937, while the C.C.P. concentrated on mobilizing peasant women, and in general called for the mobilization of working-class women, the K.M.T. merely *depoliticized* the existing urban women's movements by further institutionalizing them. Although the Guangdong (Kwangtung) branch of the K.M.T. resolved in 1927 that peasant women should be *educated,* not much action followed this announcement.[32] And it is notable that the K.M.T.'s strategy for mobilizing peasant women began with 'education' rather than land redistribution or marriage reform.

Concerned with the C.C.P.'s infiltration into women's groups, the K.M.T. accelerated its incorporation of the existing women's organizations by legalizing only those organizations which followed the 'Three People's Principles'. 'The Organizational Principles of Women's Organizations' (1930) clearly emphasized the moralistic, non-political and non-economic nature of women's organizations: '[The] improvement of knowledge and skills, the germination of morality and a healthy [and] maternal ethics and citizenship so that social progress will be accelerated.'[33]

These 'Organizational Principles' severely limited the autonomy of women's organizations in recruiting members and forming alliances among themselves.[34] Two years later, the 'Organizational Principles' were revised and women's organizations were further restricted and depoliticized by the K.M.T.[35] To supplement its efforts at incorporation, the K.M.T. decided to unify 'all' women's organizations.[36] Between 1930 and 1937, it was busy organizing different types of women's anti-imperialist activities such as training nurses, guards and self-defence teams.[37]

With respect to working-class women, the K.M.T. appears to have been interested only in changing their legal status. Some attempts had been made in Jiangsu and Guangdong to curb the old custom of discriminating against women in employment,[38] but this seems to have been restricted to white-collar women workers. On 30 December 1929, the K.M.T. declared it had passed a resolution to promote women's rights in the factories by setting regulations to protect women and girls from working in dangerous conditions, by limiting their hours of work, by giving them better maternity benefits, by restricting their age of employment, by equalizing their wages with those of men, etc.[39] This Factory Act of 1929 (revised slightly in 1932), would have provided a legal framework for the protection of working-class women *if* it had been enforced. Unfortunately, it remained a formal piece of paper without teeth and it is doubtful that working-class women received any benefit from it at all.

1937-45

The great C.C.P. drive to bring peasant women into production created a backlash.[40] In 1942, a number of women in the liberated area criticized the C.C.P. for its failure to deal with issues specific to women, and its assumption that women would play a dual role — participating in both domestic and productive labour. These criticisms were immediately countered by the C.C.P. which argued that 'full sex equality had already been established', and that their feminism was outdated and harmful.[41]

Despite this brief episode of criticism, production remained the main sphere for mobilizing women in the liberated area throughout the 1930s and 1940s. While it was reported that, during the Sino-Japanese War, women worked in the fields only when there was a shortage of manpower, handicraft industries (especially textiles) were revived and agriculture was improved through the strenuous efforts of peasant women.[42] The C.C.P. encouraged women to spin and weave since the liberated areas were very short of clothing.[43] Throughout the war period, it constantly reminded women that economic work was essential: 'Women cadres must stop looking on economic work as unimportant.' It held the position that the 'feudal oppression of women' lay in women's lack of participation in production.[44] The resolution of the C.C.P. on women's work in 1943 clearly de-emphasizes the participation of women in other campaigns, so that 'they can participate in production *en masse.*'[45]

The same resolution (1943) also specified that integrating women into production was the key task of the Women's Federation. The latter must 'penetrate into villages, educate and help peasant women to solve the problems of engaging in work on the production line'. Although the C.C.P. emphasized the significance of the role women could play in production, it realized that regional differences and familial concerns must be taken into consideration. Production work had to be related to the peasant economy. To ensure success in this policy, the C.C.P. advised the organizers of women's work to inform themselves about economics and production.[46]

Centred around the question of production were issues such as education, the war effort and family consolidation. In 1939, the C.C.P. declared the education of women to be one of its tasks.[47] Through production, peasant women not only learnt different production skills but raised their level of literacy.[48] The C.C.P. also sought to raise the political consciousness of women with respect to imperialism, as advocated in 1940 in the notice the Central Committee of the C.C.P. sent to all its branches.[49] But, once again, this political knowledge was to be transmitted through production.[50]

The C.C.P. encouraged peasant women to join the war effort not only by participating in recruitment drives and encouraging men to join the army, but also by organizing themselves into militia, such as the Women's Detachment of the Eighth Route Army, Guangxi Women's Battalion and Zhejiang Women's Guerrilla Band.[51]

As the war proceeded further inland, the C.C.P. reversed its former policy of marriage reform. Instead of talking about 'equality of the sexes' or 'free-choice marriages', the C.C.P. began to use slogans such as 'Save the Children',

'A Flourishing Family', and 'Nurture, Health and Prosperity'.[52]However, it had not completely forgotten about changing the status of women. During the war period, women had to take responsibility for the economic needs of the family when men began to join the armies. In this context, women were encouraged to join the productive sector. Thus, the call for a family-oriented programme did not violate socialist principles. It was merely a tactical change in a period of emergency. The government of the Shanxi-Chahar-Hebei border region in fact issued certain policies benefiting women cadres in 1943. Maternal leave was given to these women and kindergartens and a clothing allowance were provided for their children. In some cases, extra rations were given to women who had had miscarriages.[53]

Although the C.C.P. concentrated on *peasant* women during the Sino-Japanese War, it called for the unity of *all* women irrespective of their party affiliation and class positions.[54] The directive given by the C.C.P. in 1940 made this point especially clear: 'Try hard to absorb the progressive, educated women and progressive, working-class and peasant women into the party and increase the number of women party members. ...'[55] Between 1941 and 1942 a political campaign was launched to involve as many women as possible in the election, both as electors and candidates.[56] And throughout the whole war period, the C.C.P. tried to recruit as many women cadres as possible.[57]

Although the C.C.P. called for the mobilization of all women, it actually was only able to concentrate on peasant women. This was due to historical circumstances and the regional isolation of the C.C.P. as well as to the K.M.T. purges of radicals in the cities. But the record of the K.M.T. in mobilizing peasant and working-class women was far from satisfactory, as has been shown. It continued to neglect both groups of women during the war period, concentrating mainly on co-ordinating women's (read: 'educated women's') activities in the cities.[58]

In 1938, the K.M.T.'s 'Principles of Resistance and Nation-Building' clearly stated that the most urgent task of the K.M.T. was 'to train women to serve in social affairs so as to increase the strength of resistance'.[59] The 'Principles of Mobilizing Women to Join the Works of Resistance and Nation-Building' (1938), the 'Principles of Final Mobilization and Publicity of Women's Morals' (1939) and the 'Methods of National Mobilization' (1942) followed this document. These three announcements escalated the efforts to mobilize women, while at the same time setting the boundaries of women's resistance work.[60]

In mobilizing women during the Sino-Japanese War, the *education* of peasant women was emphasized. The K.M.T. stated in 1938: 'We should ... emphasize ... propaganda work in the countryside.[61] These educational meetings were concentrated in the war districts in Hubei and Hunan in 1938-39 and two districts in Sichuan after 1939. They included literacy classes, putting up propaganda notices and posters, giving speeches, organizing dramas and home-visiting. Even though the figures were most likely exaggerated for political reasons, they demonstrated that the proportion of peasant women involved in the K.M.T.'s educational mobilization campaing was very insignificant.[62]

In addition to its educational campaign, the K.M.T. mobilized women in the areas of recreation, production, hygiene, gathering funds and the consolation of soldiers' families in the countryside.[63] But the K.M.T.'s efforts in rural areas were minimal and it centred its energy on the cities: training women officers, providing guidance in occupational and educational choices, establishing medical services, organizing women to console soldiers, providing assistance for refugees and children, publishing women's journals, doing surveys and co-ordinating general activities for women.[64]

The K.M.T. did concern itself with the production of textile goods and silk handicrafts, but it only mobilized 52,282 women between 1938 and 1943. The number of peasant women involved in this task was quite small, since this figure includes refugees, soldiers' families and workers, as well as peasant women.[65]

The extent to which the K.M.T. succeeded in mobilizing working-class women was also minimal. The project of producing textile goods and silk handicraft mentioned above involved such a small number of people and did not reduce the rate of unemployment among working-class women in the city during the war period. The K.M.T. launched an educational campaign in the factories to raise the literacy rate of factory women, but only six factories were involved in this project. Between 1943 and 1944, only 5,366 working-class women were involved in the educational project. Judging from the small scale of these educational efforts, it is doubtful that the K.M.T.'s mobilization of working-class women was effective,[66] while the other K.M.T. activities mentioned in previous paragraphs barely touched working-class women.

Although the K.M.T. claimed to be mobilizing *all* women, it ended up just dealing with educated women. This neglect of working-class women and peasant women was criticized in the Chinese press during this period. The *Eastern Miscellany (Dongfang Zazhi),* for example, was very critical of the K.M.T.'s inattention to women in the 'lower strata'[67] Women's journals such as *Women's Life (Funu Shenghuo), United Voices of Women (Funu Gongming),* and *Kwangtung Women (Guangdong Funu)* consistently pointed out the class bias in the K.M.T.-led women's movements: the members and leaders of the movements were educated women, and there was a lack of support among the peasant and working-class women.[68] The women's literature urged greater mobilization of poor women.[69]

1945-49

At the end of the Sino-Japanese War, several drastic changes occurred in the C.C.P. policy regarding the mobilization of women. Land reform was re-introduced with great vigour. Peasant women were urged to join in mass meetings to decide the division of land, the reduction of rents and interests, the disposal of landlords' properties and the treatment of landlords. As Davin noted, in places where many men were away in the army, women played a much greater role in land reform. Peasant women could now have a share in the land,

and sometimes separate land deeds were issued to men and women.[70]

The integration of peasant women into production continued to be the central policy of the C.C.P. during this period. It has been claimed that by 1949, 50 to 70% of women in the liberated areas were working in the fields, and as many as 80% in the best organized locations.[71]

Apart from involving women in production and re-introducing land reform, the C.C.P. made a special effort to change the traditional thinking of both men and women. They urged people to treat the mobilization of women as a glorious task, and not something to be looked down upon.[72] More specifically, the C.C.P. advocated the abolition of foot-binding, infanticide, purchase marriage and the system of 'child-wives'. While these reforms paved the way for the Marriage Laws of 1950, between 1945 and 1949, they were not pushed very hard. The C.C.P. realized that 'it is work to change peasants' ideas and a long demanding job which cannot be hurried'.[73]

As early as 1946, the C.C.P. began to shift its mobilization campaigns from the countryside to the cities.[74] As in the period before 1927, it was concerned with educated women, working-class women and peasant women. By 1949, this policy was clearly stated at the All-China Women's Congress: 'Contemporary work with women, while ensuring that work with peasant women is not jeopardized, should treat the urban women's movement as its focus of concern.'[75] Consequently, the C.C.P. strategy in 1949 was to mobilize women of *all* classes.[76] The C.C.P. decided that in the previously-liberated areas, women should continue production, attack feudalistic ideas and improve levels of political education and knowledge of hygiene. In the newly-liberated areas, women should engage in interest-and-rent reduction campaigns, land reform, production, and anti-warlord movements.[77]

As the focus of the C.C.P. in 1945-49 began to shift to the urban settings, its concern with mobilizing working-class women increased. This can be seen as early as 1946 when a new woman's journal was published in Zhanjinkou (Kalgan), carrying articles on the life of working-class women and the situation of prostitutes in the town of Shijiazhuang (which had just been liberated).[78] In the same year, a woman member of the C.C.P. maintained that women cadres concerned with the mobilization of women should aim at women workers, working-class family members and destitute women of the lower strata, in addition to schoolgirls and educated women.[79]

This shift in focus was further reinforced during a conference of cadres responsible for mobilizing women in September 1948. At this conference, Zhu De, the commander-in-chief of the Communist armies, remarked, 'With the development of the revolutionary situation, the task of those who work amongst women has become more important than ever, especially now that many towns, large, medium and small, have already set up revolutionary powers, and the towns contain *thousands upon thousands of women workers.* This means there must be another change in woman-work.'[80]

The resolution adopted in 1949 by the First National Congress of the Women's Federation posited working-class women as the base, with intellectual and professional women in the towns uniting with them.[81] And, towards the end of the civil war between the C.C.P. and the K.M.T., working-class women became the key focus of the C.C.P.'s mobilization policy. The goals set by the First National Congress of the Women's Federation (1949) summed up this policy:

> Within the national boundary, [we] have to strengthen, expand, [and] penetrate into the working masses of women, [and] mobilize and unite them with the oppressed masses of women of various classes all over China, to construct and expand the united front [of the forces] which oppose American imperialist invasion, the reactionary regimes of the K.M.T., feudalism and capitalism, together [we] struggle and build an united and democratic people's republic in China.[82]

Whereas the C.C.P.'s mobilization of working-class and peasant women reached its peak after the Sino-Japanese War, this was the moment when the K.M.T. relaxed its campaign, and encouraged women to go back home to take care of children and perform household tasks.[83] The class bias of the K.M.T. women's movement in this period was revealed in an article in *Dagongbao (Shanghai)* in which Peng Lin argued that the urban women who spent most of their time organizing meetings and giving speeches to women were neglecting 'those who really needed to be liberated – the peasant women'.[84]

The above discussion illustrates the differing policies of the C.C.P. and the K.M.T. From its inception, the C.C.P. was interested in mobilizing peasant and working-class women, and its mobilization campaigns of peasants were escalated by the purges of the K.M.T. which drove the C.C.P. to the country-side. In contrast, it is doubtful that the K.M.T. was genuinely enthusiastic about mobilizing women in general, let alone working-class and peasant women. Its incorporation of existing women's efforts into its own party organization was influenced by C.C.P. activities among women. Before the Sino-Japanese War, the K.M.T. policies suggested that it had intended to depoliticize the women's movements.

Although the C.C.P. showed some interest in mobilizing working-class women, especially before 1927, it failed to formulate a specific policy for recruitment, and after 1927, when the C.C.P. was driven to the countryside, this policy was naturally not implemented. However, even after the Sino-Japanese War, when the C.C.P. had an opportunity to mobilize working-class women, it still lacked a specific policy.

Nonetheless, the C.C.P. was more articulate than the K.M.T. with regard to mobilizing peasant women, formulating policies on *marriage reform, land redistribution* and, in particular *production.* In contrast, the K.M.T. relied on *education* as a means of mobilizing peasant women. Evidence shows that, through production, the C.C.P. influenced peasant women more significantly than the K.M.T. did through its educational campaigns (which only took place in a few locations). The C.C.P. did not deny the importance of educating peasant women, but claimed that education was secondary to production, land redistribution and the removal of feudal family relationships. Besides, the C.C.P. maintained that women could be educated through production.

During the war, the C.C.P. toned down its policy of marriage reform and land redistribution in order to form a united front with the K.M.T. against the Japanese. However, after the war, these two policies re-emerged and supplemented the key strategy of production, while the K.M.T. appeared to abandon its mobilization efforts and launch a back-to-the-home ideology. The C.C.P. also changed its policy from mobilizing peasant women to mobilizing *all* women, both in the countryside and in the cities.

The failure of the K.M.T. to mobilize both working-class and peasant women was due to (1) its lack of concern for these women; and (2) its policy of working through educational reform. Peasant women constituted the majority of the female population in China, and working-class women were a significant part of the urban population. By ignoring them, the K.M.T. restricted its power-base, which, for any political party or social movement, is suicidal. Although reluctant to acknowledge this error before 1949, the K.M.T. admitted it after its defeat in Taiwan. Pi Yishu commented on this mistake, especially with respect to the neglect of peasant women:

> From the beginning and up to now, the Chinese women's movement . . . has concentrated in the cities. [It is] a career for a minority of women intellectuals, and most of the women in the countryside remain unmobilized. . . . In fact, this majority of women are suffering the most; at the same time, they constitute the most powerful . . . force, . . . [and] women's movements cannot be totally successful without them. Previous work in the women's movements on the Mainland has already given us many precious experiences and lessons.[85]

The second reason for the K.M.T.'s failure was its strategy of education. In a period in which there were natural disasters, economic crises, starvation and poverty, it was meaningless and futile to teach peasant and working-class women how to read or to tell them about the brutality of the Japanese. The exploitation and oppression that the working-class women in the cities had to experience every day was fundamental. For these women, the enemy was not the Japanese invader but the capitalists and their middlemen who beat and tortured every day. To be sure, the invasion meant extra hardship for these factory workers, but then educating them did not solve their anxiety about unemployment, poverty and brutality at work. For peasant women, destitution and hunger were their main concerns. The recurrent rice riots and peasant unrest should have been sufficient to indicate to the K.M.T. the desperation of the peasantry.[86] Food was the major issue of concern, and the C.C.P. showed that it realized this by concentrating on production and land redistribution which, in both the short and the long term, could solve the problems confronting peasant women. It is clear that the K.M.T.'s educational strategy was not capable of mobilizing peasant women, while C.C.P. strategy could.

In a world of feudalistic and authoritarian relationships within the Chinese peasant family system, illiteracy and ignorance of world affairs were *not* significant in the oppression of women. The confessions of peasant women in 'speak-bitterness meetings' testify to this.[87] The K.M.T. miscalculated in employing educational campaigns to mobilize peasant and working-class women. The C.C.P., in contrast, clearly analysed the specific milieux of peasant women (and to some extent, working-class women) — economic inde- dependence, restriction within the family and increasing desperation. Land redistribution, marriage reforms and advances in production were certainly favoured by peasant women.

Mobilization Tactics

Our discussion on policies of the C.C.P. and the K.M.T. shows a clear pattern: throughout the period from its establishment up to 1949, the K.M.T. claimed to mobilize *all* women, when, in fact, it was concerned mainly with urban bourgeois women. The C.C.P. also claimed to mobilize women of *all* classes in the 1920s and late 1940s, but no specific policies were formulated to mobilize working-class and bourgeois women. With respect to peasant women, the C.C.P. did formulate several policies for mobilizing them, especially in the 1930s and 1940s. The K.M.T. stressed educational campaigns; while the C.C.P. emphasized marriage reforms, land redistribution and production (the handicraft industry and agriculture). The question we must now ask is: how did the C.C.P. and the K.M.T. carry out their policy of mobilization? What methods did they use, and how did they use them? In this section, we will compare the organizational methods and approaches of these two parties in mobilizing women — how they structured their tasks of mobilization, and how they recruited women into their networks.

1912-27

Only one year after its formation, the C.C.P. established a Ministry of Women and a special bureau to mobilize women.[88] Its 1922 declaration stated that 'In the third conference of the Third International, it was decided that in all countries a special committee should be established in the Communist Party to lead women, a women's department be elected, and a special column for women be set up in the party newspaper. The C.C.P. decided to adopt this plan as soon as it could.'[89] Xiang Jingyu was selected as the first leader of the women's bureau of the C.C.P. in 1922. She worked to mobilize women, especially working-class women, until 1928.

The C.C.P.'s mobilization of women was based on the existing networks of women, such as women's organizations, women's bureaux and schools for adults.[90] The C.C.P. members, in fact, formed the leadership of the militant National Women's Association, which had 300,000 members.[91] Women cadres were trained to mobilize peasant women in Guangdong (Kwangtung) in 1926.[92] The C.C.P. recommended that the peasant women's movement should be based on the existing peasants' unions. The 'Emergency Notice' of

the Hubei Peasants' Union (June 1927) testifies to this format: 'Organizationally, . . . peasant women should be actively absorbed into the unions. . . .'[93]
In the same year, the C.C.P. branch in Wuhan further specified that peasant
schools and co-operatives be constructed to absorb women into the movement.[94]

Throughout the 1910s, the K.M.T. abandoned its policy of mobilizing
women as noted. It was not until 1923 that it formed the first women's
bureau.[95] By 1926, it had constructed women's bureaux in every branch of
the Party and at all levels, in order to facilitate the K.M.T.'s incorporation of
the existing women's movements and to pre-empt the C.C.P.'s efforts to
mobilize women.[96]

1927-37

By 1931, the mobilization of peasant and working-class women had
become an integrated part of C.C.P. Party work at every level of the Party in
the soviets, and in the Poor Peasants' Unions. Two short-lived women's
groups were created: the Committee to Improve Women's Lives and the
Representatives' Congress of Women Workers and Peasants. Theoretically,
they had branches in each district *(xiang)*, but in reality, some of these
branches merely existed on paper. The Committee facilitated the communication link between the C.C.P. and the masses of peasant women. It co-ordinated activities for women and implemented C.C.P. policies in the soviets.
The Congresses were meant to be held periodically in every village or district.[97]
Both groups were dissolved during the Long March, but the C.C.P. still maintained a 'Women's Work' bureau to organize women's activities.[98]

This period saw some changes in the organizational structure of the K.M.T.'s
mobilization work. As soon as the K.M.T. consolidated its power, *it removed
women's bureaux from its party structure,* and subordinated their functions
under the newly-formed Public Training Committee in 1928. Under this new
Committee and its provincial branches, 'women's sections' were created.[99]
This structural alteration implied that the mobilization of women ceased to
be part of the central 'training' programmes. It also meant that the K.M.T.
underestimated, as well as undermined, the significance of women-mobilization. In order to further control the direction of the existing women's movements, it demanded that all women's organizations be registered under the
new Public Training Committee.[100]

Like the C.C.P. in the early 1930s, the K.M.T. began to form special
women's organizations to mobilize women, and they were much more permanent than those of the C.C.P. Between 1934 and 1938, three *national*
women's organizations were created; the Women's Working Committee of
the New Life Movement (1934), the Headquarters of Chinese Women for the
Consolation of Self-Defence and Resistance Soldiers (1937) and the War-time
Childcare Headquarters (1938). The first was formed to promote Confucian
moral principles among Chinese women, but it expanded in July 1938 to
co-ordinate all women's resistance work.[101] The latter were formed in response
to the escalating attacks of the Japanese.

The distinctions between the C.C.P. and the K.M.T. in the 1920s and early 1930s were: the mobilization of women was still party work for the C.C.P., but the K.M.T. gradually abandoned such a venture, and subsumed it under the category of 'public training'. Since women were still recruited through peasants' unions instead of independent women's organizations in the C.C.P.'s areas, the C.C.P. viewed women in 'class' terms (and not as a distinct 'gender' group). In contrast, the K.M.T. saw women as a separate group in which 'gender' certainly was the key element. With the exception of the K.M.T. after 1934, neither party relied heavily on *separate* women's organizations for the task of mobilization.

1937-45

As already mentioned, the C.C.P. followed the Comintern's directive to form a Popular Front with the K.M.T. during the Sino-Japanese War. Following such a policy, there were some structural mergers of the C.C.P. and the K.M.T. in the mobilization of women. For example, one C.C.P. member was invited to the K.M.T.'s 1938 special conference for women representatives of the women's organizations.[102] However, 'co-operation' between the K.M.T. and the C.C.P. was in practice quite limited, with the exception of the War-time Childcare Association in which the women's organizations of both parties did work together.[103] In general, the C.C.P. and K.M.T. went in different directions in their mobilization of women during the war period.

For the C.C.P. the mobilization of women was directed by the Women's Committee of the Central Committee.[104] It also established the Village Women's Representatives' Organization and the All-Women's Federation above the village level as early as 1938.[105] Special women's groups were formed to promote resistance activities, such as work teams, service teams, sisters' associations, patriotic organizations, national salvation teams and resistance teams.[106] By 1939, more than 8,000 locations in northern China had already established women's national salvation teams. At the end of the war, 88% of the villages in the C.C.P.'s Border Regions had village women's organizations.[107]

Membership in these organizations had been increasing since the declaration of the Sino-Japanese War. An estimated 130,000 members belonged to these mass organizations of peasant women in 1937, and by 1943 the number had risen to 2,532,208.[108] By 1945, these mass organizations in Shaan-Ningxia and seven other liberated areas had 7,100,000 members.[109]

Although these organizations played a co-ordinating role, peasant women were actually mobilized through the grass-roots structure of production co-operatives, literacy classes, peasant unions, mutual help teams and youth organizations within each village. There were no grass-roots *women's* organizations below the village level.[110]

In 1938, the Women's Guidance Committee of the New Life Movement (formerly known as the Women's Working Committee of the New Life Movement, established in 1934) was designated as the party-organizer of women's war efforts.[111] Meanwhile, the women's bureau of the K.M.T. was finally reinstated in the party structure in 1938 (it had been abolished in 1928). It was claimed that the party branches had women's associations in every county and province.[112] The new women's bureau was later known as the Women's Movement Committee. It was subordinated to the K.M.T.'s Central Organizational Bureau in 1941 and, a year later, unified the provincial women's organizations under its management.[113]

During the Sino-Japanese War, the Women's Guidance Committee of the New Life Movement was the main co-ordinator of women's activities. This organization had 12 provincial branches and 34 women-work teams (one in each government department).[114] There were nine bureaux to carry out the tasks of officer-training, rural service, life-guidance, soldier-consolation, production, child welfare, cultural affairs, surveys and statistics and co-ordination of organizations. The branches and women-work teams each implemented some of the tasks of these bureaux. They also had their own sub-branches and sub-teams which penetrated down to the village level. The exact number of members is unknown, but it is estimated that the numbers were in the millions.[115]

The distinctions between the C.C.P. and the K.M.T. activities during the war are not obvious on the formal organizational level. Both were centrally organized, apart from the fact that the K.M.T. had separate national women's organizations to co-ordinate all work at a fairly high level of its administration. The C.C.P., however, had only one separate women's organization (that is, the All-Women's Federation) just above the village level. The other difference was that women were mobilized through a branch (or sub-branch) of a national *women's* organization under the K.M.T.'s administration, but in the C.C.P.'s areas peasant women were mobilized through the existing grass-root *peasant's* (and not specifically women's) organizations. The latter feature was simply a manifestation of the persistent priority of *class* over gender in the C.C.P. framework, and that of *gender* over class in the K.M.T.

1945-49

After the war, the C.C.P. continued to mobilize peasant women in the pre-existing poor peasants' unions, co-operatives, mutual-help teams and literacy classes, according to their social (class) backgrounds.[116] In its initial stage of land reform, the C.C.P. mobilized peasant women who worked as hired-labourers, and gradually it began mobilizing middle peasants. The extent of this mobilization may be seen in Ding Xian (in Hebei); by the end of 1947, 84% of the peasant women who were hired labourers and 74% of those who were middle peasants were incorporated into existing peasants' unions.[117]

This method of mobilizing through pre-existing peasants' groups was criticized by some C.C.P. members for neglecting unorganized peasant women, for being inefficient to the extent that memberships overlapped and for ignoring the work carried on by the various organizations. More importantly, the pre-existing organizational structure failed to concentrate on problems specific to women, such as child-care, family disputes, love and marriage, hygiene issues and feudalistic beliefs.

By 1948, the official attitude of the C.C.P. may be summarized as follows: 'The freeing of women can't be isolated from revolution. Two wrong tendencies were to be guarded against: one is to think that all would be well with women so long as general revolutionary aims were fulfilled, and there was, therefore, no need to pay special attention or to have separate women's organizations; the other was to think that women's emancipation was a cause in itself, not a part of the revolution.'[118]

In the same year, the C.C.P. published a report showing the usefulness of special organizations for women. It was argued that the mobilization of women was best done through two organizations: one for both sexes, the other exclusively for women. The latter could hold small meetings so that women could speak their minds; and these meetings would not last too long, so as to avoid interfering with familial obligations.[119]

Consequently, after some debate on this issue, the C.C.P. announced in 1948 that 'a separate women's mass organization' was necessary. The basic unit of women's organizations changed from peasants' groups to the Women's Representatives' Congress. There were women's representatives' congresses, organized under the Women's Federation of the Liberated Areas,[120] in factories, departments, voluntary associations, schools, hospitals and workers' residences in all neighbourhoods, villages, districts, counties and regions. Congresses were to be held periodically to discuss the lessons, experiences and directions of women's mobilization.[121] The women representatives' congresses were hierarchically arranged. Representatives, who were elected from each neighbourhood, village, district and county to represent the viewpoints of women in their own area, then elected leaders to attend congresses at the higher levels. For example, the leaders of the village representatives attended the district women's congresses, and so.[122]

In the cities, the organizational structure focused either on the occupational groups or on places of residence of women. It was claimed that through this organizational structure working-class women, as well as other career women, could best be mobilized.[123] Two types of organizations were set up: dependants' associations and residents' committees (or street associations). The former were set up in factories or firms and its members were mainly housewives in workers' families. These organizations were directed by trade unions. The residents' committees were mainly composed of women living in the same area or on the same street. These women — working-class and residential — met periodically to discuss the experiences and problems they confronted as women.[124] The special task of the residents' committee was to organize 'housewives' or unemployed women and introduce them to various occupations or literacy classes.[125]

In the K.M.T. areas, the Women's Guidance Committee of the New Life Movement remained the national co-ordinator of women-work. During this period, the C.C.P. competed with the K.M.T. by forming a separate national women's organization in the liberated areas.

The organizational structure of the C.C.P. and the K.M.T. were quite different: although the C.C.P. did not have a separate top-level women's organization until 1948, the K.M.T. had developed three by 1934. The C.C.P. continued to mobilize women through grass-roots, usually peasant-oriented, organizations and the K.M.T. carried out a limited mobilization through branches of the central national women's organizations. Although the C.C.P. consistently maintained a 'women's committee' within its party structure, the K.M.T. dropped such a committee between 1928 and 1938. The K.M.T. did not have special organizations for each class of women; for most of the time, the C.C.P. had several groups or organizations to mobilize peasant women. This comparison of organizational structures confirms the picture of the C.C.P. emphasis on class, while the K.M.T. thought gender to be more significant. These modes of analysis and organizational structures were mutually reinforcing and were related to the mobilization methods used by the two parties.

Mass Line Verus Elitist Strategies

The Communist Party

The approach used by the C.C.P. throughout this period may be labelled a mass line approach (see Chapter Five).[126] As Mao Zedong declared in 1934: 'The central task of [the soviet government] is *to mobilize the broad masses* to take part in the revolutionary war, overthrow imperialism and the Kuomintang [Guomindang] by means of such war, spread the revolution throughout the country, and drive imperialism out of China. . . . For revolutionary war is *a war of masses;* it can be waged only by mobilizing the masses and relying on them.'[127]

Following mass line politics, the mobilization of peasant and working-class women, according to Mao, had to 'grasp firmly the issues of immediate benefit to the women masses, mobilize [women] according to these issues [and] relate [them] to full-scale political mobilization'.[128]

This grass-roots approach became the central technique for mobilizing peasant and working-class women. As early as 1926, the C.C.P. resolved that when party members mobilized women, they must 'become one with the masses, and should not be separate themselves from the masses', because the C.C.P.'s 'central responsibility is to recruit and gain support from the masses'. In addition, the C.C.P. advocated popularizing women's publications by 'describing the immediate suffering and concrete demands of women, so that every woman can see and feel' their voice and experience in these publications.[129] This approach was revived during the Sino-Japanese War and after: 'All the women-mobilization cadres [should] penetrate deeply into the working-class women, and blend with the poor women as one.'[130]

In concluding a panel on women-mobilization in 1946, one C.C.P. cadre commented on this approach:

> In conclusion, the principle of what [one should] do is to begin with the demands of the masses according to the concrete circumstances,

and determine the things that we should do. In the past, we have had
some comrades who formulated a whole set of plans, and then went
to the masses so as to 'fulfil the plans'; this tendency should be radically
changed now. . . . We should be determined to follow this principle:
join those people whom [we] serve. To serve working-class women,
[one] has to go among working-class women and join their production,
and mix with them in their daily life, [so that] their demands can be
deeply understood. What they want determines what [we will] do
[for them]. Move one step forward in helping and educating them.
[We] should demolish the attitude that we are acting as political
cadres outside the masses.[131]

This approach was facilitated by the specially-trained cadres of the C.C.P.
In 1926, the C.C.P. began a policy of training cadres for the mobilization of
women. In that year, the C.C.P. resolved that, 'if circumstances allow, party
branches in every place should establish training classes for women or special
discussion groups on women's movements'.[132] Training cadres to mobilize
women was a continuing policy during the C.C.P.'s administration, especially
after 1937. In 1939 the C.C.P. resolved to mobilize all women cadres and
women members within the party to take up the responsibility of mobilizing
women and to try their best to recruit more women for this task.[133] In
response to this resolution, the women's groups of north-western Shanxi
determined to train one-third more cadres in three months on the village level,
and to form cadre-training classes on the county level to train at least 60
cadre leaders in three months.[134] The same resolution was operative during
the civil war period.[135]

Through 'mixing' with the masses and finding out what they wanted, the
women cadres were able to approach women in a friendly way. In fact, the
C.C.P. made sure that all its members were friendly to the masses of women.
The armies were instructed to treat the villagers with respect wherever they
went.[136] During the Long March, when the Red Army fought its way through
11 provinces, it made sure that it did not loot or plunder the villages it passed
through. Especially important was the regulation that the army could not
'take liberties with women'. This was very different from the armies of either
the warlords or the K.M.T., and is one of the reasons why the Red Army was
acceptable to the villagers.[137]

Another approach that the women cadres took was the small group 'speak-
bitterness' technique. Usually, a woman cadre gathered a few women
together in a village, a production unit or a co-operative group, and simply
invited them to talk about their lives and experiences. The cadre encouraged
them to find a means of solving their immediate problems, and attempted to
politicize them by linking their experiences with the larger political context.[138]

In the countryside, it was quite common to find women working together,
spinning, weaving, reeling, etc. This was encouraged by the C.C.P., since it
allowed the women to communicate among themselves. The women cadres
usually lived and worked with other peasant women. If they were mobilizing

destitute women who did not have work, these cadres followed their life-styles: begging for food or looking for employment. By actually living and working with their fellow women, they were able to gain their confidence and support. The cadres paid special attention to peasant women's immediate demands, such as the care of children or household tasks. Mutual-help teams were organized, especially at harvest time. The cadres introduced songs or rhythms related to production or politics to peasant women, and later to working-class women; and also taught them how to read and write elementary words related to their daily life. Women were encouraged to talk about their familial or marriage problems. They might talk about bitter experiences with their husbands or parent-in-laws, or the brutality of their masters. The whole idea behind this approach was that 'bitterness will elicit more bitterness'; the task of the women cadres was to politicize them through such confessions and link their experiences of the landlords or male chauvinism to the larger political situation.[139]

Of course, there were no standard blue-prints for the mobilization of women, and the C.C.P. did not prescribe any. It constantly cautioned women cadres that they must take into consideration the objective circumstances of the villages in which they worked, and mobilize women accordingly. However, it appears that the above approaches were general enough to apply in quite a number of places; peasant women were enabled to obtain food (thus solving their immediate problem), and also to come to the realization that marital problems, poverty, and starvation were all related to feudalism, imperialism and male chauvinism (authoritarianism).[140]

After the C.C.P.'s shift in policy in the late 1940s, these mobilization approaches were used also in the towns and cities, tailored to suit regional specificities.[141]

The Kuomintang

If the C.C.P. approach was mass line, the K.M.T. was elitist. Unlike the C.C.P. cadres, the K.M.T. women officers contacted the educated youth or well-known officials in a few selected districts or villages. Once they received their approval and acceptance, these women officers began their mobilization work in the countryside.[142] In contrast, the C.C.P. started off with the peasant women, rather than with the village elite.

The K.M.T. cadres next organized literacy classes and propaganda campaigns. Peasant women were encouraged to join the literacy classes and to learn how to read, write and sing. Speeches were made, dramas presented and posters and cartoons posted to promote anti-Japanese sentiment, knowledge of hygiene, etc. In some cases, welcoming parties, family visits, sanitary competitions, and discussion forums were carried out to promote the Party. These campaigns were expected to raise women's consciousness on such issues as women's oppression and the war.[143] Unlike the C.C.P., the K.M.T. designed 'education' and 'propaganda' materials prior to mobilization and they were used mechanically in the rural areas, irrespective of local conditions.[144] Often, literacy classes were not linked to production skills or daily necessities, and peasant women could see no point in joining them, as witnessed by the high turnover rate of participants.

During the harvest season, literacy classes were sometimes abandoned in favour of building child-care centres and carrying out surveys and censuses.[145] Skill-training was only marginally carried out.[146]

Although the K.M.T. paid lip service to mobilizing working-class women and its literature urged women officers to 'penetrate into the masses of women' and 'actively and intimately relate to the masses of women', their actions were 'formalistic, official and separate from the masses'.[147] Although the K.M.T. provided a number of services for working-class women, such as counselling, literacy classes and entertainment, it failed to put them to any immediate use. Women officers responsible for encouraging working-class women to educate themselves often found the task 'difficult', and reported that there were a number of 'stubborn' workers who refused to be educated.[148]

In summarizing the weaknesses of the women-mobilization campaigns of the K.M.T., one writer noted in 1940:

> Most of the women's organizations lack a foundation in the masses mainly because the organizations themselves fail to fit the needs of the masses. [They are run by] a few women with ambitions for leadership [and] temporary enthusiasm; [they] do not recognize their [limited] strength, or understand the needs of the masses. Since their formation, the [women's] organizations have been managed and run by a small number of people. Their recruited members usually come on the invitation of several people [in the organizations]. The members still fail to feel that these organizations are theirs . . . . Consequently, with paper membership and empty-headed leadership, organizations separate from the masses have been formed. These organizations have failed to appropriate the needs of the masses and therefore have little chance to expand their work.[149]

Thus, in mobilizing working-class women and peasant women, the K.M.T. retained the mentality of urban-educated women (who had no experience of life in the countryside or in the factories or of unemployment), while neglecting completely the concrete and immediate needs of working-class and peasant women. It is not surprising that these elitist approaches mobilized only a limited proportion of peasant women.[150]

The failure of the K.M.T.'s approach was criticized in a letter to the editors of the *Women's Life (Funu Shanghuo)*: 'If the government does not improve the lives of the poor masses, then mobilizing [them] is impossible. As long as their immediate daily needs remain unsolved, they will not be impressed by flowery speeches or statements that the country is in great peril and how painful it would be if their country is defeated.'[151]

Conclusion

The activities used to mobilize women by both the C.C.P. and the K.M.T. were similar, especially during the Sino-Japanese War: officer-training, education, production, soldier-consolation, child-welfare, military training, nursing and medical care, etc.[152] But merely comparing the *types* of activities cannot tell us why the C.C.P. was successful in enlisting peasant women in resistance and revolution, and why the K.M.T. failed. What matters most in the mobilization of peasant women is not *what* they were mobilized to do but *how* they were mobilized.

In its lack of concern with women, especially working-class and peasant women, and its fixation on mechanistic educational campaigns, the K.M.T. demonstrated its distance from the masses of women. The C.C.P., by contrast made the mobilization of peasant women and, to a lesser extent, working-class women part of its programme right from its inception. In addition, its policies of marriage reform, land redistribution and, most important of all, orientation towards production clearly show the C.C.P.'s familiarity with the poverty and oppression experienced by peasant women.

Organizationally, the K.M.T. mobilized women from the top down, through highly centralized women's organizations established to carry out the policies of the K.M.T. Peasant women were mobilized through teams of women-officers who entered villages with the approval of the village elite or local gentry and introduced educational materials developed by central women's organizations in the cities. Similarly, factory women were encouraged to learn, or join the government campaigns to defend the country. Little attempt was made to understand these women on a grass-roots level. In contrast, the C.C.P. worked its way up, using peasant organizations to recruit women. The C.C.P. tried to understand the experience of peasant women by living and working with them and relating their experiences to the larger political structures through small 'speak-bitterness' meetings or small productive units. It paid attention to their general welfare and their individual immediate needs. No blue-prints for mobilization were offered by the C.C.P., and mobilization tactics were tailored to regional or local specificities after a long period of observation and experience on the part of the women cadres. Since the C.C.P.'s strategies were more relevant to the peasant women, its mass line approach further reinforced the impetus of mobilization. Whereas the irrelevant educational policy and elitist approach of the K.M.T. finally drove peasant women and working-class women away.

The differences in policies, organizational structures and approaches between the C.C.P. and the K.M.T. are largely related to their frameworks of analysis. Throughout this period (1912-49), the C.C.P. perceived class as cutting across gender lines, while the K.M.T. insisted that gender cut across class lines. This is witnessed in the K.M.T.'s selection of an educational policy as opposed to the C.C.P.'s economic one, in their differing organizational structures, and in the K.M.T.'s choice of an elitist approach as opposed to the mass line advocated by the C.C.P. The K.M.T.'s bourgeois framework assumed that peasant and working-class women suffered from the same weaknesses as their urban-educated counterparts — namely lack of understanding, education and occupational skills — and so, in mobilizing peasant and working-class women, it formulated its strategy with a bourgeois bias. The C.C.P., however, saw that there were different classes of women, and that bourgeois women differed from peasant and working-class women in their relation to the means of production, life-experiences, mentality, needs and concerns. Based on this analysis, the C.C.P. wisely used 'economic' policies in mobilizing peasant women and, after 1945, working-class women, instead of educational ones. The organizational patterns of the two parties reflected their analyses: the K.M.T. mobilized peasant women through *women's* organizations, and the C.C.P. mobilized them through *peasant* organizations or *working-class* organizations (unions).

References

1. The C.C.P. Central Committee's Editorial and Translation Department Research Branch edition of the writings of Marx, Engels, Lenin and Stalin, *The Introduction of the Periodicals of the May Fourth Movement Era,* Vol. 1, pp.155-6.
2. Julia Kristeva, *About Chinese Women,* London: Marion Boyars, 1977, p.116.
3. Ibid.
4. *New Intellectual Currents,* 15 June 1976, p.4.
5. Luo Qiong, 'The Basic Rules of the Development of the Chinese Women's Movements', *New Chinese Women,* December 1952, pp.26-8.
6. Wang Jiamin, *A Draft of the History of the Chinese Communist Party,* Taiwan: self-published, 1965, pp.239-40.
7. *Gongjiao Zhishi,* April 1971, p.18.
8. Fang Suzhong, 'The National Father's Idea of Women's Rights', *Revolutionary Ideas Monthly,* Vol. VI, No. iii, August 1959, p.25.
9. *Shibao,* 1 April 1925, section 2, p.4.
10. *Jiangxi Funu,* 8 March 1937, pp.24-5.
11. Ibid.
12. *Shibao,* 5 December 1925, section 2, p.3.
13. Xu Hui, 'The Policies of the National Party on Women', *Funu Yuekan,* Vol. I, No. vi, February 1942, pp.21-5.
14. The K.M.T. Central Committee's Editorial Committee of Party Historical Data, *The Year-chart of Seventy Years of Important Events of the K.M.T.,* Taibei: The KMT Central Committee's Editorial Committee of Party Historical Data, 1964, p.90; *Huazi Ribao,* 6 May 1927, section 2, p.2; *Shibao,* 7 May 1927, p.7.
15. Janet Salaff and J. Merkle, 'Women in Revolution', *Berkeley Journal of Sociology,* Vol. XV, 1970, pp.166-91.
16. Kristeva, op. cit., p.119.

17. Delia Davin, *Woman-Work*, Oxford: Clarendon Press, 1976, pp.22, 26.
18. Kristeva, op. cit., p.120.
19. Davin, op. cit., p.26.
20. Ibid.
21. Delia Davin, 'Women in the Liberated Areas', in M.B. Young, *Women in China*, Ann Arbor: Center for Chinese Studies, University of Michigan, 1973, p.73-91.
22. *Guangdong Government Gazette*, Vol. VI, 18 July 1929, pp.29-32; Vol. CXXXIX, 31 December 1930, pp.28-29.
23. Wang, op. cit., p.51.
24. Ibid., p.418.
25. The exact number of women was not known, it was somewhere between 15 and 50.
26. 'The Advanced Deeds of Women Cadres', *Union Research Service*, Vol. LIX, No. 9, 1 May 1970, p.113.
27. Salaff and Merkle, op. cit., p.182.
28. Kristeva, op. cit., p.100.
29. Leslie E. Collins, 'The New Women', : A Psycho-Historical Study of the Chinese Feminist Movement from 1900 to the Present', unpublished Ph.D. dissertation, Yale University, 1976, p.645.
30. Katie Curtin, *Women in China*, Toronto: Pathfinder Press, 1975, p.31.
31. Kristeva, op. cit., p.125.
32. Huang Xiaomin, 'On Women's Movements and Guangdong Women', *Funu Zazhi*, Vol. XIII, No. 4, April 1927, p.6.
33. *Education Department Gazette*, 26 July 1930, Vol. II, p.26; 23 August 1930, pp.35-7.
34. *Jiangsu Civil Administration Gazette*, 25 February 1930, pp.1-3.
35. *Education Department Gazette (Jiaoyubu Gongbao)*, 6 November 1932, pp.68-9; 15 January 1933, pp.7-9; *Guangdong Government Gazette*, 30 November 1932, pp.62-3.
36. *Shibao*, 5 October 1931, section 2, p.6.
37. *Funu Shenghuo*, 1 May 1935, p.24; *Huazi Ribao*, 9 November 1937, section 2, p.4; 9 November 1937, section 2, p.1.
38. *Jiangsu Civil Administration Gazette*, Vol. LXVI, 24 September 1927, p.4; *Guangdong Government Gazette*, Vol. CLI-CLIII, 10 May 1931, pp.173-4.
39. Chen, 'The Changing Status of Women in the Early Republic', Taiwan: Sili Zhongghuo Wenhu Shixue Yanjusho, M.A. Thesis, 1972, pp.173-4; Gu Bingyuan, 'The Issue of Shanghai Women Workers', *Nugingnian*, Vol. VIII, No. v, May 1929, pp.4-10; Xie Zhenmin, *The Legislative History of the Republic of China*, Xianggang: Zhengzhong Shuju, 1948, pp.1356-8; Lanping, 'The Protection of Women in the Existing Legislation in our Country', *Dongfang Zazhi*, Vol. XXXIV, No. v, March 1937, pp.95-100.
40. *Liberation Weekly*, 8 March 1939, pp.2-5.
41. Davin, 'Women in the Liberated Areas', op. cit., pp.73-91.
42. Ibid., pp.19-20.
43. Lan Feng, 'Northwestern Shanxi Women's Federation First Women-Officers' Expansion Meeting', *Funu Shenghuo*, Vol. VIII, No. v, 5 December 1939, pp.19-20.

44. For more interesting details on this, see Davin, 'Women in the Liberated Areas,' op. cit., pp.76 and 78.
45. *Documents on the Women's Movements*, Xianggang: Xin minzhu chubanshe, 1949, pp.2-3.
46. The Publicity and Education Department of the All-Women's Democratic Federation of China, *Important Documents of the Chinese Women's Movements*, Beijing: Renmin chubanshe, 1953, pp.1-3.
47. *Liberation Weekly*, Vol. LXVI, 8 March 1939, pp.2-5.
48. The Publicity and Education Department of the All-Women's Democratic Federation of China, op. cit., pp.1-3.
49. *Liberation Weekly*, Vol. CI, 8 March 1940, p.1.
50. *Documents on the Women's Movements*, op. cit., pp.2-3.
51. The Publicity and Education Department of the All-Women's Democratic Federation of China, op. cit., pp.1-3; Davin, *Woman-Work*, op. cit., p.36; Collins, op. cit., p.647.
52. Davin, 'Women in the Liberated Areas', op. cit. p.76.
53. Davin, *Woman-Work*, op. cit., p.155.
54. *Liberation Weekly*, 8 March, 1939, pp.2-5.
55. *Liberation Weekly*, 8 March 1940, p.1.
56. Davin, *Woman-Work*, op. cit., p.36.
57. *Liberation Weekly*, 8 March 1939, p.1; Lan, 'Northwestern Shanxi Women's Federation First Women-Officers' Expansion Meeting', *Funu Shenghuo*, Vol. VIII, No. v, 5 December 1939, pp.19-20.
58. *Huazi Ribao*, 9 November 1937, section 2, p.4; 9 November 1937, section 1, p.1; 5 January 1938, section 2, p.2; 8 February 1938, section 2, p.2; 2 March 1938, section 2, p.1.
59. Zou Lu, *A Brief History of the K.M.T. in China*, Taibei: Shangwu Press, 1965, p.205; *Gongjiao Zhishi*, 1971, pp.13-14; *Funu Shenghuo*, 16 April 1938, p.1.
60. Tan Sheying, *Forty Years of Women's Movements*, Taiwan: publisher unknown, 1952, pp.44-5; *Funu Shenghuo*, 1 May 1939, pp.27-8; *Funu Gongming*, May 1942, p.1.
61. *Funu Gongming*, 5 April 1938, pp.5-6.
62. *Funu Xinyun*, July 1944, pp.19-44; New Life Movement Women's Directing Committee, *Women's Rural Services*, Congqing: Xin yun funu zhidao wenyuanhui, 1944, pp.5-73; *Huazi Ribao*, 5 August 1940, section 2, p.1.
63. New Life Movement Women's Directing Committee, op. cit. pp.5-73.
64. *Funu Xinyun*, July 1944, pp.19-44; *Funu Shenghuo*, 16 October 1939, pp.10-11.
65. *Funu Xinyun*, July 1944, pp.19-44; *Guangdong Funu*, 8 March 1941, pp.31-5; 25 April 1942, p.35; Luo, 'The Creation Process of Rong District and its Afterthrought', *Funu xinyu*, December 1944, pp.11-14.
66. *Funu Xinyun*, July 1944, pp.26-7.
67. Mo Yan, 'How Do Women Learn and Join the Resistance?'; *Dongfang Zazhi*, Vol. XXXV, No. 1, January 1938, pp.71-5.
68. Xiong Zhi, ' "March 8th" Women's Day', *Jiangxi Funu*, Vol. I, no. 1, 8 March 1937, pp.12-14; Zi Jiu, 'The Evaluation of Women's Work after One Year of Resistance', *Funu Shanghuo*, Vol. VI, no. vi, 20 July 1938, pp.7-8; Yuan, 'How Can Women-Officers Be Ignored?' *Guangdong*

Funu, Vol. III, Nos. 1-2, 15 October 1942, p.5.

69. Dong, 'Wish this Organization Pays More Attention . . .', pp.3-4; Liang Ying, 'Expanding Wartime Women's Work into the Countryside', *Funu Gongming,* Vol. VII, No. vi, 5 April 1938, pp.11-13.

70. Davin, 'Women in the Liberated Areas', op. cit., p.83; Editorial of the *Liberation Daily,* 'The Coming Mission of Chinese Women', *Documents on the Women's Movements,* op. cit., pp.20-3; The All-China Democratic Women's Federation Preparation Committee, *A Sketch of the Peasant Women's Movement in the Chinese Liberated Areas,* Xianggang: Xinminzhu chubanshe, 1949, pp.47-53.

71. Davin, *Woman-Work,* op. cit., p.47.

72. Ibid.

73. Davin, 'Women in the Liberated Areas', op. cit. p.82.

74. *Shidai Funu,* July 1946, pp.10-11.

75. All-China Democratic Women's Federation, *Concerning the Urban-Rural Women Representatives Conference,* Beijing: Zhongguo Quan'quo Minzhu funu lianhehui, 1950, p.1.

76. *The First National Representatives' Congress of Chinese Women,* Xianggang: Xinminzhu chubanshe, 1949, pp.2-3, 36-50.

77. Ibid., pp.87-91.

78. Davin, *Woman-Work,* op. cit., p.155.

79. 'The strategies of women's work in Zhangshi', *Shidai Funu,* Vol. I, No. 1, July 1946, pp.10-11.

80. Davin, *Woman-Work,* op. cit., p.156.

81. Ibid., pp.156-7.

82. *The First National Representatives' Congress of Chinese Women,* op. cit., pp.2-3.

83. *Guangdong Funu,* October 1945, pp.2-3; *Family,* April 1946, pp.3-4.

84. Peng Lan, 'I Suggest: March 8th Should Go to the Countryside', *Dagongbao,* Shanghai, 8 March 1948, p.7.

85. Pi Yishu, 'An Attempt to Discuss the Contemporary Women's Movement in Taiwan', *Zhongguo Funu,* Vol. I, No. i, July 1950, pp.8-9.

86. *Shibao,* 3 July 1935, p.4; 2 July 1926, section 2, p.3; 3 July 1926, section 2, p.3; *Huazi Ribao,* 2 June 1936, section 3, p.3; 3 June 1936, section 3, p.3.

87. Dymphna Cusack, *Chinese Women Speak,* Sydney: Halstead Press, 1959, pp.52-3.

88. Kristeva, op. cit., p.112; Suzette Leith, 'Chinese Women in the Early Communist Movement' in M.B. Young, *Women in China,* op. cit., p.49.

89. Leith, op. cit., p.49.

90. Dong Tingchao, 'A "March 8th" Day Thirty Years Ago', *Zhongguo Funu,* Vol. III, No. vi, 1956, p.6; Wang, op. cit. pp.239-40.

91. Curtin, op. cit., p.26.

92. Wu, 'In memory of Martyr Chen Tiejun', *Zhongguo funu,* Vol. X, No. 16, 1962, p.15.

93. Wang, op. cit., Vol. 1., p.428.

94. Wang, op. cit., Vol. 1, p.435.

95. *Shibao,* 1 April 1925, section 2, p.4.

96. *Jiangxi Funu,* 8 March 1937, pp.24-5.

97. Davin, *Woman-Work,* op. cit., pp.24-5.

98. Edgar Snow, *Random Notes on Red China, 1936-1945*, Cambridge, Mass.: Harvard University Press, 1957, p.138.
99. *Gongjiao Zhishi*, April 1971, pp.11-12.
100. *Shibao*, 1 July 1928, p.5.
101. *Funu Shenghuo*, 20 August 1938, p.19; November 1939, p.1.
102. Collins, op. cit., p.645.
103. Ibid.
104. Davin, 'Women in the Liberated Areas', op. cit., p.80.
105. Wang Yiwei, 'Women in the Resistance Mobilization of Special Districts', *Funu Shenghuo*, Vol. VI, No. ii, 20 May 1938, pp.22-3.
106. Yan'an Research Society on Current Affairs, *Chinese Wartime Politics*, pp.382-3; *Huazi Ribao*, 1 January 1939, section 2, p.2.
107. Li, 'Move one Step Forward', *Shidai funu*, Vol. I, No. 1, July 1946, pp.6-9.
108. Helen Snow, *Women in Modern China*, The Hague: Mouton, 1967, p.225.
109. Davin, *Women-Work*, op. cit., p.43.
110. *Chinese Women Stand Up*, Xianggang: Xinminzhu chubanshe, 1949, pp.4-6; *Jiefang Zhoukan*, 8 March 1939, pp.2-5; All-China Democratic Women's Federation, op. cit., pp.1-3.
111. *Funu Shenghuo*, Vol. VI, No. viii, 20 August 1938, p.19; Vol. VI, No. xi, November 1939, p.1.
112. Sheying Tan, *Forty Years of Women's Movements*, Taiwan, p.62.
113. *Guangdong Funu*, 15 July 1941, pp.19-21.
114. *Funu Xinyun*, July 1944; July 1948.
115. *Funu Shenghuo*, 20 February 1940, pp.4-6.
116. *Chinese Women Stand Up*, op. cit., pp.4-6.
117. The All-China Democratic Women's Federation Preparation Committee, *A Sketch of the Peasant Women's Movement in the Chinese Liberated Areas*, Xianggang: Xinmizhu chubanshe, 1949, pp.17-21.
118. Collins, op. cit., p.649.
119. Davin, *Woman-Work*, op. cit., pp.43-4.
120. Cusack, op. cit., pp.199-200.
121. The All-China Democratic Women's Federation, *Concerning the Urban-Rural Women Representatives*, op. cit., pp.94-101.
122. *The First National Representatives Congress of Chinese Women*, op. cit., pp.69-74.
123. Ibid.
124. Davin, *Woman-Work*, op. cit., p.157.
125. The All-China Democratic Women's Federation, *Concerning the Urban-Rural Women Representatives*, op. cit., pp.19-23.
126. Ilpynong J. Kim, 'Mass Mobilization Policies and Techniques Developed in the Period of the Chinese Soviet Republic', in A. Doak Barnett, *Chinese Communist Politics in Action*, Seattle: University of Washington Press, 1970, pp.79-80.
127. Ibid., pp.79-80. (my emphasis).
128. The All-China Democratic Women's Federation, *Concerning the Urban-Rural Women Representatives . . . .*, op. cit., p.iii.
129. Luo, op. cit., pp.26-8.
130. *The Chinese Women Stand Up*, pp.4-6.

131. 'The Strategies of Women's Work in Zhangshi', *Shidai Funu,* Vol. I, No. 1, July 1946, pp.10-11.
132. Wang, op. cit., pp.239-40.
133. *Liberation Weekly,* Vol. LXVI, 8 March 1939, p.1.
134. Lan, op. cit., pp.19-20.
135. *The First National Representatives Congress of Chinese Women,* pp.58-9;
136. *Guangdong Government Gazette (Guangdong Sheng Zhengfu Gongbao),* 31 December 1930, Vol.CXXXIX, pp.28-9.
137. Douglas Palk, *China: The Sleeping Giant,* Don Mills; Greywood, 1972, p.107.
138. Carol Tavris, 'The Speak-bitterness Revolution', *Psychology Today,* Vol. VII, No. xii, May 1974, p.49.
139. *The Chinese Women Speak Up,* pp.9-11.
140. Liu Zhi, 'The Standing Up of Women in Dingxian', The All-China Democratic Women's Federation, *A Sketch of the Peasant Women's,* op. cit., pp.17-21.
141. *Shidai Funu,* July 1946, pp.10-11.
142. Chi Zhenchao, 'The Situation of Woman's Work in Jiangxi', *Dongfang Zazhi,* Vol. XXXV, No. xvii, September 1938, pp.78-84; Guixiu, 'An Experiment in Mobilizing the Masses in the Countryside', *Funu Shenghuo,* Vol. VI, No. ix, 1 December 1938, pp.19-20; Ma; 'In the Villages', *Funu Shenghuo,* Vol. VI, No. i, 5 May 1938, pp.24-5.
143. Ma, op. cit., pp.24-5; Guixiu, 'An Experiment in Mobilizing the Masses in the Countryside', *Funu Shenghuo,* Vol. VI, No. ix, 1 December 1938, pp.19-20; Chun Shao, 'The Organizational Process of a Peasant Women's Association', *Funu Shenghuo,* Vol. VI, No.v, 5 July 1938, pp.24-5; Xu Youzhi, 'Our One Year of Peasant Service in Zhonghechang', *Funu Xinyun,* Vol. VI, No.x, December 1944, pp.5-8.
144. Chi, 'The Situation of Women's Work in Jiangxi', *Dong fang zazhi,* Vol. XXXV, No. xvii, September 1938, pp.78-84.
145. Ma, op. cit., pp.5-8.
146. Guixiu, op. cit., pp.19-20.
147. Women's Life Society *(Funu Shenghuo She), Women's Wartime Handbook,* Chongqing: Shenghuo sheju, 1939, p.24.
148. *Funu Xinyun,* Vol. VI, No. vii, July 1944, p.29.
149. Shiliang, 'My Opinion on the Present National Organization of Women, *Funu shenghuo,* Vol. VIII, No. x, pp.4-6.
150. *Funu Xinyun,* July 1944, pp.19-44.
151. *Funu Shenghuo,* 16 September 1939, p.29.
152. *Funu Xinyun,* July 1944, pp.19-44; Siu, *Fifty Years of Struggle,* Xianggang: Revomen Pub. Co., 1975, pp.157-248.

7. Lessons from the Chinese Women's Movement

The central thesis of this book is that the resistance movements of working-class and peasant women in China sprang from the encroachment of imperialism upon China, and that the women who participated in these movements played an important role in its removal. The changing structure of the capitalist economies in Britain, Japan and the U.S. forced them to seek overseas markets, cheap labour and natural resources. When these imperialist powers descended upon China in the 19th and 20th Centuries, they truncated its economic development through various military, political, economic and cultural mechanisms. As a result, the indigenous cotton textile goods handicraft industry was ruined and the Chinese factory system could not establish itself. Simultaneously, the agricultural system was severely dislocated due to the rise of cash crop farming, the shrinkage of farm size and the concentration of landownership. On top of this, the K.M.T. Government not only failed to resurrect the dying economy, but also escalated its decline through mismanagement.

This deterioration in economic conditions had major effects on Chinese women. First of all, foreign military bombardment affected the physical and social security of both working-class and peasant women. The declining handicraft industry and the worsening agrarian situation made the already miserable lives of peasant women intolerable: infanticide and the marketing of women were on the rise. Many women migrated or were sold to work in the factories in the cities. In their struggle for survival, these factory women were subjected to atrocious working conditions, starvation wages, maltreatment and harsh living conditions. Although they may not have been worse off than their counterparts in the countryside, these working-class women were certainly exploited and oppressed to an inhuman degree. The agonizing experiences of peasant and working-class women can only be meaningfully understood in the context of imperialist domination and K.M.T. mismanagement of the country.

The bitter experiences of working-class and peasant women gave them an incentive to struggle for power. Their sporadic and loosely-organized rebellions, demonstrations, protests and strikes of the 1920s changed to a systematic mobilization campaign in the 1930s and 1940s as the Japanese invasion escalated. The growing militancy among working-class and peasant women was part of a rising radicalism in the peasant and labour movements as a whole.

The history of women's resistance also shows that the C.C.P. played a very significant role in mobilizing these women. The C.C.P. viewed the class factor as stronger than the gender factor and it mainly mobilized women through existing organizations not especially designed for the mobilization of women. It followed mass line politics, mobilizing peasant women firstly through land reform and production, and secondly through marriage reforms. Thus, policies of educating women, family consolidation and involvement of women in war efforts were introduced, but in line with the primary goals of land reform and production. It was because the C.C.P. understood the necessity of eradicating feudalism and imperialism as well as the needs of peasant and working-class women that it was able to mobilize women successfully.

In comparison, the K.M.T. saw gender as more important than class, and created special women's organizations to mobilize women for resistance. Although it paid lip service to recruiting peasant and working-class women and did a minimal amount of work in educating these women, the K.M.T. followed an elitist line of approach and never got support of underprivileged women.

In fact, if one examines the history of women's resistance in China, the K.M.T. actually carried out two retrograde policies with respect to women: institutionalization and repression. The K.M.T. tried to incorporate women's activities and deradicalize them. Only in the 1930s, when the Sino-Japanese conflict intensified to such an extent that the security of the K.M.T. was threatened, did it mobilize women into support work for the fronts. However, this mobilization drive was relaxed in the K.M.T. areas after the Sino-Japanese War, when institutionalization and deradicalization failed, the K.M.T. did not hesitate to suppress militant actions by women. For that reason, the K.M.T. Government was always at odds with working-class and peasant women. But repression did not curb the advance of women's resistance: in some cases, it pushed resistance work underground, in others it only fuelled women's militancy. The 1949 Liberation demonstrated just how ineffective were the repressive measures of the K.M.T. in putting a stop to revolutionary action.

Women's resistance was further justified and legitimized through the general women's literature. Women were urged to join in resistance work and to unite with men and women all over the world to fight against fascism and imperialism. To justify women's involvement, resistance was depicted as a responsibility of citizens and human beings; women's liberation was connected with anti-imperialism. Several strategies and tactics were suggested to mobilize women: the most favoured being economic and educational strategies, while familial and legislative ones were relatively neglected. Organizationally, both the use of existing organizations and the creation of special women's groups were proposed. Tactically, both mass line (grass-roots) and elitist (top-down) approaches were suggested. In spite of the difficulty of determining the political affiliation of women's publications, some were identified as C.C.P. organs, and these tended to emphasize the involvement of women in resistance work, the connection between women's liberation and national liberation, a strategy of economic change, the mobilization of women through the existing networks and a mass line approach to recruitment.

Most of the anti-imperialist articles appeared in the 1930s and early 1940s and, on the whole, did not give special consideration to working-class and peasant women. This was partly because, as China's weakness was no longer blamed on internal problems, there was a tendency to homogenize Chinese society against external constraints; and partly because the ideas of women's resistance were primarily put forward by educated women who tended to ignore the condition of the 'lower strata'.

These, in sum, are the key arguments presented throughout this book. It will be recalled that this study of women's resistance in China began with an overall historical and global examination of economic changes in other parts of the world and how these changes affected the political economy of China. It then moved from the general level to the specific effects these structural changes had on working-class and peasant women, including the question of how women perceived their relationship to the larger society. We then looked at the activities of these women in the context of the larger radical movements, and investigated the inter-relationship between government policies and the women's movements. Finally, the question of why the C.C.P. was more successful in mobilizing working-class and peasant women was answered by comparing the policies and tactics of the two parties. Women were seen to be central agents of social change, participating in social movements aimed at eliminating imperialism and revolutionizing the country. We have made it explicitly clear that imperialism creates its own contradictions: the misery it generated for women was to come back and help destroy it.

Much can be learnt from the history of women's resistance in China. Although the pattern of social change in China before 1949 cannot be replicated, one may, nevertheless, note several features which can, with caution, be applied to other countries. The term 'with caution' must be stressed, since each situation is historically and culturally specific and there can be no blueprint of social change.

First of all, women were agents of social change. For centuries, the important contribution of women (especially that of peasant and working-class women) has been ignored. The Chinese example shows that peasant and working-class women can organize themselves to fight against imperialist invasions, landlord domination and capitalist exploitation: they forced the government to change policies, confronted the imperialist enemies with grenades, bombs, rifles and sabotage, launched campaigns for land redistribution and marriage reform, taught themselves skills and shared knowledge, became self-sufficient through production, exercised their power over production processes in the factories and fought as guerrillas and soldiers on the front. All these illustrate the contribution of working-class and peasant women to bringing about the political, economic and social change in the country. The liberation of China in 1949 would have remained a dream if working-class and peasant women had not been actively involved.

Secondly, the oppression and exploitation of women was eliminated through active organization and mass line mobilization. It has often been argued that the poor and the underprivileged cannot be easily mobilized since their basic concern is survival rather than politics. The experience of Chinese women shows otherwise. While it is true that educated women were the first to organize and fight for women's rights in the early 1900s, peasant women and, to a lesser extent, working-class women protested along with men (or sometimes by themselves) against the social injustices they experienced as peasants, as workers, and as women. Although in the early stages their struggle was sporadic and localized, at the beginning of the 20th Century, their poverty, desperation and starvation led them to become more organized. Chapter Three documents the human consequences of imperialism and mismanagement by the K.M.T. Government and shows how absolutely deprived these women were. The C.C.P., understanding the survival needs of women, approached them on the grass-roots level and linked their needs to political issues. Women were politicized through producing for their basic needs, redistribution of land, changing the patriarchal feudal relationships and resisting first the Japanese and later the K.M.T. armies. Through these activities, peasant women (and, to a lesser extent, factory women) were mobilized and organized.

The third lesson is that class is stronger than gender in the mobilization process. Many contemporary feminists would argue that the gender is equally as strong, if not stronger than, class and that the oppression of women takes similar forms in all cultures and historical periods. The experience of Chinese women puts this perspective in doubt. Although both peasant and working-class women were oppressed and exploited, the forms of their oppression and exploitation varied: peasant women were restricted by the strong feudal system of child-wives, the decline of the handicraft industry and of farming and their incapacity to control the grain market. Working-class women were exploited by the capitalist system and experienced sexual discrimination at work. Working-class women in the city had close contact with the imperialist powers, while peasant women experienced the feudal landlord system prevalent in the countryside. Educated women — a group which is of peripheral concern in this book — experienced patriarchal restraint, but they were not, for instance, sold as child-wives nor did they work in the fields or in the factories, or experience unhealthy living conditions or the extremes of humiliation by imperialist powers. Their different experiences were manifested in their concerns and interests: where working-class women emphasized working conditions and job security, where the peasant women struggled around land and production, the educated women fought for personal liberation and Chinese nationalism.

The erosive effects of imperialism also undermined the livelihood of both men and women. The declining peasant economy affected all peasants in China, men and women. It was on the basis of this understanding that the C.C.P. appealed so successfully to both men and women in the fields and factories. There were some special 'women's issues', but these could be

181

largely traced back to feudalism, capitalism and imperialism, which were the underlying bases of their oppression. Hence, the C.C.P. mobilized women primarily according to their class background, and only secondarily on the basis of their gender. For a long time, women were mobilized through the existing peasant and workers' organizations. The K.M.T. made the mistake of seeing women as a homogeneous group with no class distinctions; it perceived peasant and working-class women's concerns as being similar to those of educated women. Consequently, it never got the support of peasant and working-class women.

Finally, our study illustrates the inability of repression and institutionalization to contain women's movements. It appears that the development of a social movement is contingent on the later structural context and not just on government policies of institutional change and social control. These three factors — social movements, government policies and structural context — are inter-related; changes in one affect the development of the others. In the case of China, the larger structural context — namely, imperialist advance and domination — could not be controlled by the Chinese Governments. Women recognized the governments' weaknesses and used the imperialist advances as a rationale for mobilizing.

Under the domination of imperialism, the government was then caught in a double bind: on the one hand, if it failed to fulfil the women's movements demands it had to confront the problem of subduing the movements. On the other hand, if the government gave in, it ran the risk of challenging the imperialist powers which it was too weak to fight. Besides, in some cases, governments had much to gain by co-operating with the imperialist powers.

Under these circumstances, the government usually followed a two-pronged strategy: repression and institutionalization, that is, suppressing the radicals and co-opting the moderates. The K.M.T. Government had little success with this strategy because the larger structural context of imperialism remained unchanged. Institutionalization did change the nature of women's resistance, in the K.M.T. areas, from militant boycotts, demonstrations and marches to work for the Party but, as was to be expected, this mainly affected educated bourgeois women; peasant and working-class women, in being largely ignored, escaped from this institutionalization process. It took strong repression to silence their movements (for example, in the mid-1910s and in 1927-28), and even so this was not for long.

The repressive measures used in China are similar to those used today in many Third World countries, such as Bolivia, Peru, the Philippines or South Korea. Governments are, on the whole, more coercive than those in Western capitalist countries. The explanation for this lies partly in the fact that these countries still maintain strong feudalistic traditions, reinforced by the foreign powers who often founded their governments, and partly in the fact that the Western capitalist powers have the necessary funds to satisfy the growing demands of the masses. (And this is also to say that the present economic crisis makes it much more likely that the governments of Western capitalist countries will use increasingly repressive methods to curb unrest.) Governments subjected to colonialism and imperialism require strong repression to secure their power bases and the interests of foreign powers. Since external constraints do not allow puppet governments much flexibility in making political/economic decisions, coercive measures are used to cope with internal crises.

Institutionalization is a politically 'safer' method of containing dissent. So far it has not been extensively used to control the women's movement in the West, but governments are beginning to recognize its potential. Many governments in capitalist countries are forming women's commissions, councils and bureaux and holding conferences; different projects relating to women are being funded, and governments are actively recruiting a few token women into the bureaucracies. All these are methods of institutionalization which were employed by the K.M.T. in China. Clearly, governments are not politically neutral in their actions but aim to change the nature of the women's movement and contain conflict. However, one can argue that, although institutionalization may change the forms that protests take and the direction of the movements, whether or not it succeeds in eliminating dissatisfaction among women depends on the structural context. As long as the structural sources of women's discontent remain, and only certain women benefit from the government institutional changes — as was the case of China before 1949 — the women's movement will continue.

Statistical Appendix

Table A
British Foreign Investment in China, 1875-1950 (£ millions)

Year	Amount
1875	1,400
1890	2,000
1910	3,500
1913	4,000
1929	3,738
1938	3,788
1945	2,417
1949	2,038
1950	2,020

Source: Wu Chengming, *The Investments of Imperialist Countries in Old China*, Beijing: Renmin Chubanshe, 1956, p.9.

Table B
U.S. Mergers in Manufacturing and Mining, 1895-1907

Year	Consolidations	Disappearance by Acquisition and Consolidation	Capitalization of Consolidation ($ million)
1895	5	43	34.50
1899	106	1,201	2,038.90
1903	15	143	144.25
1907	10	87	53.30

Source: M. Weinberg, 'American Economic Development', in V.B. Singh, *Patterns of Economic Development*, New York: Allied Pub., 1970, p.178.

Table C
U.S. Average Annual Rates of Per Capita Growth during 1839-89 and
1899-1939

Period	Agriculture	Mining	Manufacturing
1839-1889	0.3	16.5	6.7
1899-1939	−0.2	2.8	3.0

Source: Weinberg, 'American Economic Development', p.184.

Table D
Rates of Profit of U.S. Manufacturing Industry, 1889-1919

	Constant Capital				Rate
Year	Fixed	Circulating	Wages	Profits	of Profits (%)
1889	350	5,160	1,891	1,869	26.6
1899	512	6,386	2,259	1,876	20.5
1909	997	11,783	4,106	3,056	18.1
1919	2,990	36,229	12,374	8,371	16.2

Source: Mandel, *Marxist Economic Theory,* London: Merlin Press, 1971, p.66.

Table E
Shares of World Industrial Output, 1920-50

	Percentage of Total Output	
Year	U.S.	Soviet Union
1920	47	1
1937	35	17
1950	39	25

Source: Weinberg, 'American Economic Development', p.185.

Table F
Production Controlled by the Mitsui Trust, 1900-43 (%)

	1900	1920	1943
Petrol	50	50	90
Iron	90	95	92
Paper	50	50	90
Wool	10	15	30

Source: Mandel, *Marxist Economic Theory,* p.409.

Table G
The Big Four Japanese Corporate Groups

	Companies Directly Controlled	With Capital in 1939 (million yen)	With Capital at the end of 1942 (million yen)
Mitsui Group	233	2,784	3,747
Mitsubishi Group	180	2,202	2,827
Yasuda Group	137	930	1,030
Sumitomo Group	53	601	783

Source: Mandel, *Marxist Economic Theory,* p.417-18.

Table H
Concentration of National Wealth in Japan, 1887-1939

Year	Share of Upper 10% of the Population
1887	37.82
1891	38.66
1895	37.14
1900	35.04
1907	37.85
1912	37.68
1919	44.62
1925	42.01
1929	42.55
1935	42.08
1939	47.43

Source: P. Banerji, 'Economic Development of Japan', in V.B. Singh, *Patterns of Economic Development,* p.310.

Table I
Growth of the Protestant Church in China, 1889-1919

	1889	1906	1919
Foreign missionaries	1,296	3,833	6,636
Ordained Chinese	211	345	1,065
Total Chinese workers	1,657	9,961	24,732
Communicants claimed	37,287	178,251	345,853
Students in missionary schools	16,836	57,683	212,819

Source: A. Feuerwerker, *The Foreign Establishment in China in the Early Twentiet. Century,* Ann Arbor: Center for Chinese Studies, University of Michigan, 1976,p.42

Table J
Protestant Missionary Schools and Enrolment, in China, 1919

	Mission Schools	Enrolment in Mission Schools		
		Boys	Girls	Total
Lower primary	5,637	103,232	48,350	151,582
Higher primary	962	23,490	9,409	32,899
Middle	291	12,644	2,569	15,213

Source: Feuerwerker, *The Foreign Establishment in China in the Early Twentieth Century,* p.51.

Table K
Effects of the Treaty of Nanjing on Chinese Tariff Rates

Commodities	Rates before 1843	Rates in 1843	% Reduced
Cotton	24.19	5.56	77.02
Cotton yarn	13.38	5.56	58.45
1st class white cotton cloth	29.93	6.95	76.78
2nd class white cotton cloth	32.53	6.95	78.64

Source: Yan Zhongping, et al., *Selection of Statistical Materials on the History of the Modern Chinese Economy,* Beijing: Kexue Chubanshe, 1955, p.59.

Table L
Chinese Imports of British Machine-Made Cotton Cloth and Yarn 1829-42

Years	Cotton Cloth (yds.)	Cotton Yarn (lbs.)
1829	910,000	500,000
1830	600,000	380,000
1831	1,732,000	955,000
1832	2,262,776	383,000
1833	4,492,563	400,000
1834	5,699,106	901,000
1835	10,356,047	2,344,482
1836	13,049,250	3,155,769
1837	10,567,120	1,845,977
1838	23,063,784	3,733,580
1839	20,567,207	1,588,500
1840	21,355,763	3,419,560
1841	22,541,855	2,914,250
1842	19,358,120	4,485,856

Source: Yan Zhongping, *A Draft on the History of the Chinese Cotton Textile 1289-1937,* Beijing: Kexue Chubanshe, 1963, p.44.

Table M
Chinese Imports of British Machine-Made Cotton Products, 1843-56

Years	Dyed & Printed Cottons (rolls)	Cotton Yarn (lbs.)
1843	169,521	6,210,024
1844	242,197	3,110,074
1845	100,615	2,640,090
1846	81,150	5,324,050
1847	81,010	4,454,210
1848	90,100	4,553,390
1849	88,030	3,200,980
1850	126,970	3,011,970
1851	233,599	3,842,870
1852	366,970	6,871,652
1853	154,680	5,244,187
1854	95,059	3,486,550
1855	198,105	2,867,970
1856	281,784	5,579,600

Source: G.W. Cooke, *China: 'The Times' Special Correspondence from China in 1857-1858,* as quoted in Peng Zeyi, *Materials on the Modern Chinese Handicraft Industry, 1840-1949,* Beijing: Zanlian Shuju, 1957, Vol I, p.491.

Table N
Price and Quantity Indices of Imported Cotton Yarn and Cloth (1872 as base)

	Imported Yarn		Imported Cloth	
	Price	Quantity	Price	Quantity
Years	Index	Index	Index	Index
1872	100.0	100	100.0	100
1876	77.2	226	75.5	97
1880	79.6	304	68.5	110
1884	70.8	524	72.3	91
1888	83.8	1,368	77.7	152
1890	75.6	2,164	76.6	127

Source: The Chinese Maritime Customs Decennial Reports, Appendix XX; Decennial Reports, 1922-1931, Vol. I, pp.113 and 182. As quoted in Yan Zhongping: *A Draft on the History of the Chinese Cotton Textile, 1289-1937,* p.58.

Table O
Rates of Exploitation and Profit in the Chinese-Owned Cotton Textile
Factories, 1932

Marxist Categories	Cotton Yarn* (Chinese $/bag)	Cotton Cloth** (Chinese $/pi)
Total value of the commodity (T)	233.245	9.693
Constant capital (C)	173.661	7.257
Variable capital (V)	18.516	0.817
Surplus value (S)	41.068	1.619
Rate of exploitation (S/V)	221.80 %	198.16 %
Rate of Profit (S/C=V)	21.37 %	20.05%

* Based on five yarn factories in Shanghai.
** Based on several cloth factories in Jiangsu.

Source: Yan Zhongping, et al., *Selection of Statistical Materials on the History of the Modern Chinese Economy,* p.170.

Table P
Spindles and Looms in Chinese- and Foreign-Owned Cotton Textile
Factories, 1897-1947*

	Spindles		Looms	
Years	Chinese	Foreign	Chinese	Foreign
1897	59.3	40.7	100.0	—
1900	67.7	32.3	100.0	—
1905	65.8	34.2	100.0	—
1910	69.7	30.3	100.0	—
1914	54.0	46.0	49.9	50.1
1920	58.1	41.9	51.0	49.0
1925	55.9	44.1	53.8	46.2
1930	57.2	42.8	49.5	50.5
1935	56.8	43.2	47.8	52.2
1947	99.0	1.0	100.0	**

* 1915, 1940, and 1945 figures are not available.
** Less than 0.05.

Source: Yan Zhongping, et al., *Selection of Statistical Materials on the History of the Modern Chinese Economy,* p.136.

Table Q
Comparison of Japanese and British Spindles and Looms in China, 1915-36*

	Japanese Factories		British Factories	
	Yarn-making factories	% of spindles in China	Yarn-making factories	% of spindles in China
1915	4	20.6	5	23.1
1925	45	37.3	4	5.7
1936	48	44.1	4	4.1
	Cloth-making factories	% of looms in China	Cloth-making factories	% of looms in China
1915	–	30.4	–	20.2
1925	25	31.4	4	10.3
1936	27	49.5	4	6.9

* The Japanese yarn-making factories' 1915 figure includes one German-owned factory, and the British yarn-making factories of the same year include on British/German-owned factory.
The 1936 figures do not include those factories in the northeastern China.

Source: Wu Chengming, *The Investments of Imperialist Countries in Old China,* p.102.

Table R
Non-Tenant Peasants Owning Land in Inner Mongolia and Northwestern China, Northern China, Central and Southern China, 1936.

Districts	No. of Xian	Non-Tenant Peasants (average %)
Inner Mongolia & Northwestern China	36	51
Northern China	483	67
Central & Southern China	601	30
Average		*46*

Source: Yan Zhongping, et al., *Selection of Statistical Material on the History of the Modern Chinese Economy,* Beijing: Kexue, Chubanshe, 1955, p.262.

Table S
Privatization of Public Lands

Periods	Public Lands (%)	Private Lands (%)	Total (%)
End of 16th Century	50.0	50.0	100.0
1887	16.8	81.2	100.0
1929-33	6.7	93.3	100.0

Source: Yan Zhongping, et al., *Selection of Statistical Materials on the History of the Modern Chinese Economy,* p.275.

Table T
Number of Chinese Chambers of Commerce and Their Membership, 1912-18

Years	Number of Chambers of Commerce	Number of Members
1912	794	196,636
1913	745	192,589
1914	1,050	203,020
1915	1,242	245,728
1916*	1,158	193,314
1917*	1,148	206,290
1918*	1,103	162,490

* Numbers in these years are incomplete.

Source: Chow Tse-tung, *The May Fourth Movement,* Cambridge, Mass.: Harvard University Press, 1960, p.380.

Table U
Seasonal Prices of Rice, Wheat, Kaoliang and Yellow Beans in Four Districts, 1936 (Lowest price index = 100, L = lowest, H = highest)

Districts	Rice L	Rice H	Wheat L	Wheat H	Kaoliang L	Kaoliang H	Yellow Beans L	Yellow Beans H
Jingle (Shanxi)	—	—	100	219.2	100	151.8	100	146.4
Zhengding (Hebei)	100	125.8	100	177.2	100	144.3	100	142.1
Xiuxian (Anhui)	100	122.3	100	171.4	100	143.8	100	137.1
Funchuan (Guangxi)	100	167.7	—	—	—	—	—	—

Source: Yan Zhongping et al., *Selection of Statistical Materials on the History of Modern Chinese Economy,* p.336.

Table V
Changing Pattern of Money-Lenders, 1938-46 (%)

Years	Banks	Native Banks	Pawn-shops	Village Stores	Co-oper atives	Co-oper- ative Ware- houses	Merchants, Landlords, & Rich Peasants	Total
1938	8	3	13	14	17	2	43	100
1939	8	2	11	13	23	2	41	100
1940	10	2	9	13	26	2	38	100
1941	17	2	9	11	30	4	27	100
1942	19	2	8	10	34	6	21	100
1943	22	2	7	8	32	5	24	100
1944	21	3	8	13	27	4	24	100
1945	22	4	9	18	19	3	25	100
1946	24	5	9	20	19	2	21	100

Source: Yan Zhongping et al., *Selection of Statistical Materials on the History of Modern Chinese Economy,* p.346.

Bibliography

English Sources

Ambrose, Stephen, *Rise to Globalism: American Foreign Policy since 1938,* Harmondsworth: Penguin, 1971.

Ayscough, Florence, *Chinese Women,* Boston: Houghton Mifflin, 1938.

Banerji, P., 'Economic Development of Japan' in V.B. Singh, *Patterns of Economic Development,* New York: Allied Pub. 1970.

Belden, Jack, 'The Land Problem' in Franz Schurmann and Orville Schell, *Republican China,* New York: Vintage Books, 1967.

Belden, Jack, 'Stone Wall Village', in Franz Schurmann and Orville Schell, *Republican China,* New York: Vintage Books, 1967.

Bisson, T.A., 'Increase of Zaibatsu Predominance in War-time Japan', in Jon Livingston et al., *Imperial Japan, 1802-1945,* New York: Pantheon Books, 1973.

Boggs, Lucinda P., *Chinese Womanhood,* Cincinnati: Jennings and Graham, 1913.

Buck, J.L., *Land Utilization in China,* New York: Council on Economic and Cultural Affairs, 1956.

Chesneaux, Jean, *Secret Societies in China in the Nineteenth and Twentieth Centuries,* Xianggang: Heinemann Educational, 1971.

Chesneaux, Jean, *Peasant Revolts in China, 1840-1949,* London: Thames and Hudson, 1973.

Chow Tse-tung, *The May Fourth Movement,* Cambridge, Mass.: Harvard University Press, 1960.

Cole, G.D.H. and Raymond Postgate, *The Common People, 1746-1946,* London: Methuen, 1966.

Collins, Leslie E., 'The New Women: A Psycho-historical Study of the Chinese Feminist Movement from 1900 to the Present', unpublished Ph.D. dissertation, Yale University, 1976.

Crowley, James, 'Creation of an Empire, 1896-1900' in Jon Livingston, *Imperial Japan, 1800-1945,* New York: Pantheon, 1973.

Curtin, Kate, *Women in China,* Tornto: Pathfinder Press, 1975.

Cusack, Dymphna, *Chinese Women Speak,* Sydney: Halstead Press, 1959.

Davin, Delia, 'Women in the Liberated Areas', in M.B. Young, *Women in China,*

Ann Arbor: Center for Chinese Studies, University of Michigan, 1973.

Davin, Delia, *Woman-Work*, Oxford: Clarendon, 1976.

Downs, Ray F., *Japan: Yesterday and Today*, New York: Bantam Books, 1976.

Endicott, Stephen Lyon, *Diplomacy and Enterprise: British China Policy, 1933-1937*, Vancouver: University of British Columbia Press, 1975.

Esherick, Joseph, 'Harvard on China: the Apologetics of Imperialism', *Bulletin of Concerned Asian Scholars*, Vol. IV, No. iv, 1972.

Esherick, Joseph, *Lost Chance in China*, New York: Vintage Books, 1974.

Feuerwerker, A., *The Chinese Economy, 1912-1949*, Ann Arbor: Center for Chinese Studies, University of Michigan, 1968.

Feuerwerker, A., *The Chinese Economy, ca. 1870-1911*, Ann Arbor: Center for Chinese Studies, University of Michigan, 1969.

Feuerwerker, A., *Rebellion in the Nineteenth Century*, Ann Arbor: Center for Chinese Studies, University of Michigan, 1975.

Feuerwerker, A., *The Foreign Establishment in China in The Early Twentieth Century*, Ann Arbor: Center for Chinese Studies, University of Michigan, 1976.

Hadley, Eleanor, 'The Zaibatsu and the War', in Jon Livingston et al., *Imperial Japan, 1800-1945*, New York: Pantheon Books, 1973.

Hart, Robert, 'The Boxers: 1900' in Franz Schurmann and Orville Schell, *Imperial China*, New York: Vintage Books, 1967,

Headland, Isaac Taylor, 'The Nu Erh Ching; or Classics for Girls', translated from the Chinese', *The Chinese Recorder*, Vol. XXVI, No. xii, December 1895.

Hill, Christopher, *The Pelican History of Britain, 1530-1780*, Harmondsworth, Penguin Books, 1969.

Ho, Kan-chih, 'Rise of the Chinese Working-Class Movement. The Working-Cl Class Movement in Hunan. The Big Political Strike of the Peking-Hankow Railway Workers' in Franz Schurmann and Orville Schell, *Republican China*, New York: Vintage Books, 1967.

Hommel, R.P., *China at Work*, New York: John Day, 1937.

Hou, Chi-ming, *Foreign Investment and Economic Development in China, 1840-1937*, Cambridge: Harvard University Press, 1965.

Kim, Ilpynong J., 'Mass Mobilization Policies and Techniques Developed in the Period of the Chinese Soviet Republic' in A. Doak Barnett, *Chinese Communist Politics in Action*, Seattle: University of Washington Press, 1970.

Kristeva, Julia, *About Chinese Women*, London: Marion Boyars, 1977.

Landy, Laurie, *Women in the Chinese Revolution*, Highland Park: International Socialist Pub., 1974,

Leith, Suzette, 'Chinese Women in the Early Communist Movement', in M.B. Young, *Women in China*, Ann Arbor: Center for Chinese Studies, University of Michigan, 1973.

Lenin, V.I., *Imperialism, the Highest Stage of Capitalism*, Beijing: Foreign Language Press, 1970.

Levy, Marion J. (Jr.), *The Family Revolution in Modern China*, New York:

Octagon Books, 1971.

Lieberman, Sima, *Europe and the Industrial Revolution,* Cambridge, Mass.: Schrenkman Pub., 1972.

Livingston, Jon et al., *Imperial Japan, 1800-1945,* New York: Pantheon Books, 1973.

Lockwood, William, 'Trade, Armaments, Industrial Expansion, 1930-1938', in Jon Livingston et al., *Imperial Japan, 1800-1945,* New York: Pantheon Books, 1973.

Mandel, Ernest, *Marxist Economic Theory,* London: Merlin Press, 1971.

Marshall, Jonathan, 'Opium and the Politics of Gangsterism in Nationalist China, 1927-1945', *Bulletin of Concerned Asian Scholars,* Vol. VIII, No. iii, 1976.

Martin, R.M., 'Minute on the British Positions and Prospects in China', 19 April 1845, Xianggang in Rhodes Murphy, *Nineteenth-Century China: Five Imperialist Perspectives,* Ann Arbor: Center for Chinese Studies, University of Michigan, 1972.

Mayo, Marlen, 'Attitudes towards Asia and the Beginnings of Japanese Empire' in Jon Livingston et al., *Imperial Japan, 1800-1945,* New York: Pantheon Books, 1973.

Murphey, Rhodes, *The Treaty Ports and China's Modernization: What Went Wrong?* Ann Arbor: Center for Chinese Studies, University of Michigan, 1970.

Murphey, Rhodes, *Nineteenth-Century China: Five Imperialist Perspectives,* Ann Arbor: Center for Chinese Studies, University of Michigan, 1973.

Nathan, Andrew J., 'Imperialism's Effects on China', *Bulletin of Concerned Asian Scholars,* Vol. IV, No. iv, 1972.

Norman, E.H., 'Early Industrialization' in Jon Livingston et al., *Imperial Japan, 1800-1945,* New York: Pantheon Books, 1973.

O'Connor, James, 'The Meaning of Economic Imperialism' in Robert I. Rhodes, *Imperialism and Underdevelopment: A Reader,* New York: Monthly Review Press, 1970.

O'Hara, Albert R., *The Position of Women in Early China,* Xianggang: Orient Pub., 1955.

Orchard, John, 'The Effect of the World War on Industrialization' in Jon Livingston et al., *Imperial Japan, 1800-1945,* New York: Pantheon Books, 1975.

Palk, Douglas, *China: The Sleeping Giant,* Don Mills: Greywood Pub., 1972.

Plumb, J.H., *England in the Eighteenth Century,* Harmondsworth: Penguin Books, 1971.

Rankin, M.B., 'The Emergence of Women at the End of the Ching: the Case of Ch'iu Chin' in M. Wolf and R. Witke, *Women in Chinese Society,* California: Stanford University Press, 1975.

Rhodes, Robert I., *Imperialism and Underdevelopment: A Reader,* New York: Monthly Review Press, 1970.

Salaff, Janet and J. Merkle, 'Women in Revolution', *Berkeley Journal of Sociology,* Vol. XV, 1970.

Schrecker, John F., *Imperialism and Chinese Nationalism: Germany in Shantung,* Cambridge, Mass.: Harvard University East Asian Series, No. 58, 1971.

Schurmann, Franz and Orville Schell, *Imperial China,* New York: Vintage Books, 1967.

Schurmann, Franz and Orville Schell, *Republican China,* New York: Vintage Books, 1967.

Siu, Bobby, *Fifty Years of Struggle,* Xianggang: Revomen Pub., 1975.

Smith, Arthur H., *Village Life in China,* London:Oliphant, Anderson and Ferrier, 1900.

Snow, Edgar, *Random Notes on Red China, 1936-1945,* Cambridge, Mass.: Harvard University Press, 1957.

Snow, Helen, *The Chinese Labour Movement,* New York: John Day, 1945.

Snow, Helen, *Women in Modern China,* The Hague: Mouton, 1967.

Stokes, Gwenneth and John Stokes, *The Extreme East: A Modern History,* London: Longman, 1971.

Tavris, Carol, 'The Speak-Bitterness Revolution', *Psychology Today,* Vol. VII, No. xii, May 1974.

Thompson, E.P., *The Making of the English Working Class,* Harmondsworth, Penguin Books, 1976.

Tsing, Ting-fu, 'The English and the Opium War,' in Franz Schurmann and Orville Schell, *Imperial China,* New York: Vintage Books, 1967.

Tugendhat, Christopher, *The Multinationals,* Harmondsworth: Penguin Books, 1976.

Van Gulik, R.H., *Sexual Life in Ancient China: A Preliminary Survey of Chinese Sex and Society from ca. 1500 B.C. till 1644 A.D.,* Leiden: E.J. Brill, 1961.

Wakeman, Frederick, 'Rebellion and Revolution: the Study of Popular Movements in China', *Journal of Asian Studies,* Vol. XXXVI, No. ii, 1977.

Wedemeyer, Albert C., 'Summary of remarks . . . before joint meeting of State Council and All Ministers of the National Government, August 22, 1947' in Franch Schurmann and Orville Schell, *Republican China,* New York: Vintage Books, 1967.

Weinberg, M., 'American Economic Development' in V.B. Singh, *Patterns of Economic Development,* New York: Allied Pub., 1970.

Wolf, M. and R. Witke, *Women in Chinese Society,* California: Stanford University Press, 1975.

Wolseley, G.J., 'War with China', in Franz Schurmann and Orville Schell, *Imperial China,* New York: Vintage Books, 1967.

Woodruff, W., *Impact of Western Man,* New York: St. Martin Press, 1967.

Wright, Mary C., 'Introduction: The Rising Tide of Change' in *China in Revolution: The First Phase, 1900-1913,* New Haven: Yale University Press, 1968.

Young, M.B., *Women in China,* Ann Arbor: Center for Chinese Studies, University of Michigan, 1973.

Chinese Sources

All-China Democratic Women's Federation Preparation Committee *(Quanguo Minzhu Funu Lianhehui Choubei Weiyuanhui), A Sketch of the Peasant Women's Movement in the Chinese Liberated Areas (Zhongguo jiegangqu nongcun funu dafanshen yundong sumino),* Xianggang: Xinminzhu chubanshe, 1949.

All-China Democratic Women's Federation *(Quanguo Minzhu Funu Lianhehui), Concerning the Urban-Rural Women Representatives Conference (Guanyu chengxiang funu daibiao huiyi),* Beijing: Zhongguo Quan'quo Minzhu funu lianhehui, 1950.

Baishuang, 'Sincerely Unite, Express Democratic Spirit:. *(Jingcheng tuanjie, fahui minzhu jingshen), Funu Shenghuo,* Vol. VI, No. viii, 20 August 1938.

Bao, Jialin, 'The Trend of Women's Thought during the Period of the 1911 Revolution, 1898-1911' *(Xin-Hai geming shiqi de funu sixiang, 1898-1911), Zhonghua Xuebao,* Vol. I, No. vi, January 1974.

Biyun, 'The Misfortunes of Contemporary Career Women', *(Xiandai zhiye funu de eyun), Dongfang zazhi,* Vol. XXXIII, No. xv, August 1936.

Biyun, 'An Examination of the Contemporary Women's Labour Issues' *(Xiandai funu laodong wenti zhi jianshi), Dongfang zazhi,* Vol. XXXIII, No. xxiii, December 1936.

Biyun, 'The Situation of Women in the Island' *(Gudao shang de funu shenghuo), Dongfang zazhi,* Vol. XXXV, No. xiii, July 1938.

Bolin, 'The Issue of Women Labour from the Medical Perspectives' *(Yixue shang de funu laodong wenti),* in Mei Sheng, *A Collection of Discussion Papers on the Issue of Chinese Women (Zhongguo funu wenti taolunji),* Vol. 1, Shanghai: Xinwenhua Shushe, 1929.

Cao, Mengjun, 'Secure the Obtained Democratic Rights' *(Baowei yide de minzhu quanli), Zhongguo funu,* September 1957.

C.C.P. Central Committee's Editorial and Translation Department/Research Branch edition of the writings of Marx, Engels, Lenin and Stalin *(Zhonggong Zhongyang Makesi Liening Sidalin Zhuzuo Bianji Bianyi ju Yanjiushi), The Introduction of the Periodicals of the May Fourth Movement Era (Wu-Si Shidai qikan jieshao),* Beijing: Renmin chubanshe, 1958.

Chen, Biyun, 'The Sufferings of Women and Children of Shanghai under the Japanese Invasion' *(Rijun qinlue xia Shanghai furu suo zaoshou dao de jienan), Dongfang zazhi,* Vol. XXXV, No. i, January 1938.

Chen, Chongguang, 'The Changing Status of Women in the Early Republic' *(Min'guo chuqu funu diwei de yanbian),* Taiwan: Sili Zhongguo Wenhu Xueyuan Shixue Yanjiusho, M.A. thesis, 1972.

Chen, Huili, 'Apprentice' *(Yangcheng gong),* Li Yuqing, *The Calamity of the Old China (Ku'nan de jiu Zhongguo),* Xianggang: Zhaoyang chubanshe, 1971.

Chen, Ying, 'Women in the Four Years of Resistance' *(Kangzhan di nian lai de funu), Guangdong funu,* Vol. XXI, No. xi-xii, 15 July 1941.

Chen, Yubai, 'Production for the Salvation of the Country' *(Shengchan jiuguo), Nuzi yuekan,* Vol. I, No. ii, 1933.

Chen, Zonglic, 'The Sexual Equalization of Landownership', *(Nan-nu diquan zhi pingjin), New Women (Xin Nuxing),* Vol. I, No. ii, 1927.

Cheng, Fangqu, 'The C.C.P. and the Liberation of Chinese Women' *(Zhongguo gongchandang yu Zhongguo funu jiefang'), Shidai funu,* Vol. I, No. i, 1946.

Cheng, Wanzhen, 'Research on New Industries, I' *(Xin gongye yanjiu), Funu zazhi,* Vol. VIII, No. viii, August 1922.

Chi, Zhenchao, 'The Situation of Women's Work in Jiangxi' *(Jiangxi funu gongzuo de shikuang), Dongfang zazhi,* Vol. XXXV, No. xvii, September 1938.

Chinese Women Stand Up (Zhongguo Funu Dafanshen), Xianggong: Xinminzhu chubanshe, 1949.

Chun, Shao, 'The Organization Process of a Peasant Women's Association' *(Yige nongcun funu tuanti de zuzhi jingguo), Funu shenghuo,* Vol. VI, No. v, 5 July 1938.

Daiming, 'The Women that are Mostly Needed in Contemporary China' *(Zhongguo jinri suoxuyaode funu), Nuzi Yuekan,* Vol. I, No. i, 22 February 1933.

De'en, 'Elementary Education and Training and Women of Our Country' *(Qianshi beji vu woguo funu), Funu zazhi,* Vol. XV, No. 1, January 1929.

Deng, Yingchao, 'How To Organize Peasant Women [?]' *(Zenyang zuzhi nongcun funu), Funu shenghuo,* Vol. V, No. xii, 16 April 1938.

Deng, Yingchao, 'Anti-Japanese Invasion and Chinese Women' *(Fandue rikou qinlue yu Zhongguo funu) Zhou Enlai and Deng Yingchao (Zhou Enlai yu Deng Yingchao),* Hankou: Yixing shuju, 1938.

Deng, Yingchao, 'Land Reform and the New Tasks of Women's Work' *(Tudi jaige yu funu gongzuo de xin renwu), Documents of the women's movements (Funu yundong wenxian),* Xianggang: Xin minzhu chubanshe, 1947.

Ding, Fengjia, 'From What I Observed on the Life-Styles of Women in this Place' *(Wo suojian zhi bendi funu shenghuo xianzhuang), Funu zazhi,* Vol. I, No. ix, September 1915.

Documents on the Women's Movements (Funu yundong wenxian), Xianggang: Xin minzhu chubanshe, 1949.

Dong, Shiyin, 'Hope That This Organization Emphasizes Peasant Women' *(Yuan Benhui Duozhuyi Xiangcun Funu), Jiangx funu,* Vol. I, No. i, 8 March 1934.

Dong, Tingchao, 'A "March 8th" Day Thirty Years Ago' *(Sanshinian gian de yici 'San Ba' jie), Zhongguo Funu,* Vol. III, No. vi, 1956.

Editorial of the *Liberation Daily (Jiefang Riba shelun),* 'The Coming Mission of Chinese Women' *(Zhongguo funu jinhou de renwu)* in *Documents on the Women's Movements (Funu yundong wenxian),* Xianggang: Xin minzhu chubanshe, 1949.

Fan, Baichuan, 'The Experience and Fate of the Chinese Handicraft Industry after the Invasion of the Foreign Capitalism' *(Zhongguo shougongyu zai*

waizuo zibanzhuyi qinruhou de zauyu) Historical Research (Lishi yanjiu),
Vol. III.

Fang, Suzhong, 'The National Father's Idea of Women's Rights' *(Guofu de nuquan sixiang), Revolutionary Ideas Monthly (Geming sixiang yuekan),* Vol. VI, No. iii, August 1959.

First National Representatives Congress of Chinese Women, (Zhongguo funu diyici quanquo daibiao da hui), Xianggang: Xin minzhu chubanshe, 1949.

Fu, Boashen, 'The Facts on the Situation of Peasant Women in Our Country and the Duties of the Y.W.C.A.' *(Woquo xiangcun funu shenghuo de shikuang yu nuqingnianhui de zeron), Young Women (Nugingnian),* Vol. IX, No. ix, November 1930.

Fu, Menglan, 'On the Necessity of Speedy Improvement Plans of Women's Industries' *(Funu shiye yi shuchou gailiang zhi fangfa lu), Funu shibao,* Vol. X, 25 May 1913.

Fu, Xuewen, *Contemporary Women (Xiandai funu),* Shanghai: Shangwu yinshuguan, 1946.

Gao, Nengcheng. 'The Theory and Practice of Organizing Women's Production Co-operatives' *(Zuzhi funu shengchan hezuoshe zhi lilun yu shiji), Funu Gongming,* Vol. X, No. v, July 1941.

Gao, Yufen, 'How to Liberate the Peasant and Working-Class Women in China[?]' *(Zenyeng caikeyi jiefang Zhongguo de nong-gong funu), Nuzi yuekan,* Vol. I, No. ii, 1933.

Ge, Qiu, 'The Women's Liberation Movement in the Anti-Fascist War' *(Fan-faxisi zhanzheng zhong de funu jiefang yundong), Guangxi funu,* Vol. XXI, 15 January 1942.

Gongdu, 'The Issue of Chinese Women Workers' *(Zhongguo nugong wenti), Funu zazhi,* Vol. XV, No. ix, September 1929.

Gu, Bingyuan, 'The Issue of Shanghai Women Workers' *(Shanghai nugong wenti), Nugingnian,* Vol. VIII, No. v, May 1929.

Guan, Meirong, 'How to Organize Peasant Women [?]' *(Zenyang dongyuan nongcun funu [?]', Funu shenghuo,* Vol. V, No. xii, 16 April 1938.

Guixiu, 'How to Go About with the Education of Peasant Women's Education During War Time', *(Zenyang jinxing zhanshi xiangcun funu jiaoyu), Funu shenghuo,* Vol. VI, No. iii, 5 June 1938.

Guixiu, 'An Experiment in Mobilizing the Masses in the Countryside' *(Dongyuan nongcun minzhong de yige shiyan), Funu shenghuo,* Vol. VI, No. ix, 1 December 1938.

Guo, Zhenyi, 'The Greater Shanghai Plan Should Note a Few Issues on Women' *(Da Shanghai jihua zhong ying zhuyi de jige funu wenti), Dongfanf zazhi,* Vol. XXXI, No. v, March 1934.

Guo, Zhenyi, *The Issue of Women in China, (Zhongguo funu wenti),* Shanghai: Shangwu yinshuguan, 1937.

He, Ganzhi, *The Contemporary Revolutionary History of China, (Zhongguo xiandai geming shi),* Beijing: Gaodeng jiaoyu chubanshe, 1956.

Hefa, 'The Labour Legislation and the Protection of Women' *(Laodong lifa yu nugong baohu), Nugingnian,* Vol. IX, No. viii, October 1930.

He-Zhang, Yazhen, 'Women and Industry' *(Funu yu shiye)*, *Women's Times (Funu shibao)*, Vol. IX, 25 February 1913.

Hu, Ziying, 'The Mobilization of Women for Production During the War' *(Kangzhan shiqi zhong de funu shengchan dongyuan)*, *Funu shenqhuo*, Vol. VI, No. ix, 1 December 1938.

Hu, Ziying, 'Several Methods of Mobilizing Women to Participate in Production' *(Dongyuan funu canjia shengchan de jige banfa)*, *Funu shenghuo*, Vol. VI, No. x, 16 December 1938.

Hu, Ziying, 'Industrial Women Workers of Chongqing' *(Chanye nugong zai Chongqing)*, *Funu shenghuo*, Vol.VIII, No. x, 20 February 1940.

Huachen, 'The Narrative of a Woman Worker' *(Yige nugong de zishu)*, *Funu zazhi*, Vol. XVII, No. vi, June 1931.

Huang, Junlue, 'The Wage System of China' *(Zhongguo gongqian zhidu)*, *Dongfang zazhi*, Vol. XXIV, No. xviii, September 1927.

Huang, Suxin, 'Expanding the War Time Women's Work into the Villages' *(Kuoda zhanshi funu gongzuo dao nongcun)*, *Funu gongming*, Vol. VII, No. vii, 5 April 1938.

Huang, Suxin, 'How to Carry on the Tasks of Women's Movement in the War Districts . . . Through the Industrial Co-operative Movement to Proceed the Tasks of Women's Movement' *(Zenyang zai zhanqunei jinxing fuyun gongzuo . . . tongguo gongye hezue yundong tuijin fuyun gongzuo)*, *Funu gongming*, Vol. VIII, Nos. v-vi, 15 October 1938.

Huang, Xiaomin, 'On Women's Movements and Guangdong Women' *(Lun funu yundong yu Guangdong de funu)*, *Funu zazhi*, Vol. XIII, No. iv, April 1927.

Hubei Federation of Philosophy and Social Sciences Learned Societies *(Hubei Sheng Zhexue Shehuikexue Xuehui Lianhehui)*, *A Collection of Papers Celebrating the 50th Anniversary of the 1911 Revolution (Xin-Hai geming wushi zhounian jinian luwei ji)*, Beijing: Zhonghua shuju, 1962.

Hui, 'Another Bloody Account' *Monshi yipian xue zhang) Funu shenghuo*, Vol. VI, No. i, 5 May 1938.

Hui, 'The Women of Xinhui' *(Xinhui de funu)*, *Family Weekly (Jiating xinggu)*, Vol. I, No. xlvii, October 1946.

Jian, Pu, 'The Goal and Direction of the Contemporary Chinese Women's Movement' *(Dangqian Zhongguo fuyun de mubiao he fangxiang)*, *Guangxi funu*, Vol. XXI, 15 January 1942.

Jiangsu Federation of Women *(Jiangxi Sheng Funu Lianhehui)*, *The Stories of Jiangxi Women's Revolutionary Struggle (Jiangxi funu geming douzheng gushi)*, Beijing: Zhongguo funu zazhishe, 1963.

Jianyue, 'Xingning women' *(Xingning de funu)*, *New Women (Xin nuxing)*, Vol. III, No. vii, July 1928.

Jieyu, 'The Women of the Slum in Nanchang City' *(Nanchang shi pinminqu de funu)*, *Jiangxi Women (Jiangxi funu)* Vol.I, No. i, January 1937.

Jihong, 'How to Do Extracurricular Work [?]' *(Zenyang congshi keyu gongzuo [?]*, *Funu shenghuo*, Vol. III, No. iv, 1 September 1936.

Jihong, 'An Interview with Jiang Yixiao, a Woman Reporter' *(Nu jizhi Jiang*

Yixiao fangoren ji), Funu zazhi, Vol. IV, No. ii, 1 February 1937.

Jihong, 'An Account of the Visit to the Labour School of the Y.W.C.A.' *(Canguan nuqingnianhui laogong xuexiao ji), Funu shenghuo,* Vol. IV, No. vi, 1 April 1937.

Jihong, 'The Wuhan Women Workers in the War Time' *(Kangzhan zhong de Wuhan nugong), Funu shenghuo,* Vol. VI, No. i, May 1938.

Jihong, 'The Path of the Liberation of Chinese Working-Class Women' *(Zhongguo laodong funu jiefang de tujing), Funu shenghuo,* Vol. VII, No. vi, 1 May 1939.

Jihong, 'Interviewing Madam Hu Lan'gui . . . Two Years [of History] of the Working-Class Women's War-Zone Service Teams' *(Fang Hu Lan'gui nushi . . . liangnian lai de laodong funu zhandi fuwutuan), Funu shenghuo,* Vol. VII, Nos. xi-xii, 1 September 1939.

Jihong, 'The Women's Textile Handicraft Industry is Expanding in Bishan of Sichuan' *(Funu shoufang tuiguang zai Sichuan Bishan), Funu shenghuo,* Vol. IX, No. i, 1 July 1940.

Jin, Er, 'A Letter to [My Mother]' *(Gei muqin de xin), Funu shenghuo,* Vol. III, No. iii, 16 August 1936.

Jin, Qihua, 'How to Call upon the Women in the Countryside [?]' *(Zenyang huanqu nongcun li de funu [?]) Funu gongming,* Vol. VII, No. vi, 5 April 1938.

Jin, Zhonghua, 'Talking National Affairs with Women' *(Yu funutan quoshi), Funu zazhi,* Vol. XVII, No. xii, December 1931.

Jingyu, 'The Future of Chinese Women's Citizen Revolutionary Movement' *(Jinhou Zhongguo funu de guoming geming yundong), Funu zazhi,* Vol. I, No. x, January 1924.

KMT Central Committee's Editorial Committee of Party Historical Data *(Zhongguo Guomindang Zhongyuang Weiyuanhui Dangshi Shiliao Biansuan Weiyuanhui), The Year-Chart of Seventy Years of Important Events of the KMT (Zhongguo Guomindang qi shinian dashi nianbiao),* Taibei: The KMT Central Committee's Editorial Committee of Party Historical Data, 1964.

Lan, Feng, 'Northwestern Shanxi Women's Federation First Women Officers' Expansion Meeting' *(Jingxibei fulian diyici kuoda ganbuhui), Funu shenghuo,* Vol. VIII, No. v, 5 December 1939.

Lanping, 'The Protection of Women in the Existing Legislation in Our Country' *(Woguo xianxingfa shang zhi funu baohu), Dongfang zazhi,* Vol. XIV, No. v, March 1937.

Li, Aizhen, 'The Situation of Women of Songgou' *(Songgou funu de zhuangkuang), Funu zazhi,* Vol. XIV, No. i, January 1928.

Li, Baoguang, 'Move One Step Forward' *(Geng qianjiu yibu), Shidai funu,* Vol. I, No. i, July 1946.

Li, Baoguang, 'Women Should Enthusiastically Join the Liberation Movement' *(Funu yao ralie canjia fanshen yundong), Shidai funu,* Vol. I, No. ii, August 1946.

Li, Changnian, 'Female Infanticide and the Issue of Unequal Ratios of the

Sexes in China' *(Nuying shahai yu Zhougguo liangxiang bujun wenti)*, *Dongfang zazhi*, Vol. XXXII, No. xi, June 1935.

Li-Wang, Limeng, *The Chinese Women's Movements (Zhongguo funu yundong)*, Shanghai: Shangwu yinshuguan, 1934.

Liang, Ying, 'Expanding War Time Women's Work into the Countryside' *(Kuoda zhanshi funu gongruo dao nongcun)*, *Funu gongming*, Vol. VII, No. vi, 5 April 1938.

Liang, Ying, 'Visits and Publicity in the Countryside' *(Nongcun fangwen yu xuanchuan)*, *Funu gongming*, Vol. VII, No. vi, 5 April 1938.

Lin, Hao, 'The Chinese Women's Liberation Movement' *(Zhongguo funu zhi jiefang yundong)*, *Nuzi Yuekan*, Vol. I, No. viii, 15 October 1933.

Lin, Xiaoqing, 'The Situation of Women of Meixian' *(Meixian de funu shenghuo)*, *Funu zazhi*, Vol. XIV, No. i, January 1928.

Lin, Yilun, 'Women's Handicraft Should not Ignore Embroidery' *(Nuzi gongyi bukefei xiu lun)*, *Funu zazhi*, Vol. I, No. iv, April 1915.

Liu, Chengfu, 'Elementary Education and Training and Women's Occupation' *Qianshi beji yu funu zhiye)*, *Funu zazhi*, Vol. XV, No. i, January 1929.

Liu, Gu, 'The Maid Servants of Guizhou' *(Guizhou de nube)*, *Women's Weekly (Funu xunkan)*, Vol. XIX, No. v, February 1935.

Liu, Hengjing, 'War and Women' *(Kangzhan yu funu)*, *Funu gongming*, Vol. XI, No. i, March 1942.

Liu, Quiying, 'The Sufferings of Child-Wives' *(Tongyangxi de tongku)*, *Jiangxi funu*, Vol. I, No. i, March 1937.

Liu, Zhi, 'The Standing Up of Women in Dingxian' *(Dingxian funu da fanshen)* in All-China Democratic Women's Federation, *A Sketch of the Peasant Women's Movement in the Chinese Liberated Areas (Zhongguo jieganggu nonqcunfunu da fanshen yundong sumino)*, Xianggang: Xin minzhu chubanshe, 1949.

Liying, 'The Situation of Child-Wives of Min-Nam' *(Min-Nam tongyangxi de shenghuo)*, *Funu shenghuo*, Vol. III, No. iii, 8 August 1936.

Lou, Yiwen, 'Speaking for Peasant Women' *(Wei nongcun funu huyue)*, *Funu Yuekan*, Vol. III, No. i, July 1943.

Lu, Kun, *The House Rule of Women's Chambers (Guifan)*, Ming keben duplicate copy *(Yingyin Ming keben)*, *1927*.

Lu, Yunzhang, 'How to Organize Peasant Women's Movement [?]' *Zenyang zuo nongcun yundong [?])*, *Funu gongming*, Vol. XI, No. iii, May 1942.

Luo, Heng, 'The Creation Process of Rong District and its Afterthought' *(Rong Qu chuangshe jingguo ji ganxiang)*, *Funu xinyun*, Vol. VI, No. x, December 1944.

Luo, Qiong, 'The Rural Working Women in Northern Jiangsu' *(Jiangsu beibu nongcun zhong de laudong funu)*, *Dongfang zazhi*, Vol. XXXII, No. xiv, July 1935.

Luo, Qiong, 'The Basic Rules of the Development of the Chinese Women's Movements' *(Zhongguo funu yundong fazhan de jiben guilu)*, *New Chinese Women (Xin Zhongguo funu)*, December 1952.

Luo, Shuhe, 'The Situation of Women of Tainpu' *(Tainpu nuzi zhi zhuang-kuang), Funu zazhi,* Vol. I, No. vii, July 1955.

Luo, Shuzhang, 'Dedicated to Those Working Comrades who Relocate Women Workers' *(Xiangei shusan nugong de gongzuo tongshi mui) Funu shenghuo,* Vol. VI, No. viii, 20 August 1938.

Luo, Shuzhuo, 'The Materialization of an Ideal Refugee Women's Factory' *Yige lixiang nu nanmin gongchang de shishi), Funu shenghuo,* Vol. VI, No. v, 5 July 1938.

Luxing, 'The Women Labour Legislation in Labour Legislation' *(Laodong lifa zhong de funu laodong fa)* in Mei Shang, *A Collection of Discussion Papers on the Issue of Chinese Women (Zhongguo funu wenti taolunji),* Shanghai: Xinwenhua shushe, 1929, Vol. I.

Ma, Chaojun, et al., *The History of Labour Movement in China (Zhongguo laogong yundong shi),* Taibei: Zhongguo laogong Fuli chubanshe, 1959, Vol. I.

Ma, Jin, 'In the Villages' *(Zai xiangcun li), Funu shenghuo,* Vol. VI, No. i, 5 May 1938.

Mei, Shang, *A Collection of Discussion Papers on the Issue of Chinese Women (Zhongguo funu wenti taolunji)* Shanghai: Xinwenhue shushe, 1929.

Meng, Qingshu, 'Concerning the Opinions on the Wuhan Working-Class Women's Movement' *(Guanyu Wuhan nugong yundong de yijian), Funu shenghuo,* Vol. VI, 5 May 1938.

Meng, Ru, 'The Illiteracy of Chinese Women' *(Zhongguo zhi wenmang), Dongfang zazhi,* Vol. XXXI, No. i, January 1934.

Meng, Xianzhang, *Teaching Materials for the History of Chinese Modern Economy, (Zhongguo jindai jingji shi jiaocheng),* Shanghai: Zhonghua shudian, 1951.

Miaoran, 'The Issue of Women Labour' *(Funu laodong wenti),* in Mei Shang, *A Collection of Discussion Papers on the Issue of Chinese Women (Zhongguo funu wenti taolunji),* Shanghai: Xinwenhua shushe, 1929, Vol. I.

Mo, Yan, 'How Do Women Learn and Join the Resistance' *(Funu zenyang renshi kangzhan yu zenyang ganjia kangzhan), Dongfang zazhi,* Vol. XXXV, No. i, January 1938.

New Life Movement Women's Directing Committee *(Xin Yun Funu Zhidao Weiyuanhui), Women's Rural Services (Funu xiangcun fuwu),* Congqing: Xin yun funu zhidao wenyuanhui, 1944.

Pan'gu 'Guo-gong Zhenzheng Jishi' Bianxiezu, *The Great Transformation: Record of KMT-CCP Internal War, 1945-1949 (Tianfan difu kai er kang: guo-gong zhangzheng jishi, 1945-1949),* Xianggang: Pan'qu chubanshe, 1975.

Peng, I, 'The Rural Women of Yunnan' *(Yunnan de nongcun funu), Funu shenghuo,* Vol. VIII, No. ii, October 1939.

Peng, Lan, 'I Suggest: March 8th Should Go to the Countryside' *(Wo tiyi: Sanyue bari yingdao xiangcun qu), Dagongbao,* Shanghai: March 8th 1948.

Peng, Zeyi, *Materials on the Modern Chinese Handicraft Industry, 1840-1949 (Zhongguo jindai shougongye ziliao, 1840-1949),* Beijing: Zanlian shuju, 1957.

Pi, Yishu, 'An Attempt to Discuss the Contemporary Women's Movement in Taiwan' *(Shilun dangqian Taiwan de funu yundong), Zhongguo funu,* Vol. I, No. i, July 1950.

Pin, Xin, *The History of the Chinese Democratic Constitution Movement (Zhongguo xianzheng yundong shi),* Shanghai: Jinbu shuju, 1946.

Publicity and Education Department of the All-China Democratic Women's Federation *(Zhongguo Quanguo Minzhu Funu Lianhehui Xuanchuan Jiao-yubu) Important Documents of the Chinese Women's Movements (Zhongguo funu yundong de Zhongguo wenjian),* Beijing: Renmin chubanshe, 1953.

Qi, Yun and Ji Qian, 'Women of Jiaodong Enthusiastically Support the People's Liberation War' *(Jiaodong funu relie zhiyuan renmin jiefang zhanzheng)* in All-China Democratic Women's Federation *(Quanguo Minzhu Funu Lianhehui), Women's Movement for Participation in War in the Liberated Areas of China, (Zhongguo jiefanggu funu canzhan yundong),* Xianggang: Xin minzhu chubanshe, 1949.

Qianshao, 'The Tasks of the Chinese Working-Class Women's Celebration of May 1st Day' *(Zhongguo laodong funu jinian wu-yi jie de rewu), Funu shenghuo,* Vol. VI, No. i, 5 May 1938.

Qin, Liufang, 'How to Carry Out the Textile Handicraft Industry of Peasant Women' *(Zenyang tuijin nongcun funu de shoafang zhiye), Funu shenghuo,* Vol. VI, No. v, 5 July 1938.

Qiufang, 'The Obstacles in Work' *(Gongzuo zhong de zhang'ai), Funu shenghuo,* Vol. VI, No. ii, 30 May 1938.

Selu, 'The International Women Labour Union and the Chinese Women' *(Guoji funu laodonghui yu zhongguo funu), Funu zazhi,* Vol. VII, No. xi, November 1921.

Shang, Mu, 'The Foci of Women's Liberation' *(Funu jiefang zhi zhuolidian), Funu zazhi,* Vol. XIII, No. v, May 1927.

Shanghai Renmin Chubanshe, *The Sinful Old Society (Zuie de jiu shehui),* Shanghai: Renmin chubanshe, 1966.

Shanghai Tongshe, *Materials for the Research on Shanghai: Supplement (Shanghai yanjiu ziliao xuji),* Taibei: Zhongguo chubanshe, 1973.

Shijin, 'Wish This Association Can Pay More Attention to Peasant Women' *(Yuan benhui due zhuyi xiangcun funu), Jiangxi funu,* Vol. I, No. i, 8 March 1937.

Shi, Jingxiang, 'Indentured Workers' *(Baoshen gong)* in Li Yuqing, *The Calamity of the Old China (Ku'nan de Jiu Zhongguo),* Xianggang: Zhaoyang chubanshe, 1971.

Shi, Jingxing, 'The Deduction of Wages' *(Fa gongqian)* in Li Yuqing, *The Calamity of the Old China (Ku'nan de jiu Zhongguo),* Xianggang: Zhaoyang chubanshe, 1971.

Shiliang, 'My Opinion on the Present National Organization of Women' *(Quanguo funu zuzhi xianzhuang yu wojian), Funu shenghuo,* Vol. VIII, No. x, 20 February 1940.

Shi, Renru, 'The Training Situation of Spinning-Research Classes' *(Fansha yanjiuban xunlian gaikuang), Guangdong funu,* Vol. II, No.11-12, 15 July 1941

Shuying, 'Several Views on the Publicity and Organization of Peasant and Working-Class Women' *(Dui xuanchuan he zuzhi nongfu ji nugong de jidian yijian) Funu gongming,* Vol. X, No. v, July 1941.

Si, Ding, 'The Liberation of Women and the Revival of Nation' *(Funu jiefang yu minzu fuxing), Zhongguo funu,* Vol. II, No. i, December 1940.

Si, Qi, 'The Women of Guizhou Panxian' *(Guizhou Panzian de funu), Shenbao Monthly (Shenbao yuekan),* Vol. IV, No. iv, April 1935.

Situ, Yan, 'The Student Unrest in the University of Zhejiang' *(Xuechao zai Zheda), Xiandai funu,* Vol. IX, No. iii, June 1947.

Song, Qingling, 'Concerning the Call for Assisting Guerrilla Fighters ... the Speech Made in the International Day Meeting in Xianggang' *(Quanyu yuanzhu youjidui zhanshi dehuyu . . . zai xianggang quoji funujie jihui shang suozuo de yanshuo), The Collected Work of Song Qingling (Song Qingling xuanji),* Xianggang: Zhonghui shuju, 1967.

Song, Qingling, 'The Chinese Women Demand Freedom of Struggle' *(Zhongguo funu zhenggu de douzheng), The Collected Work of Song Qingling (Song Qingling xuanji),* Xianggang Zhonghui shuju, 1967.

Tan, Sheying, *Forty Years of Women's Movements (Fuyun Sichinian),* Taiwan: Publisher unknown, 1952.

Tang, Caichang, *A Reader of Xiangbao (Xiangbao leizuan),* Shanghai: Zhongguo bianyi yinshuguan, 1902.

Tang, Guozhen, 'How to Help Women and Children During the War' *(Zenyang jiuyi zhanshi furu), Funu gongming,* Vol. VIII, No. i, 20 January 1938.

Tao, Fen, 'The Women's Question and Men' *(Funu wenti he nanzi), Funu shenghuo,* Vol. III, No. iii, 16 August 1936.

Wang, Jiamin, *A Draft of the History of the Chinese Communist Party (Zhongguo gongchandang shiquo),* Taiwan: self-published, 1965.

Wang, Minyi, 'Celebrating "March 8th" Day' *(Jinian 'san Ba' jie), Jiangxi funu,* Vol. I, No. i, 8 March 1937.

Wang, Pingling, 'The Labour-Training of Women During the War' *(Kangzhan shiqi de funu laodong xunlian), Funu gongming,* Vol. VII, No. vii, 20 April 1938.

Wang, Rusheng, 'Textile Women Workers Talked of the Past and Present' *(Fangzhi nugong hua jinxi), Zhongguo funu,* January 1963.

Wang, Yi, 'The Situation of Child-Wives' *(Tongyangxi de shenghu), Dongfang zazhi,* Vol. XXXII, No. xv, August 1935.

Wang, Yiwei, 'Women in the Resistance Mobilization of Special Districts' *(Tequ kangzhan dongyuan zhou de funu), Funu shenghuo,* Vol. VI, No.ii, 20 May 1938.

Wangli, 'Women and Production Co-operative' *(Funu yu shengchan hezuoshe), Funu shenghuo,* Vol. IX, No. iii, 16 September 1940.

Wenna, ' "March 8th" Day and Village Work' *('San-Ba jie yu xiangcun gongzuo), Funu gongming,* Vol. VII, No. iv, 5 March 1938.

Women's Life Society *(Funu Shenghuo She), Women's War-Time Handbook (Zhanshi funu shouce),* Chongqing: Shenghuo sheju, 1939.

Wu, Chengming, *The Investments of Imperialist Powers in Old China (Diquozhuyi zai jiu Zhongguo de touzi),* Beijing: Renmin chubanshe, 1956.

Wu, Naiyin, 'In Memory of Martyr Chen Tiejun' *(Ji Chen Tiejun lieshi), Zhongguo funu,* Vol. X, 1962.

Wu, Yuzhang, 'The Chinese Women Have Been on the Path of Independent Liberation During the May Fourth Movement' *(Zhongguo funu zai Wu-Si yundong zoushangle ziji jiefang zhi daolu), Documents on the Women's Movements (Funu yundong wenxian),* Xianggang: Xin minzhu chubanshe, 1949.

Wu, Yuzhang, *On the 1911 Revolution (Lun Xin-Hai geming),* Beijing: Renmin chubanshe, 1972.

Xia, Yingzhe, 'The Pioneer Call for the Investigation of the Women's Work on the National Level' *(Quanguo funu gongzuo zongjianqing de xiaosheng), Funu shenghuo,* Vol. IX, No. iii, 16 September 1940.

Xie, Kang, 'The Traditional Views on Women's Education in Chinese Families' *(Zhonghua jiating chuantong de nujiao guannian), Journal of Zhongshan Academy and Culture (Zhongshan xueshu wenhua jikan),* Vol. VI, November 1970.

Xiong, Zhi, ' "March 8th" Women's Day' *('San-Ba' funu jie janyan), Jiangxi funu,* Vol. I, No. i, 8 March 1937.

Xiuling, 'I Am Also a Woman Worker' *(Wo ye shi yige nugong), Women's Circle (Funujie),* Vol. VIII, No. ix, March 1941.

Xu, Hui, 'The Policies of the National Party on Women' *(Zhongguo Guomindang de funu zhengce), Funu yuekan,* Vol. I, No. vi, February 1942.

Xu, Yasheng, 'Peasant Women's Elementary Education and Training' *(Nongjia funu de qianshi boji xuelian), Funu zazhi,* Vol. XV, No. i, January 1929.

Xu, Youzhi, 'Our One Year of Peasant Service in Zhonghechang' *(Yinian lai women zai Zhonghechang de xiangcun fuwu gongzuo), Funu xinyun,* Vol. VI, No. x, December 1944.

Xuejian, 'The Situation of Haifang Women and Their Movement' *(Haifeng funu de shenghuo jiqi yundong), Funu zazhi,* Vol. XIV, No. xii, December 1928.

Yan, Zhongping, 'Examples of the Provincial Official Encouragement of Textile Industry in the Ming and Qing Dynasties' *(Ming-Qing liangdai difangguan changdao fangzhiye shili), Dongfang zazhi,* Vol. LX, No. viii, April 1946.

Yan, Zhongping, *A Draft on the History of the Chinese Cotton Textile, 1289-1937 (Zhongguo mianfanqzhi shigao, 1289-1937,* Beijing: Kexue Chubanshe, 1963.

Yan, Zhongping, et al., *Selection of Statistical Materials on the History of the Modern China (Zhongguo jindai jingjishi tongji ziliao xuanji),* Beijing: Kexue chubanshe, 1955.

Yan'an Research Society of Current Affairs *(Yan'an Shishi Wenti Yanjiu Hui), Chinese Wartime Politics (Kangzhan zhong de Zhongguo zhengzhi),* Yan'an: Jiefangshe, 1940.

Yao, Lan, 'The Marching Song of Women' *(Funu jinxingqu) Funu shenghuo,* Vol. VI, No. xi, 1 January 1939.

Ye, Chusheng, 'A Short History of "March 8th"' *('San Ba' jianshi), Jaingxi funu,* Vol. I, No. i, 8 March 1937.

Ye, Yuying, 'May 1st Labour Day and the Future of the Issue of Women's Labour' *(Wu-yi laodongjie yu funu laodong wenti zhanwang), Funu gongming,* Vol. VIII, No. viii, 20 April 1938.

Yin, Falu, 'The Direct Destruction of Imperialism on the May Fourth Movement' *(Diguozhuyi dui Wu-Si yundong de zhijie bohuai),* The Central China's Technical College Materials Room on Marxism and Leninism *(Huazhong gongxueyuen makesi-liening zhuyi ziliaoshi), Collected Work on May Fourth Movement (Wu-Si yundong wenji),* Wuhan: Renmin chubanshe, 1957.

Yinqiu, 'What Can Peasant Women Do?' *(Nongcun funu neng zuoxia shenme?') Funu gongming,* Vol. VII, No. vi, 5 April 1938.

Yinqiu, 'Working Women Should Stand on the Front Line of National Defence' *(Laodong funu yinggai zhanzai guofang diyixian), Funu gongming,* Vol. VII, No. vii, 20 April 1938.

Ying, 'The Issue of Women's Farming in the Fields' *(Tan funu xiatian gengzhong wenti), Funu gongming,* Vol. X, No. v, July 1941.

Yuan, 'How to Expand the Working-Class Women's Movement?' *(Zenyang kaizhan laodong funu yundong?), Funu gongming,* Vol. VII, No. vii, 20 April 1938.

Yuan, 'How Can Women Officers be Ignored?' *(Fugan girong hushi), Guangdong funu,* Vol. III, Nos. 1-2, 15 October 1942.

Zeng, Wan, 'The Improvement of Women's Situation During the War' *(Kangzhan qi zhong funu shenghuo de gaishan), Dongfang zazhi,* Vol. XXXV, No. xiii, July 1938.

Zhang, Chuanhong, 'The Body-Search System' *(Chaoshen zhi)* in Li Yuqing, *The Calamity of the Old China (Ku'nan de jiu Zhongguo),* Xianggang: Zhaoyang chubanshe, 1971.

Zhang, Hui and Bao Cun, *The Revolutionary History of Shanghai in the Last Hundred Years (Shanghai jin bainian geming shihua),* Shanghai: Renmin chubanshe, 1963.

Zhang, Peifan, *The Issue of Women (Funu wenti),* Shanghai: Shangwu yinshuguan, 1922.

Zhang, Shen, 'The Voices of Women Workers' *(Nugong de hua), Funu shenghuo,* Vol. VII, No. vi, 1 May 1939.

Zhang, Xiuxia, 'Awake! Dear Women Compatriots!' *(Xingxingba! Qin'aide funu tongbao!), Nuzi Yuekan,* Vol. I, No. viii, 15 October 1933.

Zhen, Li, 'Portrait of the Women's Life Styles in Western Jiangxi' *(Jiangxi funu shenghuo xiezhen), Shenbao yuekan,* Vol. IV, No. vii, July 1935.

Zhennong, 'Organize the Large Masses to the Anti-Japanese Front Line' *(Zuzhi guangda de qunzhong dao kangri zhanxian shang lai), Jiefang zhoukan,* Vol. I, No. xii, August 1937.

Zhong, Tiemou, *The Peasant Movement of Hailufeng (Hailufeng nonqmin yundong)*, Guangdong: Renmin chubanshe, 1957.

Zhou, Jingchu, 'Women and Agriculture' *(Furen yu nongye)*, *Funu shibao*, Vol. XI, 20 October 1913.

Zhu, Yingmei, 'The Ways to Improve the Livelihood of Peasant Women' *(Gaijin Zhongguo nonggong funu shenghuo de tujing)*, *Funu zazhi*, Vol. XVII, No. xi, January 1931.

Zhuang, Ming, 'The Marching Song of Women' *(Funu jinxingqu)*, *Women's Life (Funu shenghuo)*, Vol. IV, No. vi, 1937.

Zhujing, 'The Shanghai Women Workers are in Struggle' *(Shanghai nugong zai douzheng zhongi)*, *Funu shenghuo*, Vol. IX, No. iv, 16 October 1940.

Zi, 'Let Us Use Indigenous Cloth' *(Dajia lai fuyang tu bu)*, *Funu shenghuo*, Vol. V, No. xii, 16 April 1938.

Zi, 'The Present Stage of Working Women' *(Xianjieduan de laodong funu men)*, *Women's Voices of Xianggang (Xianggang Nusheng)*, Vol. I, No. i, May 1947.

Zi, Jiu, 'Concerning Visits of Labour Families' *(Guanyu laodong jiating fangwen)*, *Funu shenghuo*, Vol. VI, No. iii, 16 February 1937.

Zi, Jiu, 'The Evaluation of Women's Work After One Year of Resistance' *(Kangzhan yi nian lai funu gongzuo de jiantao)*, *Funu shenghuo*, Vol. VI, No. vi, 10 July 1938.

Zou, Lu, *A Brief History of the KMT in China (Zhongguo Guomindang shilue)*, Taibei: Shangwu Press, 1965.

Zuo, Songfen, 'The Two Key Issues of the Work Among Rural Women' *(Xiangcun funu gongzuo zhong de liang da wenti)*, *Funu shenghuo*, Vol. VIII, No. viii, 20 January 1940.